CW00969775

Developing Groundwater

Developing Groundwater
A Guide for Rural Water Supply

Alan MacDonald, Jeff Davies,
Roger Calow and John Chilton

ITDG
PUBLISHING

Published by ITDG Publishing
Schumacher Centre for Technology and Development
Bourton Hall, Bourton-on-Dunsmore, Warwickshire CV23 9QZ, UK
www.itdgpublishing.org.uk

© NERC 2005

First published in 2005

ISBN 1 85339 596 X

All rights reserved. No part of this publication may be reprinted
or reproduced or utilized in any form or by any electronic, mechanical,
or other means, now known or hereafter invented, including photocopying
and recording, or in any information storage or retrieval system,
without the written permission of the publishers.

A catalogue record for this book is available from the British Library.

The contributors have asserted their rights under the Copyright Designs and
Patents Act 1988 to be identified as authors of their respective contributions.

ITDG Publishing is the publishing arm of the Intermediate Technology
Development Group. Our mission is to build skills and capacity of people in
developing countries through the dissemination of information in all forms,
enabling them to improve the quality of their lives and that of future generations.

Illustrations by Gill Tyson.

Typeset by RefineCatch Limited, Bungay, Suffolk
Printed in Great Britain by Ashford Colour Press Limited, Gosport, Hants

Contents

CONTENTS

Figures, tables and boxes

Tables

Boxes

Plates

Foreword

The 2002 World Summit on Sustainable Development (WSSD) in Johannesburg made an important advance when it placed poverty reduction at the heart of efforts to achieve sustainable development. Priority actions highlighted by the UN Millennium Development Goals have allowed countries to focus their efforts on addressing poverty and to pursue sustainable development. The WSSD reiterated the importance of tackling complex issues and the need to develop new approaches to water and sanitation provision.

Water is a key ingredient in generating rural livelihoods, growing food, providing sanitation and drinking water, improved health benefits, producing energy, encouraging industrial growth and ensuring ecosystem integrity and the goods and services they provide. The challenge now is to respond to the growing need for improved water services.

Developing groundwater, an output from DFID's Engineering Knowledge and Research Programme, adds valuable and practical information and techniques to the existing knowledge base for implementing rural water supply projects in sub-Saharan Africa and Asia. The manual is unique in that it has been developed in consultation with people from 29 countries who helped to design the structure and scope of the contents. It contains information to improve our understanding of groundwater resources, on techniques to locate and construct water points, and to appreciate water quality issues, together with ideas on community management and resource requirements.

It is a valuable contribution to help those working on projects, and also enhances the effectiveness of our efforts in the development community.

Peregrine Swann
Senior Water Adviser
Department for International Development, UK
January 2005

Acknowledgements

Many individuals have contributed in some way to the development and production of this book. Not only has this enhanced its value (ensuring that the contents and style were more appropriate for general use), but made the process of developing the manual more enjoyable and less solitary. The manual benefited from collaboration with WaterAid – particularly in the early stages.

We are grateful to all who contributed ideas and insights through workshops or by email (apologies to any who have slipped off the list): Ian Acworth, Matin Ahmed, Boniface Aleobua, Catherine Allen, Jim Anscombe, Edwin Arthur, Kwabena Asante, Peter Ball, Sohrab Baghri, Ron Barker, Andy Bastable, Charles Batchelor, Erich Baumann, Nega Bazezew, Eberhard Braune, Fanie Botha, Nick Burn, Clive Carpenter, Richard Carter, Ben Cobbing, Jude Cobbing, Aidan Cronin, Bob Elson, Bill Fellows, Peter Fenning, Stephen Foster, Ian Gale, Martin Gillespie, Sam Godfrey, Joe Gomme, Herbert Kashililah, Steven King, Kitka Goyol, Hilary Grimes, John Hackett, Philip Hankin, Jonathan Harris, Peter Harvey, Robin Hazell, Ray Heslop, Guy Howard, Peter Howsam, Mark Hughes, Simon Hughes, Craig Hutton, Euan Hyslop, Viju James, Mikael Joergensen, Richard Kellet, Stephen King, Kurt Klitten, Chris Leake, Hervé Levite, Valerian Makusaro, John Marsh, James Montgomery, Brian Morris, Godfrey Mpangala, Gordon Mumbo, Ricky Murray, Emmanuel Naah, Ilka Neumann, Alan Nicol, Amaka Obika, Jeremy Ockelford, Brighid Ó Dochartaigh, Comfort Olayiwole, Emmanuel Ongaji, Roger Peart, Orlando Rovira Pérez, Serge Puyoô, John Petrie, Niall Roche, Bryan Robson, Dinesh Shrestha, Nick Sinclair, Nigel Smith, Steve Sugden, Chris Thomas, Simon Trace, Richard Treves and Susan Wagstaff.

Once written, the chapters of the book were improved by careful reviews. Thanks to those who were involved in the review process: Dotun Adekile (Water Surveys, Nigeria), Eberhard Braune (DWAF, South Africa), Willie Burgess (University College London), Richard Carter (Cranfield University), Othniel Habila (UNICEF), Mikael Joergensen (Carl Bro International), Michael Kehinde (University of Lagos), Roger Peart (BGS), Nick Robins (BGS), Ian Tod (independent consultant) and Pauline Smedley (BGS).

Many thanks to Gill Tyson for her diligence and patience in drafting the illustrations. The technical photographs of rock specimens shown in the Appendix are from the BGS image collection and were mostly taken by

Fergus McTaggart under the geological direction of Euan Hyslop. Other photographs (unless otherwise attributed) were taken by the authors.

The book has benefited from the guidance and careful management of staff at DFID, BGS and ITDG Publishing. In particular we thank James Dalton at DFID, Denis Peach & Donna Keane at BGS, and Helen Marsden & Sarah Silvester at ITDG Publishing. We also acknowledge the help of other colleagues at BGS, for sharing with us their experiences and insights.

The manual is an output from DFID's Knowledge and Research Programme (project number R8162); much of the material in the book has come from previous BGS projects in Africa and Asia, supported by DFID. The views expressed are not necessarily those of DFID. The book is published by permission of the Executive Director of the British Geological Survey (NERC).

1 Introduction

1.1 The need for a manual

In 2004 there were still at least 1 100 000 million people across the world who did not have access to safe, clean drinking water. Many of these people live in rural areas and are among the poorest and most vulnerable to be found anywhere in the world. Without clean water, people's health and livelihoods can be severely affected; the education of children (particularly girls) suffers as the daily tasks of survival take precedence over all other concerns. Faced with this depressing reality, the international community has set ambitious Millennium Development Goals to reduce by half the number of people without clean water by 2015 (United Nations 2000).

In this context, the need for sustainable development and management of groundwater cannot be overstated. Across large swathes of Africa, South America and Asia, groundwater provides the only realistic water supply option for meeting dispersed rural demand (Foster et al. 2000). Alternative water resources can be unreliable and expensive to develop: surface water (if available) is prone to contamination and often seasonal; rainwater harvesting can be expensive and requires good rainfall throughout the year. Groundwater, however, can be found in most environments if you look hard enough with the appropriate expertise. It generally requires no prior treatment since it is naturally protected from contamination; it does not vary significantly seasonally and is often drought resistant. Also it lends itself to the principles of community management – it can be found close to the point of demand and be developed incrementally (and often at low cost).

Yet many projects spend large amounts of money installing water sources without trying to understand the groundwater resources on which these sources depend. As a result, many supplies are unsuccessful or perform poorly. Successfully developing groundwater resources sustainably and cost-effectively on the scale required to help achieve the Millennium Development Goals is not trivial. The challenge is more than just providing extra drilling rigs to the worst-affected countries: technology, software and hardware must all be appropriate to the nature of the groundwater resources in the project area. For example, in sub-Saharan Africa alone, up to 300 million rural people live in areas where finding groundwater resources is difficult, and special techniques are required to help locate groundwater close to a community (MacDonald and Davies 2000). Because of their history of failed water supply interventions, these areas are often highest priority for reducing poverty and improving health.

Information and expertise on groundwater resources is therefore fundamental to extending rural water supply to the poorest and most vulnerable. However, trained and experienced groundwater specialists are rare and expertise is not often available to projects. Hence the reason for this manual. The discipline of understanding the occurrence and behaviour of groundwater is called **hydrogeology**; and those with these skills are called **hydrogeologists**. This manual introduces the hydrogeological techniques and knowledge that are required for undertaking rural water supply projects. The aim is to take some of the magic and mystery out of hydrogeology so that those working on rural water supply projects will be able to apply some of the science of hydrogeology to improve the success of their projects.

The idea for this manual first came about in 1997 during a WaterAid project in rural Nigeria. This project was in an area where different techniques were required to site wells and boreholes across the project area. Training courses and workshops were run for the project engineers and hydrogeologists working in the area and a file of useful field techniques developed. This file was further developed to form a simple technical manual as part of a project funded by the UK Department for International Development (DFID), helping WaterAid projects in Ethiopia, Tanzania and Ghana (MacDonald et al. 2002). This first manual was produced in 2002 and distributed both on CD and via the Internet. The unexpectedly high level of interest in this technical manual, and in particular a demand to have it enlarged to include more techniques, led to a new project funded by DFID to produce the current manual. This project has involved widespread consultation on both the style and content of the manual – over 80 people from 29 countries have contributed ideas, either through workshops or by email. Their help is greatly appreciated and the acknowledgments page lists individuals who have contributed.

1.2 Who is the manual for?

The manual is aimed at the **implementers** of rural water supply projects in sub-Saharan Africa and Asia. In particular, those faced with the challenge of actually trying to site water points, design boreholes, judge whether the source will supply the required yield at the required quality, and estimate the likely sustainability of the supply, will find much in this book to guide them. This group comprises a wide range of skills and disciplines. It includes hydrogeologists, water engineers, geophysicists and general technicians working within, or for, rural water supply projects and their client communities; all of them are referred to as project engineers or hydrogeologists in this manual. In addition, those charged with the design, oversight and management of rural water supply projects will find the manual useful, and a necessary reminder of the need to invest in resource assessment and waterpoint design, as well as source management and financing arrangements. The manual could also be useful to help benchmark the hydrogeological input required on projects. Such knowledge will facilitate local control of contractors or in judging the success and cost-effectiveness of projects.

1.3 The scope of the manual

The content of this manual was decided by a group of about 80 people from 29 countries. Two workshops and much email correspondence helped refine what subjects the manual would cover and what would be left out. One of the main decisions from this group was that the manual should be designed to help projects that are developing springs, wells or boreholes with low capacity: i.e. sources that will sustain the yield of a handpump (less than $10 \, m^3/day$).

This manual primarily deals with one part of rural water supply: the techniques used to help understand the groundwater resources and thereby help to increase the success and the sustainability of boreholes, wells and springs. These techniques are not presented in isolation, but have been put in the wider context of rural water supply, particularly ideas of community management and participation. The scope of the manual was further broadened during the consultation and review process to include information about the construction of water points and detailed information on water quality aspects of rural water supply.

The manual provides a resource of tried and tested techniques that together can help to increase the chance of obtaining successful water sources. All the techniques have been successfully applied to rural water supply projects across the world. To a trained hydrogeologist many of the techniques should be well known and familiar, although their specific application to rural water supply issues may be less well known. A computer is not needed to carry out any of the techniques described here – hydrogeology is a field science, and the use of a computer can sometimes reduce the quality of science rather than improve it.

The geographical emphasis of the manual is rural sub-Saharan Africa, where coverage of clean and safe water supplies is low and dispersed community water supplies through handpumps and shallow wells are a common solution. Many of the techniques will also be directly relevant to rural Asia and South America, where similar conditions apply. However, other groundwater issues prevalent in Asia, such as resource management due to overpumping, are not addressed in detail in this manual.

A word of caution: scientists may have devoted their working lives to studying just one small aspect of hydrogeology – this manual just scratches the surface of that knowledge and expertise. In many cases, the techniques described here will prove sufficient for the small yields required for rural water supply. In some areas, however, where the hydrogeology is complex, more rigorous science may need to be applied and the experts will have to be called in.

1.4 The contents of the manual: a roadmap

This manual is not meant to be read cover to cover, nor is it meant as a blue print for guaranteed successful projects. Rather, it provides information and techniques that a project engineer should find useful to help understand the groundwater resources available to a community and design appropriate water points. Although many different techniques are described, the manual cannot be exhaustive, so further resources to be consulted are given at the end of each chapter.

Chapter 2: Groundwater. An introduction to groundwater, what it is and how it occurs. The main hydrogeological environments encountered in the world are described and illustrated with schematic diagrams. A summary is also given of the many different methods used to access groundwater around the world.

Chapter 3: Projects and communities. This chapter sets groundwater development in the wider context of rural water supply. The current approaches to rural water supply provision are described (e.g. community management and demand responsive approaches) and the impact that complex groundwater resources can have on these principles. The project cycle is introduced, and where groundwater expertise is required within this cycle. Information is also given on how to assess the cost-effectiveness of different technologies and the various skills required within a project.

Chapter 4: Reconnaissance. This short chapter describes the important steps needed for pre-project reconnaissance: where to find important data, who to talk to, how to carry out a reconnaissance visit and finally how to use all this information to create a rough groundwater development plan.

Chapter 5: Finding groundwater. Introduces all the different techniques used to help site wells and boreholes in communities – from geophysics to dowsing. A general framework is introduced to help decide which technique is appropriate in which situation and the general principles for using more complex techniques, such as geophysics. Techniques for helping to integrate communities into this process are also described. The chapter then describes three common siting techniques in detail: electrical conductivity, resistivity and magnetics. Information is given on how to carry out surveys and interpret the data in common hydrogeological environments.

Chapter 6: Designing and constructing water points. Describes the role of the project engineer/hydrogeologist in supervising the construction of the water points. After introducing different drilling methods, detailed information is given on what data should be recorded from the construction process and then how this should be used to help design the water point. Different standard designs of borehole are given along with a standard well and spring design.

Chapter 7: Assessing the yield of a source. Several methods are given for assessing the yield of a borehole. Three pumping tests of different complexity are explained: a simple airlift, a bailer test and a constant rate test. Detailed descriptions of how to carry out each test and interpret the data are given. The chapter also suggests a simple method for assessing the performance of hand-dug well.

Chapter 8: Water quality aspects of rural water supply. This chapter describes the important aspects of water quality in rural water supply. After introducing international guidelines on drinking water quality, both microbiological contamination and inorganic (chemical) quality are discussed. Techniques are given for how to assess the risk of microbiological contamination both through the aquifer and through local routes. The occurrence and effect of arsenic, fluoride, nitrate and iron and manganese are described in detail, and some general guidance given on how to take water samples. The chapter also introduces a general framework for assessing the risk of pollution.

Chapter 9: Learning lessons. This chapter brings the manual to a close by emphasizing the need for holding on to all the hydrogeological data collected during rural water supply projects and putting it to good use.

1.5   Don't panic, you are not alone

Finally, in this introduction, two words of encouragement – don't panic. The hydrogeological community is small and generally friendly. If there are groundwater resource issues that this manual does not cover adequately, or the experience of your project does not match up to that described here, get in touch. Email has genuinely made the world smaller. There are a number of resource centres that can be called on, such as the British Geological Survey (BGS) in the UK, the IRC International Water and Sanitation Centre in the Netherlands or the family of hydrogeologists known as the International Association of Hydrogeologists (IAH). The science of hydrogeology is advancing all the time and new ways of finding usable groundwater resources in inhospitable environments are being routinely found.

References, further reading and resources

British Geological Survey: http://www.bgs.ac.uk

Foster, S.S.D., Chilton, J., Moench, M., Cardy, F. and Schiffler, M. (2000) Groundwater in Rural Development. World Bank Technical Paper No. 463. World Bank, Washington, DC. Available at: http://www-wds.worldbank.org/

International Association of Hydrogeologists: http://www.iah.org

IRC International Water and Sanitation Centre: http://www.irc.nl

MacDonald, A.M. and Davies, J. (2000) A brief review of groundwater for rural water supply in sub-Saharan Africa. BGS Technical Report WC/00/33. Available at: http://www.bgs.ac.uk/hydrogeology/ruralwater/

MacDonald, A.M., Davies, J. and Ó Dochartaigh, B.É. (2002) Simple methods for assessing groundwater resources in low permeability areas of Africa. British Geological Survey Technical Report CR/01/168. Available at: http://www.bgs.ac.uk/hydrogeology/rural-water/

United Nations (2000) Millennium Development Goals. Available at: http://www.un.org.millenniumgoals

2 Groundwater

2.1 Groundwater – a mysterious resource

The importance of groundwater is often overlooked. It is a mysterious resource – out of site and out of mind. However, some 97 per cent of all freshwater found on the Earth is stored underground (excluding frozen water in glaciers). Over 1.5 billion people depend on it for their drinking water, and many more will in the future if the Millennium Development Goals are to be met. The resource is naturally fairly resistant to drought, storing up water in times of plenty, and releasing it in times of need; also the quality of the water tends to be good and is much less vulnerable to contamination than surface water. However, the resource is not invulnerable: with the ability to pump out huge quantities of water, and the advent of particularly persistent contaminants, the resource needs to protected and managed. Table 2.1 summarizes the advantages of groundwater for rural water supply, with some qualifications.

One of the main purposes of this book is to take some of the mystery out of groundwater. In this chapter some of the basics of groundwater are covered and the main environments in which groundwater occurs described. The

Table 2.1 Advantages and limitations of groundwater

Advantage of groundwater	Qualifying limitations
Often available close to where it is required	Considerable effort may be needed in some situations to locate suitable sites
Can be developed relatively cheaply and progressively to meet demand with lower capital investment than many surface water schemes	As overall coverage increases, the more difficult areas which are left can become more costly to supply
Generally has excellent natural quality, and is usually adequate for potable supply with little or no treatment	Constraints on naturally occurring quality are becoming more widely observed (see Chapter 8)
Generally has a protective cover provided by the soil and unsaturated zone	As development increases more rapidly, the threat of pollution from human activities needs to be assessed in relation to the nature of the protective cover

chapter concludes with a description of the main ways that groundwater resources can be accessed and exploited.

2.2 Groundwater in the hydrological cycle

Groundwater is part of the Earth's natural **hydrological cycle** (see Figure 2.1). The cycle is driven by the energy of the sun and takes water from the large reservoir of the oceans and transfers it through the atmosphere back to the oceans through various routes. When rain falls onto the land surface, a component infiltrates into the soil with the remainder evaporating, or running off to rivers. Water stored as soil moisture can be taken up by plants and transpired, or flow quickly (a few days to a year) as interflow to a river channel. However, some of the water will infiltrate more deeply, eventually accumulating above an impermeable bed, saturating available pore space and forming an underground reservoir. This water is now called **groundwater** (or **ground water** if you are American). The rocks that store and transmit groundwater are called **aquifers**. Groundwater is rarely static, but flows slowly towards rivers or the sea. Rocks that do not easily transport groundwater (such as clays) are known as **aquitards**. The natural hydrologic cycle has been modified by human activity: rivers are dammed, water used for irrigation and groundwater abstracted.

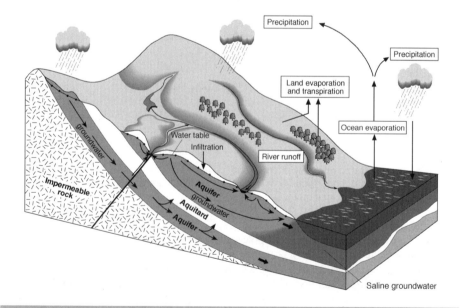

Figure 2.1	Groundwater in the hydrological cycle.
	Source: adapted from Morris et al. 2003.

2.3 Groundwater: basics and definitions

Since groundwater is stored and transmitted by rocks, the resource can only be understood and managed with some appreciation of geology. This is emphasized by the name given to the study of groundwater – **hydrogeology** (meaning water in rocks). Some basic geology is given in Box 2.1, and more detailed discussions with photos are given in Appendix 1.

BOX 2.1 Geology basics: the different types of rocks

Sedimentary rocks are formed by deposition of material, usually under water from lakes, rivers and the sea, and more rarely from the wind. In unconsolidated granular materials, such as sands and gravels, the spaces between the grains are called voids or **pores**. These may become consolidated physically by compaction and chemically by cementation to form typical sedimentary rocks such as **sandstones** (consolidated sand and gravel), **limestones** (consolidated fossil shells) and **mudstones** (consolidated clay). The process of consolidation significantly reduces the pore spaces between grains.

Igneous rocks are formed from molten geological material rising from great depths and cooling to form crystalline rocks either below the ground or at the land surface. Igneous rocks that cool below the surface can occur in huge bodies many kilometres across to form rocks like **granite**, or can be squeezed up fractures less than a metre across to form dykes or sills. Igneous rocks that cool at the land surface are formed from various types of volcanic eruptions and include lavas and ashes. Most igneous rocks are strongly consolidated and, being crystalline, usually have no pores between the grains.

Metamorphic rocks are formed by deep burial, compaction, melting, alteration or recrystallization of igneous or sedimentary rocks during periods of intense geological activity. Metamorphic rocks include **gneisses** and **slates** and are also normally consolidated, with few pore spaces in the matrix between the grains.

Groundwater is stored within pore spaces and fractures in rocks (see Figure 2.2). The proportion of voids in a rock is the porosity and is generally expressed as a percentage. Where the pores and fractures are joined up, water can flow easily and the rocks are said to be **permeable**. The rock characteristics determine how much groundwater can be stored and how productive an aquifer is. Unconsolidated granular sediments, such as sands or gravels contain large amounts of pore space between the grains. The water content in these aquifers can exceed 30 per cent of their volume. However, the porosity progressively reduces both with the proportion of finer materials such as silt or clay and with consolidation. In highly

Primary porosity

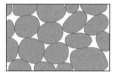

High porosity
unconsolidated sand or
gravel

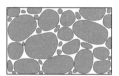

Porosity reduced by
cementation or the
presence of clays and silts

Secondary porosity

Consolidated crystalline rock
rendered porous by the
presence of fractures
(e.g. crystalline basement)

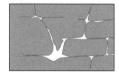

Consolidated fractured
rock with porosity
increased by dissolution
(e.g. limestones)

Figure 2.2 Rock texture and porosity for typical aquifers. Primary porosity refers to porosity from between grains; secondary porosity refers to porosity from fractures.

consolidated sedimentary rocks, the porosity may reduce to less than 10 per cent. In crystalline rocks, such as igneous and metamorphic rocks, groundwater is found only in fractures and rarely exceeds 1 per cent of the volume of the rock mass. However, where the rocks are soluble (such as limestones) these fractures may become enlarged, by dissolution and preferential flow, to form fissures and caverns. Even then the total storage is relatively small compared with unconsolidated aquifers.

The deeper the rocks are the more compressed they become, and pores and fractures close up. It is difficult to estimate the depth at which usable groundwater can be found. Some has been found at a depth of 10 km! In most cases, however, 1 km is usually taken as the deepest that groundwater will naturally circulate; and for rural water supply only groundwater at depths of less than 50 m, perhaps sometimes 100 m, can be practically and economically exploited.

When a hole is dug in an aquifer, at a particular level water begins to flow in. The surface of that water is called the **water table**. Above the water table is the **unsaturated zone** where water still occurs but the pores are generally not fully saturated.

All freshwater found underground must have had a source of **recharge**. This is normally precipitation (rainfall or snowmelt), but can also sometimes be seepage from rivers, lakes or canals. The recharge typically travels vertically downwards through the unsaturated zone to the water table. Once below the water table groundwater can flow horizontally, according to pressure gradients, until water reaches the land surface where it flows from the ground as springs or seepages, providing the dry-weather flow (or **baseflow**) of lowland rivers. Thus the aquifer becomes saturated to a level where the outflow matches recharge.

Shallow aquifers in recharge areas are generally **unconfined**, that is the water table is within the aquifer and at atmospheric pressure (see Figure 2.3). Groundwater, however, is often **confined** by low permeability rocks (an **aquitard**). Under confined conditions water may be encountered under pressure, and when wells are drilled, water rises above the top of the aquifer, sometimes even above ground surface, to a level called the **potentiometric** surface.

The ability of an aquifer to transmit groundwater is usually described by its hydraulic properties, hydraulic conductivity, thickness, porosity, transmissivity and storage coefficient. **Porosity** is the total void space within a rock and, therefore, usually defines the total amount of groundwater stored in an aquifer. The **hydraulic conductivity** of a rock (measured in m/day) describes the velocity that groundwater would flow through the rock if there was a pressure gradient of 1 m per metre. **Transmissivity** (measured in m²/day) describes the ability of an aquifer to transmit volumes of groundwater and is calculated by multiplying the hydraulic conductivity by the aquifer thickness. The **storage coefficient** is a truer measure than porosity of the amount of groundwater stored in an aquifer. It is defined as the amount of groundwater released from storage within the aquifer when

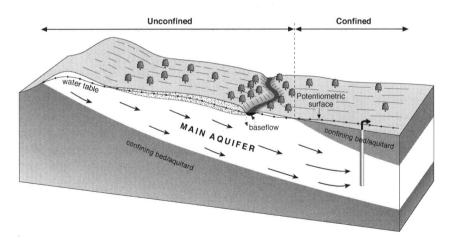

| Figure 2.3 | A basic groundwater system. |

the water table falls by 1 m. Pumping tests are the most common method for measuring hydraulic properties, and give estimates of the storage coefficient and transmissivity (see Chapter 7).

Groundwater has excellent natural microbiological quality and generally adequate chemical quality for most uses. Nine major chemical constituents (sodium, calcium, magnesium, potassium, bicarbonate, chloride, sulphate, nitrate and silicon) make up 99 per cent of the solute content of natural groundwaters. The proportion of these constituents reflects the geology and history of the groundwater. Minor and trace constituents make up the remaining 1 per cent of the total, and their presence (or absence) can occasionally give rise to health problems or make them unacceptable for human or animal use. Much more detailed information on groundwater quality is given in Chapter 8.

There is an ongoing project to provide a simplified hydrogeological map of the world at a scale of 1:25 million (1 cm on the map = 250 km). The project should be completed by 2006 (the web address is given at the end of this chapter). Figure 2.4 is taken from an early version of this map. The world is divided into three types of environment: (1) major aquifers; (2) areas with important by complex aquifers and (3) areas of low permeability with local minor aquifers.

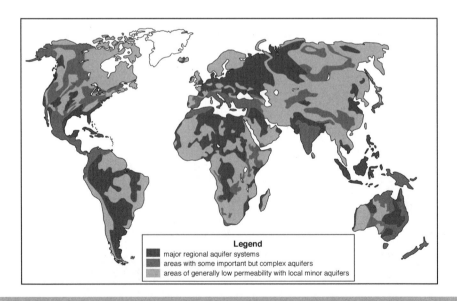

Legend
■ major regional aquifer systems
■ areas with some important but complex aquifers
■ areas of generally low permeability with local minor aquifers

Figure 2.4 Simplified hydrogeological map of the world.
Source: based on Foster and Chilton (2003). Reproduced with permission of the German Federal Institute for Geosciences and Natural Resources BGR, 2003.

2.4 Different hydrogeological environments

2.4.1 Overview

As discussed above, the availability of groundwater depends primarily on the geology. Although almost all geological materials contain some water and many different rocks can form useful aquifers, it is possible to develop a summary of the most common aquifer types and hydrogeological environments (Table 2.2). Such a broad classification inevitably involves some simplifications of the true breadth of subsurface geological variation and complexity: many hundreds of scientific papers have been written on each environment, and some workers have devoted their lives to understanding just one environment. That being said, a brief summary of each environment and subdivision is given below. Figure 2.5 shows the

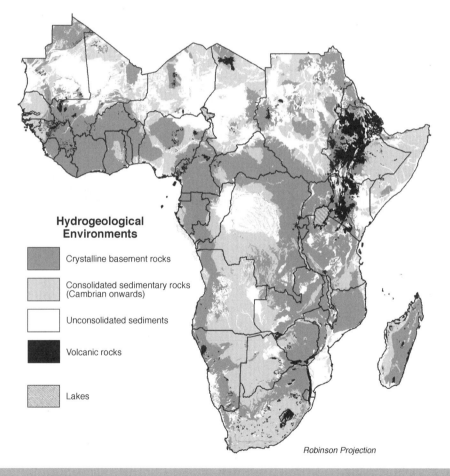

Hydrogeological Environments

- Crystalline basement rocks
- Consolidated sedimentary rocks (Cambrian onwards)
- Unconsolidated sediments
- Volcanic rocks
- Lakes

Robinson Projection

| Figure 2.5 | A simplified hydrogeological map of sub-Saharan Africa. |

Table 2.2 The groundwater potential of the main hydrogeological environments

	Hydrogeological sub-environment	Description	Groundwater potential and average yields (in litres/second)	Groundwater targets
Crystalline basement rocks	Highly weathered and/or fractured basement	Ancient crystalline and metamorphic rocks can be highly fractured. They can also decompose to form a mantle of weathered material tens of metres thick, which can be gravelly and fractured	Moderate 0.1–1	Fractures at the base of the deep weathered zone Vertical fracture zones
	Poorly weathered or sparsely fractured basement	Ancient crystalline and metamorphic rocks, where they have not been weathered or fractured. Groundwater may be very difficult to find	Low 0.1–1	Widely spaced fractures and localized pockets of deep weathering
Consolidated sedimentary rocks	Sandstones	Sands and gravels that have been compacted and are often cemented to form consolidated rocks. The degree of consolidation generally varies with age	Moderate – High 1–20	Coarse porous or fractured sandstone
	Mudstones and shales	Silt and clay that has been consolidated. More consolidated mudstones can be fractured; softer mudstones tend not to be fractured. Often interbedded with sandstone or limestone layers	Low 0–0.5	Hard fractured mudstones Igneous intrusions or thin limestone/sandstone layers
	Limestones	Remains of shell fragments, aquatic skeletons and reefs that were deposited in seas and cemented to form consolidated rocks. These rocks are slightly soluble in rainwater, therefore fractures can be enlarged to form well developed conduits and fracture systems (karst features)	Moderate – high 1–100	Fractures and solution-enhanced fractures (dry valleys)

	Recent coastal and calcareous island formations	Coral limestones and shell banks found in coastal areas and coral islands. Often loosely cemented with high porosity and permeability	High 10–100	Proximity of saline water limits depth of boreholes or galleries. High permeability results in water table being only slightly above sea level
Unconsolidated sediments	Major alluvial and coastal basins	Sands, gravels and clay deposited by major rivers, deltas or in shallow seas. These deposits can be kilometres thick. Sands and gravels have both high porosity and permeability	High 1–40	Sand and gravel layers
	Small dispersed deposits, such as river valley alluvium and coastal dunes deposits	Alluvium is found near many modern-day rivers. Very mixed and can comprise cobbles, gravels, sands, silts clays and mixtures. Coastal deposits are usually sandy due to the high energy environment of deposition	Moderate 1–20	Thicker, well-sorted sandy/gravel deposits Coastal aquifers need to be managed to control saline intrusion
	Loess	Windblown deposits comprising fine sand and silt. Generally has low permeability and is only several metres thick – but can be extensive and thick in some areas (e.g. eastern and central Asia)	Low – Moderate 0.1–1	Areas where the loess is thick and saturated, or drains down to a more permeable receiving bed
	Valley deposits in mountain areas	In mountainous areas valley sides and bottoms can be filled with poorly sorted rock fragments, sands gravels and cobbles. Where the mountains are (or have been) volcanic, they can also contain ashes and volcanic debris, ashes and lava flows	Moderate – High 1–10	Stable areas of sand and gravel; river-reworked volcanic rocks; blocky lava flows

Table 2.2 —*cont.*

	Hydrogeological Sub-Environment	Description	Groundwater potential and average yields (in litres/second)	Groundwater targets
Volcanic Rocks	Extensive volcanic terrains	Lava flows from volcanoes which can form extensive plateaus, sometimes dissected to form mountainous terrains. Often volcanic terrains are made up of layers of lava and pyroclastic rocks (volcanic material, commonly ash, which is blown into the atmosphere by explosive volcanic activity). Can form complex multilayered aquifers	Low – High Lavas 0.1–100 Ashes and pyroclastic rocks 0.5–5	Generally little porosity or permeability within the lava flows, but the edges and flow tops/bottom can be rubbly and fractured; flow tubes can also be fractured Ashes are generally poorly permeable but have high storage and can drain water into underlying layers

distribution of these hydrogeological environments across sub-Saharan Africa.

2.4.2 Crystalline basement rocks

Precambrian crystalline basement rocks are present over large parts of Africa and Asia. They comprise ancient igneous and metamorphic rocks over 550 million years old. Unweathered basement rock contains negligible groundwater, but significant aquifers develop within the weathered overburden and fractured bedrock (Wright and Burgess 1992).

Because these ancient rocks occupy stable continental shield areas, there has been plenty of opportunity for prolonged periods of weathering, and the zone of weathering tends to be better developed and thicker in tropical regions where such processes are more active. As a result, the weathered zone can be as much as 60 m thick, but more commonly in the range of 20–30 m. Below this zone the rock becomes progressively less weathered and more consolidated until fresh fractured bedrock is reached (see Figure 2.6). Porosity generally decreases with depth; permeability, however, has a more complicated relationship, depending on the extent of fracturing and the clay content (see Figure 2.7). In the soil zone, permeability is usually high, but groundwater does not exist throughout the year and dries out soon after the rains end. Beneath the soil zone, the rock is often highly weathered and clay rich, so permeability is low. Towards the base of the weathered zone, near the fresh rock interface, the proportion of clay significantly reduces. This horizon, which consists of fractured rock, is often permeable, allowing water to move freely.

Deeper fractures within the basement rocks are also an important source of groundwater, particularly where the weathered zone is thin or absent. These deep fractures are tectonically controlled and can sometimes provide

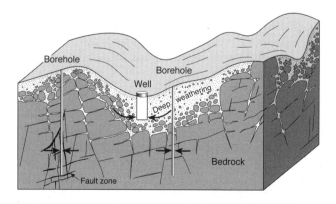

Figure 2.6 How groundwater occurs in weathered basement.

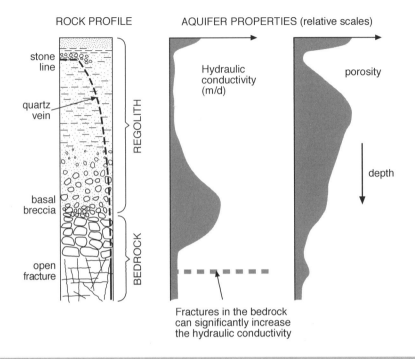

ROCK PROFILE   AQUIFER PROPERTIES (relative scales)

Figure 2.7 Porosity and permeability variations with depth in weathered basement.
Source: Chilton and Foster 1995.

from basement rocks and deposited in valleys as alluvium can also be important sources of groundwater; these are discussed in section 2.4.4.

2.4.3 Consolidated sedimentary aquifers

Sedimentary rocks comprise sandstone, limestone, siltstone and mudstone: rocks formed from fragments of pre-existing material (see Box 2.1). The most prolific aquifers are found within sandstones and limestones. Mudstones are the least productive group and unfortunately make up more than half of all sedimentary rocks. Figure 2.8 summarizes how groundwater can occur in sedimentary areas.

Younger **sandstones** usually retain a primary porosity (the pore spaces between sand grains). These rocks contain large resources of groundwater and also allow groundwater to move easily throughout the rocks – they are excellent aquifers. In older, more-cemented formations, the primary porosity is highly variable and, depending on the degree of cementation, may not exist at all. In these cases it is the secondary (fracture) porosity which provides the aquifer permeability and storage and groundwater occurs in a similar way to crystalline basement rocks. Sandstone aquifers are important sources of water in Western Europe and North America, in North Africa (the Nubian sandstone), Southern Africa (the Karroo

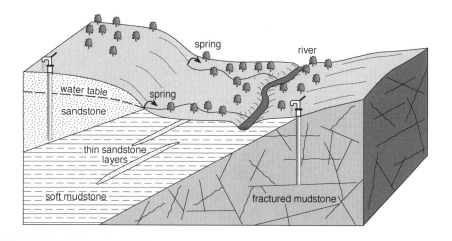

Figure 2.8 How groundwater occurs in sedimentary areas.

sandstone), in northern India (Tertiary sandstones), in South America (the Guarani complex) and in Australia (the Great Artesian Basin).

Limestones are widespread and can be prolific aquifers. They are particularly important in China where they cover an area of 2.2 million km². Limestones generally have little usable primary porosity, and water is stored and transmitted in fractures. Because they are soluble, many of the fractures are enlarged by dissolution to form conduits centimetres or even metres across (see Figure 2.9). This is usually called **karst**. Karst limestones are unpredictable environments to work in. Boreholes drilled several metres apart may have very different yields. Also borehole yields can vary considerably throughout the year. Large springs are common in karst limestone environments.

Although **mudstone** and siltstone are poor aquifers, small amounts of groundwater can often be found in these environments with careful exploration (see Figure 2.10). Mudstones are clays that have become consolidated through compaction and heating. The pore spaces are too small for water to move through easily, so usable groundwater is only found in fractures. In soft mudstones there are no open fractures, and groundwater can only be found if there are thin interlayers of sandstone or limestone. Where the mudstone is slightly harder, fractures can remain open and usable groundwater resources exist. Mudstones are the most common sedimentary rock and are found throughout the world.

Recent coastal calcareous formations are important local aquifers in several parts of the world, including Jamaica, Cuba, Hispaniola and numerous other islands in the Caribbean; the Yucatán peninsula of México; the Cebu limestone of the Philippines; and the Jaffna limestone in Sri

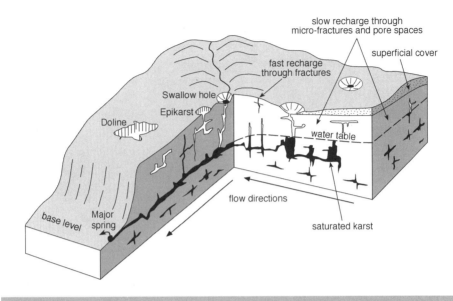

Figure 2.9 A cross section through groundwater flow in karst limestones.

Lanka. They provide important sources of potable water for the people living there and for irrigation. These highly porous formations are made up of weakly cemented shelly limestones and sandstones. They can also be fractured and karstic. Groundwater flow in these environments is rapid, and infiltration can be so high that there are few streams or rivers. Since they are found next to the sea, the intrusion of saline water into the aquifer is a constant problem.

2.4.4 Unconsolidated sedimentary aquifers

Unconsolidated sediments are deposited in different environments such as rivers and deltas by various combinations of physical processes. The sediments are all relatively young and as the name suggests, the material is still loose and groundwater is stored and transmitted through pore spaces, not fractures. They comprise a range of materials, from coarse gravel and sand to silt and clay. At one end of the scale are extensive sequences of coastal, river and deltaic alluvium, sometimes hundreds of metres or even kilometres thick. At the other end of the scale can be a thin covering of alluvium next to a small river.

Major alluvial and coastal basin sediments form some of the most important aquifers in the world, in which very large volumes of groundwater are stored and from which large quantities of water are pumped for water supply and irrigation. Examples include the Lower Indus, Ganges–Brahmaputra, Mekong, Tigris–Euphrates and Nile valleys. Aquifers in

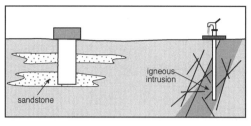

In soft, sticky mudstones there is no usable water within the clay. The only water in these areas is found in thin sandstone layers or small igneous intrusions

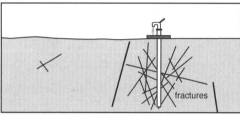

If the mudstone has been buried and altered to become slightly harder, usable groundwater can be found in large fractures and faults. Faults and fractures however, may be far apart.

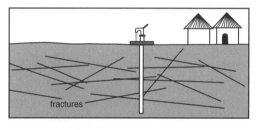

Where mudstones have been altered to comprise hard shales, fractures are widespread and groundwater is easily found.

Figure 2.10 Groundwater occurrence in mudstones.
Source: MacDonald et al. 2005.

unconsolidated strata are rarely simple homogeneous systems but typically consist of alternating permeable layers of productive sands and gravels separated by less permeable aquitard layers of clay and silt, reflecting the complex history of deposition (Figure 2.11). In such sequences, the shallow aquifers are the easiest and cheapest to exploit, but are likely to be the most vulnerable to pollution. The presence of aquitards may produce complex groundwater flow patterns, but the permeable horizons may still have a degree of hydraulic continuity, such that pumping from one layer will affect the others, producing significant vertical head gradients and consequent leakage. Deeper groundwater in thick alluvial sequences is derived from recharge several hundred to several thousand years ago, and the term **fossil** has sometimes been used to describe deep, old groundwater.

Small **riverside alluvium and other deposits** can form locally important aquifers. Shallow floodplains, less than 100 m wide and with less than 10 m thickness of sediments can be a valuable resource, particularly where the underlying bedrock has little potential for groundwater (Carter and Alkali 1996). In these deposits groundwater is close to the surface, so pumping lifts are small; also, the proximity to the rivers offers a reliable source of recharge

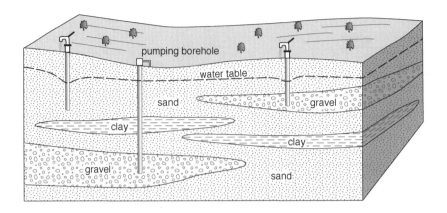

| Figure 2.11 | Groundwater occurrence in major alluvial basins. |

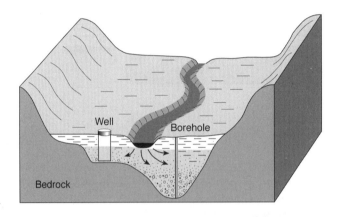

| Figure 2.12 | Groundwater occurrence in riverside alluvium. |

(Figure 2.12). In southern Africa, sand-rivers are important sources of water for domestic use and stock watering. These rivers rarely contain surface water, but the thick sediment within the river channel can contain significant quantities of groundwater. Deposits from glaciers and glacial streams can form important aquifers at altitude in mountain ranges of the Andes and Himalayas. Ice-transported sediments are commonly unsorted mixtures of all grain sizes from clay to boulders, and they typically have low permeabilities, acting as aquitards/aquicludes. In contrast, water-sorted sediments, laid down from glacial meltwaters, often comprise sands and gravels and form highly productive aquifers.

Sediments which infill the troughs in mountain regions are known as **intermontaine deposits**. Interlayering with volcanic ashes and lavas may also occur, often with reworking of erupted material. There are numerous examples of these systems in Central America (such as the aquifers that underlie Mexico City, Chihuahua, León and Guatemala City), and beneath Kathmandu (Nepal) and Sana'a (Yemen). Aquifer permeability and porosity are generally high, but variable. The deposits are recharged both from rainfall and surface water flowing down from the surrounding mountains. The interlayering of volcanic and sedimentary rocks can also generate productive spring systems, and occurs widely at sandstone/lava junctions in the Rift Valley basalts of Ethiopia.

Fine windblown deposits, called **loess**, can form important aquifers. Although loess is found elsewhere, such as in Argentina and north of the Black Sea, thick deposits are almost entirely restricted to north central China where they cover an area in excess of $600\,000\,km^2$ and can be between 100 and 300 m thick. Loess deposits comprise fine round sand and silt grains, usually uniformly deposited. The distinctive geomorphological features and geological characteristics produce a complex groundwater system. The loessic plateau aquifers are frequently cut through by gullies and ravines, so that the plateaux form a series of independent water circulation systems.

2.4.5 Volcanic terrains

The groundwater potential of volcanic rocks varies considerably, reflecting the complexity of the geology. Individual lava flows can be up to 100 m thick, and although the more massive flows are often impermeable, extensive jointing can allow water to infiltrate and move through them (see Figure 2.13). The junctions between flows can form highly productive aquifers: cracks and joints develop as the lava cools rapidly; also rubble zones often develop as a new lava flow covers the rough weathered surface of an existing flow and the base of the flow cools rapidly. Where they exist, flow tubes in the lava can be targeted for groundwater supplies. Flow tubes are often highly fractured and contain rubbly lava.

Other volcanic materials are thrown out as volcanic clouds, which sometimes settle as ash deposits or become welded tuffs. The mineralogy and chemistry of the volcanic rocks and their viscosity and gas content determine the precise nature of the volcanic eruptions and resulting rocks. Alternating sequences of ashes and lavas, in which the lavas act as conduits for groundwater flow and the intervening ashes provide the storage, characterize the important aquifer systems of Costa Rica, Nicaragua and El Salvador.

The main targets for groundwater development in volcanic rocks are (Kehinde and Loehnert 1989):

- thick paleosoils or loose pyroclastic material between lava flows
- joints and fractures due to the rapid cooling of the tops of lava flows
- contact between lava flows and sedimentary rocks or earlier volcanic material
- lava flows with significant gas bubbles, and porosity within ashes and agglomerates.

One of the largest and most important areas of volcanic lava flows occurs in the central and western parts of India, where the Deccan basalts cover more than $500\,000\,km^2$ (Kulkarni *et al.* 2000). Other extensive volcanic terrains occur in North and Central America and East Africa, and many islands are entirely or predominantly of volcanic origin, such as some of the Caribbean islands.

2.5 Accessing groundwater

There are many different ways of accessing groundwater – from tapping water from springs to drilling deep boreholes, or even horizontal boreholes. In many cases, the methods used to access groundwater depend on the nature of the resource itself; for example shallow hand-dug wells cannot readily be used to access groundwater that is 50 m below the ground surface. However, in some hydrogeological environments, different methods can be

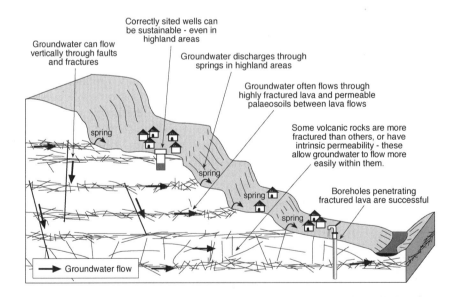

Figure 2.13 Schematic of how groundwater can exist in upland volcanic terrains.

used, and in those cases other factors, such as cost or community wishes can be given a higher priority.

Below we describe some of the many methods used to access groundwater – some of them are not now used very often. The three most common are boreholes, hand-dug wells, and springs. Pumping methods are not described – there are several other manuals and resources which go into detail about pumps.

2.5.1 Springs

A spring is a place where groundwater flows naturally from the rock or the soil onto the land surface; it is essentially an overflow from the aquifer. No equipment is required to make a spring – it is there already. Springs are dependent on the nature and relationship of rocks, especially the layering of permeable and impermeable rocks, the presence of faults, the position of the water table and changes in slope (see Chapter 6 for more details on springs). The yield of springs also varies enormously, from mere seepages of less than 0.1 l/s to huge flows of thousands of litres per second.

Springs can be highly vulnerable to contamination (particularly from activity around the spring itself) and susceptible to drought or even several months with no rainfall. To try to protect the spring, and maximize the yield from it, a collection chamber can be built away from the eye of the spring and the water collected from a controlled tap (see Figure 2.14).

2.5.2 Hand-dug wells

Wells have been dug to access groundwater for millennia. Wells are dug by hand, and therefore need to be constructed in soft material, such as weathered basement, sands and gravels, or limestone and chalk. They are generally less than 20 m deep and 1–2 m in diameter, although there are several instances of wells more than 100 m deep or with a diameter of more than 4 m. Little or no specialized equipment is required to construct a well – just something to dig with, and a way of getting the spoil out of the well. Wells often need to be lined to keep them open. Bricks, stones, concrete

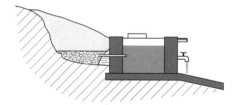

| Figure 2.14 | Improved spring. |

rings, steel and even tractor tyres have all been used as lining materials. Like springs, hand-dug-wells are vulnerable to contamination from activity around the top of the well. In an attempt to minimize this, hand-dug wells are generally improved by installing a concrete apron around the top (Figure 2.15).

The main advantage of a well is its large storage. A well that is 10 m deep and 1.5 m in diameter has over 17 m³ of storage space (although generally less than half of this will be used, because of the depth of the water table). The large storage allows water to accumulate overnight (while the well is not in use) to be emptied in the morning at a time of high demand. In this way wells can be successful even in weakly permeable aquifers.

A well is fairly susceptible to drought, and can also dry up towards the end of a normal dry season. There are three main reasons for this:

- they often tap only shallow groundwater
- they are often located in poorly permeable aquifers which don't allow the well to recover completely when demand is high
- hand digging often only allows penetration to previous drought-time water levels, unlike a borehole which can go deeper.

2.5.3 Boreholes

A borehole is a narrow-diameter tube drilled into the ground at a controlled angle (usually vertical). This is the most common type of water source used on rural water supply projects. Boreholes started to be constructed in earnest with the invention in the nineteenth century of the steam-driven

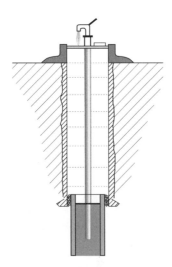

| Figure 2.15 | Improved large-diameter well. |

drilling machine. Nowadays, powerful diesel-driven rigs are used to construct boreholes, although in some places hand drilling can be effective (see Chapter 6). Boreholes for rural water supply are generally drilled to a depth of between 20 and 100 m, although in some situations where the aquifers are very shallow or very deep they can lie outside this range. They are often between 100 and 300 mm in diameter. In Asia they are often referred to as **tube wells**, and by Americans just as **wells**.

Boreholes have several advantages:

- they are quick to construct, if the right equipment is available
- they can be drilled deep and can therefore tap deeper, often more sustainable, groundwater
- they can be drilled in very hard rock
- effective sanitary seals can easily be constructed.

However, borehole drilling is expensive, and requires a specialized drilling rig, which is expensive to maintain and run. A well-trained crew is required to drill boreholes and it is difficult to involve communities directly in the process.

A borehole is partially or fully lined with casing to keep it from collapsing (see Figure 2.16). At the water-bearing horizons, perforated casing is used to allow the water to flow into the borehole. Since a borehole is narrow in diameter, pumps are required to abstract the water – a bucket is too big to fit down. These pumps require maintenance and can break down if

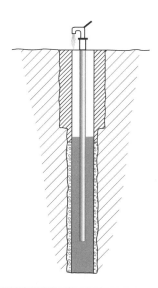

| Figure 2.16 | Cross-section through a typical borehole. |

inappropriate for the job, ill-used or incorrectly installed. There are many different designs of hand pumps, each with different qualities and strengths.

2.5.4 Collector wells

A collector well (or Ranney well as it is sometimes known) is a well that has been modified by drilling horizontal boreholes radially below the water table (Figure 2.17). Collector wells are most often constructed in alluvium or weathered basement. In alluvium they are located next to rivers (or sand rivers) and radials drilled under the river to tap water from the stream. Where constructed within weathered basement, radials are drilled out into the weathered zone to increase the seepage area from the base of the weathered zone and increase the chance of intersecting a vertical fracture. Collector wells have proved more drought resistant than unmodified hand-dug wells or individual boreholes.

To construct a collector well, a central shaft is first constructed and lined with concrete rings, brick or corrugated steel. The radial perforated pipes are drilled or jacked hydraulically into the formation. Fine material around the pipes is removed by washing during construction. This is a sophisticated and expensive method of well construction, requiring the use of specialist machinery, and is not in widespread use. The method combines the attributes of infiltration galleries with the storage characteristics of hand-dug wells. Such systems have been installed in Zimbabwe, Malawi, Sri Lanka and Botswana.

2.5.5 Qanat

A qanat (foggara, karez or kanat) is an ancient, sophisticated way of abstracting groundwater and transporting it to the point of demand. They are still used today in Oman, Yemen, Afghanistan and Iran. A qanat comprises a mother well, usually in alluvial deposits at the edge of a mountain, and a

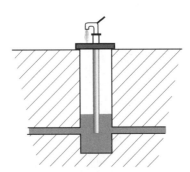

Figure 2.17 Collector well.

gently inclined underground channel which allows the groundwater to flow downhill from the edge of the mountains to the village area for both domestic and irrigation (see Figure 2.18). Since the channel is covered, evaporation is minimized. Construction of a qanat involves the combined excavation (often by hand) of horizontal tunnels (or galleries) and vertical shafts.

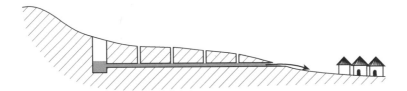

Figure 2.18   Cross section of a qanat.

2.5.6 Infiltration gallery

An infiltration gallery is a horizontal drain constructed to abstract shallow groundwater. They are particularly useful for abstracting water from alluvium, windblown deposits or sand rivers. They are simply constructed by excavating a trench to 2–3 m below the dry season water table. To do this, the sides may have to be shored up with timber and a dewatering system installed. Plastic drainage pipe is then put in the trench and surrounded by a washed gravel, before backfilling the trench. A sump is then located at either end of the trench from which the water is pumped (see Figure 2.19).

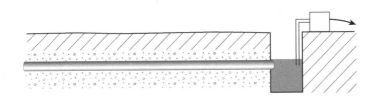

Figure 2.19   Infiltration gallery.

References, further reading and resources

Carter, R.C. and Alkali, A.G. (1996) Shallow groundwater in the northeast arid zone of Nigeria. *Quarterly Journal of Engineering Geology*, **29**, 341–356.

Chilton, P.J. and Foster, S.S.D. (1995) Hydrogeological characterisation and water-supply potential of basement aquifers in tropical Africa. *Hydrogeology Journal*, **3**, 36–49.

Fetter, C.W. (2001) *Applied hydrogeology* (4th edition). Prentice-Hall, Englewood Cliffs, NJ. One of the best-selling textbooks on groundwater and hydrogeology – aimed at university students.

Foster, S.S.D. and Chilton, P.J. (2003) Groundwater: the process and global significance of aquifer degradation. *Philosophical Transactions of the Royal Society of London* B, **358**, 1957–1972.

Freeze, R.A. and Cherry, J.A. (1979) *Groundwater.* Prentice-Hall, Englewood Cliffs, NJ. Despite its age, still an excellent overview of the science of groundwater – aimed at university students.

Kehinde, M.O. and Loehnert, E.P. (1989) Review of African groundwater resources. *Journal of African Earth Sciences*, **9**, 179–185.

Kulkarni, H., Deolankar, S.B., Lalwani, A., Josep, B. and Pawar, S. (2000) Hydrogeological framework of the Deccan basalt groundwater systems, west-central India. *Hydrogeology Journal*, **8**, 368–378.

MacDonald, A.M., Kemp, S.J. and Davies, J. (2005) Transmissivity variations in mudstones. *Ground Water*, **43**, 259–269.

Morris, B.L., Lawrence, A.R., Chilton, P.J., Adams, B., Calow, R.C. and Klinck, B.A. (2003) Groundwater and its susceptibility to degradations: a global assessment of the problem and options for management. Early warning and assessment report series, RS. 03–3. United Nations Environment Programme, Nairobi, Kenya.

Price, M. (1996) *Introducing groundwater* (2nd edition). Chapman & Hall, London. A good all-round introduction to groundwater, readable and accessible.

USGS Publications http://water.usgs.gov/pubs

WHYMAP http://www.iah.org/whymap/ Information about the World Hydrogeological Mapping and Assessment Programme. including the world hydrogeological map.

Wright, E.P. and Burgess, W.G. (eds) 1992. *The hydrogeology of crystalline basement aquifers in Africa.* Special Publication No. 66, Geological Society, London.

3 Projects and communities

3.1 Introduction

The aim of this chapter is to review the wider context in which groundwater development for rural water supply fits. The discussion is pitched at the manager, or team leader, of a rural water supply project. The project manager has a vital role to play in ensuring the success of any rural water supply investment. While the manager may not be involved in the day-to-day detail of community–project interaction, s/he is responsible for setting the terms of reference for such interaction, within the broader framework of rural water supply objectives, standards and policies set by government.

More specifically, the aims of this chapter are to:

- Summarize **where we are now** in terms of approaches to rural water supply provision, highlighting some basic concepts and principles that underpin the design and implementation of projects. In particular, the need for community participation in decision-making about service provision and management is highlighted, reflecting a shift in emphasis away from top-down planning to a more **demand-responsive** approach.
- Locate groundwater development for rural water supply within the broader project cycle, recognizing that current approaches to service provision do not prescribe options and service levels for communities, but rather promote **informed choices**. In other words, groundwater supply from wells or boreholes may be one of a number of supply options that need to be discussed with communities, along with levels of service, the location of water points, management and cost-sharing arrangements. For this reason we do not limit discussion in this chapter to groundwater development only.
- Explore the role of the project manager in strategy development – a key management responsibility and an essential starting point for project design. By strategy development, we mean a strategy for the project. This will be guided by wider government policies but the project manager is likely to have some flexibility in deciding how a project is to be implemented according to local conditions, within the **enabling framework** set by government.

Discuss the implications of more participatory approaches to service provision for the project team, focusing particularly on the changing role of the project engineer, or technician.

Before proceeding, it is important to note that this chapter provides a **summary** of rural water supply issues and guidance for the project manager, rather than detailed insights or an implementation roadmap. A comprehensive discussion covering the topics raised here could easily run to several hundred pages, and is beyond the scope of this book. Suggestions for further reading are provided at the end of the chapter.

3.2 Basic principles and concepts in rural water supply

3.2.1 What is rural water supply?

Investment in rural water supply is about providing communities with access to clean, reliable water supplies. Water for drinking, cooking and basic hygiene is normally the top priority, though a household's 'domestic' needs may also include water for minor productive uses, such as brick-making, garden irrigation and livestock watering. A key objective is the provision of potable water on a **continuous** basis: security of supply across seasons, and between wet and dry years, is essential if health and wider poverty alleviation benefits are to be met and sustained. Most countries have developed water supply targets, based on coverage and quantity–quality norms. Most projects, operating within such guidelines, are tasked with meeting these targets.

3.2.2 The benefits of improved rural water supply

Rural communities typically place a high priority on improved water supply. This is because access to safe water is fundamental to health and poverty reduction.

The direct health benefits of improved rural water supply, especially when integrated with sanitation initiatives, are well known. They derive mainly from the safe disposal of human excreta, the effective use of water for hygiene purposes (washing, cleaning, etc.), and the satisfaction of basic drinking needs with clean water. However, the full range of health benefits may only be realized through intensive community sensitization campaigns around water, sanitation and health. Unlike demand for a better water supply, demand for improved sanitation facilities is often weak or non-existent. It may therefore need to be stimulated before it can be responded to.

More recently, greater attention has been paid to the broader **livelihood** benefits of rural water supply, looking beyond direct links between improved water supplies and public health (UNICEF 1999; Nicol 2000; Calow et al. 2002; Moriarty and Butterworth 2003). A focus on the multiple uses and benefits of domestic water supplies (see Box 3.1) has important implications for the way projects are conceived, designed and implemented. Water may

BOX 3.1 Beyond basic needs: the wider benefits of improved rural water supply

The benefits of improved water supplies can extend well beyond links with health. An impact assessment exercise carried out by the NGO WaterAid to establish the long-term effects of water supply interventions in Ghana, Ethiopia, Tanzania and India highlighted the following:

Direct benefits – relatively quick changes at individual-household level

■ Time and energy savings, particularly for women and children. Savings can be 'invested' in new income-earning opportunities; school enrolment and attendance – particularly for girls – increases.
■ Reduced sickness especially among children, reduced expenditure on medicines and care and increases in the number of working days.
■ Expenditure savings – because of reduced expenditure on more expensive water from vendors, for example.

Indirect benefits – longer term, more diffuse

■ Development and diversification of the local economy as productive water use increases (e.g. for brick-making, tea shops), and money/time is invested in industrial and service enterprises.
■ Development of management and negotiation skills in village communities which can be deployed in other areas. Particularly important where decentralization policies are placing new demands on local institutions.
■ Household and community empowerment through taking control of important decisions relating to the selection and management of water systems.
■ Improved food security and greater resilience to shocks such as drought.

Source: WaterAid (2001); (2004)

be used in a variety of productive uses, generating important sources of income (cash and non-cash) for households. Productive uses may include cultivation (e.g. small garden irrigation of vegetables), livestock watering (chickens, goats, cattle), cottage industries (e.g. brewing, brick-making) and services (e.g. tea shops). Ignoring such uses during project design (by assuming demand is for basic needs only, for example) may result in the well or borehole being unable to meet demand in terms of the quantity, reliability and location of water needed for different uses. Exploring how water is used (or could be used) by the community, and by different households **within** the community, is therefore essential.

Of course an improved water supply does not automatically lead to poverty alleviation. In order to maximize water-related benefits, interventions in other areas or sectors may be required. For example, an improved water supply combined with microenterprise development may enable women to use time savings to their best advantage, creating new sources of income for the household. Conversely, projects in non-water sectors may only fulfil their objectives with complementary investment in rural water supply. Research on drought and water security in Ethiopia, for example, has shown how food and water security are intimately linked. Water supply interventions – rehabilitation, repair, well deepening and so on – coordinated with food security/asset rebuilding efforts, can help sustain income, production and consumption in the early stages of drought, or in the aftermath of a bad year (Calow et al. 1997; DFID 2001; Calow et al. 2002).

3.2.3 The need for multidisciplinary approaches

Successful and sustainable rural water supply projects require both good technical design and installation, **and** substantial investment in community sensitization, mobilization and participation. Ignoring either technical or social factors will compromise the sustainability of the water supply. If communities do not regard the system as theirs, and management and cost-sharing arrangements are not adequately dealt with, the system is more likely to fail. If a well or borehole is poorly constructed, or developed and sited with little regard to the geology beneath, the chances of mechanical breakdown or the source drying up will also increase.

Yet discussion around sustainability is often polarized. In the past it was often true that technical considerations dominated in many projects: engineers were trained to take important decisions on behalf of communities, using their knowledge to decide what was in a community's best interests. Consultation, if there was any, was often token – communities effectively rubber-stamped the decisions of sector professionals. A welcome retreat from this position, however, has not always led to more balanced approaches. Those who now maintain that technical and environmental issues are unimportant, and that sustainability is determined only by the quality of project 'software' are equally misguided. The key to good project design lies in recognizing the multiple dimensions of sustainability, not in engineering **or** social dogma. Box 3.2 gives examples of two projects where the environmental dimensions of sustainability were important.

3.2.4 From community participation to community management

The need for community participation in the planning and implementation of rural water supply projects became increasingly apparent in the 1980s. Governments and donors realized that that they could no longer afford centralized operation and maintenance systems, and that existing top-down approaches were not creating sustainable water supply systems. As a consequence, the idea that beneficiaries, or users, needed to be involved with

BOX 3.2 The technical and environmental dimensions of sustainability are important

In a project in West Africa, the water supply choices offered to communities by an international NGO were predetermined according to social criteria. Since the construction of shallow, hand-dug wells offered more scope for community involvement and payment in kind (labour and materials), only this option was pursued. By the dry season, however, most of the wells had dried up, leaving communities reliant on the distant, poorer-quality sources they used before.

Lessons? Shallow wells in this hydrogeological environment were inappropriate. By ignoring the technical and environmental dimension of sustainability, the programme failed to achieve its objectives and investment in community mobilization and participation was undermined. In these circumstances, it will be more difficult to win community support for follow-up projects based on community management and cost-sharing.

An international donor funded a major rural water supply programme aimed at bringing potable water to isolated rural communities in East Africa. Only one technical package was considered – hand-dug wells equipped with a certain type of handpump – and then implemented across a diverse range of hydrogeological environments. This was because of a decision taken centrally to promote the package on health grounds: sealed systems were thought to lower the risk of well-head contamination. Within a few years, however, most of the pumps had broken, and communities had become disillusioned with a cycle of breakage and temporary repair (see Figure 3.2).

Lessons? In this case an option was fixed centrally and implemented according to a standard design across different geological areas. These particular pumps broke because they were inappropriate for the shallow lift required from the hand-dug well. By not allowing flexibility in design related to local hydrogeology, people living in a drought-prone area were left with no improved water supplies at all, and a wider legacy of frustration with community-based management.

the ongoing **maintenance** of systems began to be more widely discussed. Hence, ideas about community participation were initially fairly restricted: most attention was focused on trying to get communities to raise funds to help with the upkeep of their water systems.

Community **management** in rural water supply, however, goes some way beyond participation (see Box 3.3). There is no fixed definition or simple formula, but a key feature is the nature and breadth of decision-making, and the responsibility for executing those decisions being more with the community. Community management, as opposed to **participation**, therefore implies (after UNICEF 1999):

- The community has legitimate authority and effective control over management of the water supply system and over the use of water.

Figure 3.1 Women and girls bear the brunt of water carrying in Africa and Asia. Photo: © Selina Sugden.

- The community commits resources towards both the implementation and upkeep of the system(s).
- Supporting agencies provide advice and technical support, but key decisions about participation in a project, and about the type, level and location of services, are made **with** the community – i.e. with the community rather than by the community or project team alone. Decisions need to be informed by an understanding of technical, environmental and other constraints. Projects and other supporting agencies have a vital role to play in this respect, providing information and screening options.
- Development of people – individual and community empowerment – is a parallel goal. Community management is people-centred: the principal concern is with people's livelihoods, not the resources they use or the technologies employed.

Despite its obvious appeal, however, community management is more complex than might first appear. Community decision-making, for example, does not always reflect the interests of poorer, more marginalized groups; hence community management does not, in itself, guarantee that the needs of all households are met. Why is this so? A key point is that communities

Figure 3.2   Collecting water from the side of a hand-dug well because the sealed pump is broken. Photo: BGS, © NERC 1999.

BOX 3.3   Lessons from successful community management

A study of 122 completed rural water supply projects from around the developing world studied the factors within projects that helped successfully increase the level of participation and community management. These are the factors they found most important:

- The development of clear project goals, strategies and rules, based on a consensus of agency (government, NGO) and community views.
- The development of flexible project strategies, with a high degree of decentralized control and decision-making powers.
- Strong commitment by project managers to a more participatory planning process, and willingness to respond positively to both community views, and the views of field staff.
- Extensive use of local knowledge, and extensive forms of local organization.
- Project approaches which fit comfortably into existing social and cultural contexts.
- A wider (higher level) framework of policies, institutions and laws that promotes popular participation and control.

Sources: Evans and Appleton (1993); UNICEF (1999)

are not homogeneous, in terms of the interests, expectations and power of different individuals to influence community decisions. Care therefore needs to be taken to ensure that the needs of all groups – especially women, children and the poor who may have little or no community voice – are factored into decisions on service provision. A project has an important role to play here in making sure that these voices are heard.

3.2.5 Decentralization and service delivery

The reliability and sustainability of community-based systems depends on a series of technical, financial and management support networks, all of which operate within a policy and legal framework. Understanding this framework, and the roles and responsibilities of different stakeholders in the delivery of rural water supply, will help the project manager design and oversee interventions that have the greatest chance of sustainable service delivery.

In many countries this framework has undergone, or is undergoing, major change. In particular, decentralization policies have devolved decision-making powers to lower levels of administration and the state has shed some of its responsibilities. In the rural water sector, partnership arrangements between government departments, the private sector, community-based organizations and NGOs have become common. The precise nature of these arrangements, and the responsibilities of different groups, are not always clear. However, some general trends and relationships can be identified (World Bank-BNWP 2002):

- **National agencies**, such as government ministries, are increasingly acting as advisers, facilitators and trainers to local governments and, sometimes, communities themselves. In addition, national agencies are generally responsible for devising the broad policy framework for rural water supply, defining targets, the process for reaching them, and the roles and responsibilities of different actors. National agencies may also define quality norms, procurement standards and, possibly, training programmes for equipment and service suppliers.
- **Local government**, usually at the regional or district level, may provide more direct support to local communities in planning, procurement of equipment and services, and training. In some cases, local government may do this directly, on behalf of communities or groups of communities within a project or programme area.
- **Communities**, under community-based, demand-led policies, become the owners of water supply infrastructure, with responsibilities that may include the procurement of equipment and services, and the setting and collection of user fees for (at least) operation and maintenance. The objective is financial sustainability. Also, communities themselves take on a responsibility for articulating demand for improved rural water supply in the first place – usually with some assistance (see below).

■ The **private sector** is increasingly seen as the community client: contracted by communities, local government or a project on their behalf, to provide a range of support services for rural water supply. These may include the supply of equipment and spare parts, well or borehole siting, drilling, operation and maintenance and organizational support and training. In many countries, however, this remains a goal rather than a reality. Support services are more frequently provided directly by projects and/or government agencies.

3.2.6 Water as a social and economic good

Many of the current changes in approaches to the delivery of rural water supply services suggested above derive from a change in thinking about the nature of water. In the past, many viewed water as a social good only. As the social value of extending services was assumed to be always higher than the cost of provision, the emphasis was on extending coverage, meeting prescribed needs (based on a minimum level of service) and government provision as a public good. Governments often assumed that communities would manage their facilities, once installed, without building capacity or commitment to do so.

During the 1990s, a new global consensus emerged around water as **both** a social and an economic good. Water should be treated as an economic good, so the argument goes, because it has a value. Some uses are valued more highly than others, and some communities value the provision of rural water supply more highly than other communities. Therefore, it makes sense to give priority to investments in these communities, on the basis that **an expression of demand is an expression of value**. Allowing communities to self-select for projects, under widely understood rules, is one of the underlying principles of the demand-responsive approach outlined below.

3.2.7 Demand-responsive approach

Drawing on the above, a demand-responsive approach to rural water supply allows consumer demand to guide key investment decisions. In other words, a project is more or less demand responsive to the degree that users make choices and commit resources to support these choices. The approach has gained widespread and rapid acceptance (albeit with some caveats – see below) on the basis that

> water supply services which are more demand responsive are more likely to be sustainable at the community level than services which are less demand-responsive (Sara and Katz 1997).

Box 3.4 summarizes some of the issues.

The approach is based on three underlying principles:

BOX 3.4 How do we know if a project is demand-driven?

The term **demand-responsive approach** is now used almost routinely in many countries. But is it being seriously devalued through overuse and vagueness? And is it being used to add credibility to policies and projects which are not demand responsive at all? The answer is, almost certainly, yes.

A key point is that all projects (or programmes, or activities) are to some degree demand-driven. Whether a project is supply or demand-driven is relative, not absolute. However, the degree to which it is demand-driven depends on **who makes the decisions** about the type and level of service, and **what range of decisions** the users make, instead of having decisions made on their behalf. A project is therefore likely to be more demand-orientated if:

- the decision to participate is made locally rather than through an external determination of need
- decisions about which type and level of service to build, and over what time period, are based on user preferences
- negotiated arrangements for cost-sharing are reached locally, again based on user preferences and ability to pay (but bearing in mind there is no magic ratio for cost-sharing).

More detailed indicators of demand which can be used to assess whether a project is responding to (and meeting) demand throughout the project cycle are outlined in Box 3.7.

- Firstly, **prioritization**. In terms of which communities should receive services first, priority is given to those communities that are actively seeking improvements to their water services. Demand can be expressed in a number of different ways, and different indicators or demonstrations of demand can be used to establish a community's commitment to a project, from initial selection for support onwards (see Box 3.7).
- Secondly, **willingness to pay**, based on the link between the type and level of service people want, and how much they are willing to pay for these services. In other words, people's willingness to pay or contribute in some way to a project is used as a barometer of demand. This contrasts with the 'old' approach to demand assessment based on an assumed level of affordability for narrowly defined water provision.
- Thirdly, the idea of **informed choice**, whereby individuals or groups make decisions about the type, level and location of services (and about how, when and by whom services are delivered and sustained) with a clear understanding of the implications of such decisions. Implications may relate to individual or group responsibilities (e.g. contributions towards capital and/or recurrent costs), expected

participation in planning and implementation, and the expected availability of and access to water. This highlights the need good information and good communication between the project team and community members.

So much for the theory. What about its translation into practice?

The translation process depends crucially on the development of project rules, and on the capacity of rural water supply stakeholders to support and implement them. Rules create the incentives that make a demand-responsive project work as intended, creating a framework through which demand can be expressed and interpreted. They cover areas such as community eligibility to receive support, the selection of service options, cost-sharing arrangements and responsibilities for investment support. When these are unclear, poorly thought through or not widely understood by stakeholders, problems emerge. Some commentators have also raised concerns about the intrinsic weaknesses of using demand to guide project design in the first place (Box 3.5). Key concerns relate to:

- The assumed link between the value of water to users, or an improved water supply to a community, and willingness to pay. Many would argue that willingness to pay depends largely on the ability to pay. Hence, even with the same basic need for or value of water, the rich will get more and the poor less (Perry et al. 1997).
- The capacity to implement the demand-responsive approach, given the speed with which this approach is being scaled up in many countries and the demands it makes on institutions grappling with new mandates.
- The ability of some (perhaps more remote) communities to articulate their demand for improved services in the first place and, once a community is selected, the ability of poorer households within it to express their particular needs.
- Related to this, underlying assumptions about the nature of communities and community decision-making. Communities are often far from homogeneous and altruistic in outlook, and community decision-making may be biased in favour of richer or more influential households.

3.3 Project–community interaction in the project cycle

3.3.1 Introduction

The question we now ask is: what steps are involved in a project process, or cycle, that reflect the principles of community management and demand responsiveness outlined above? In particular, what is the relationship between the community, a project and other stakeholders in the development of sustainable rural water supplies?

BOX 3.5 Some common problems with the implementation of demand-responsive approaches

In many countries demand-responsive approaches to the provision of rural water supplies have quickly overtaken traditional, supply-driven approaches. However, rapid scaling up, institutional upheaval and a lack of local capacity to put policy into practice can create problems:

- Pushing a policy forward before procedures are in place for community self-selection, for example, can mean that government continues to drive investment and make decisions on behalf of communities. *The result? More top-down provision, not less.*
- Offering communities choice places major logistical and administrative demands on those charged with offering it. The process of informing, assessing and responding to demand is a challenging and time-consuming process, and may not be very attractive to service providers striving to meet narrowly defined coverage targets. *The result? Community dialogue and choice can be minimal, or non-existent.*
- Leaving decisions entirely in the hands of communities can re-inforce existing inequalities based on caste, gender and wealth. *The result? The new community standpipe ends up in the compound of the village leader.*
- Cost-sharing and financing arrangements may discriminate against the poor, who may not have the regular cash income required to pay for service fees. Moreover, where different households select different service levels, but user fees remain the same, the poor cross-subsidize the rich. *The result? Poorer households opt out of new schemes, or fund the choices of others.*
- Since the demand-responsive approach focuses on the development and management of individual **sources**, there is a danger that the bigger **resource** picture is missed. *The result? In some hydro-geological environments, ad hoc development of water points can result in interference between community sources and, potentially, over-exploitation of the resource.*

Sources: based on BGS field experience in Tamil Nadu, Rajasthan and Gujarat (India); Ariyabandu and Aheeyar (2004); Joshi (2004)

Figure 3.3 identifies the steps involved. Interaction between the project and community is highlighted, with potential supporting roles played by the private sector, NGOs and other stakeholders. It is the interaction between the community and other stakeholders, with the community at centre stage in decision-making, that defines a demand-responsive approach to rural water supply.

In the discussion below we provide an overview of the complete process, summarizing the rationale for the steps identified and what, and who, might

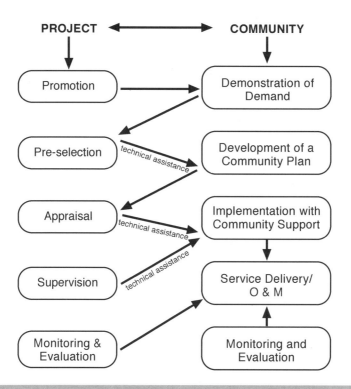

PROJECT ⟷ **COMMUNITY**

Promotion → Demonstration of Demand

Pre-selection *technical assistance* Development of a Community Plan

Appraisal *technical assistance* Implementation with Community Support

Supervision *technical assistance* Service Delivery/ O & M

Monitoring & Evaluation → Monitoring and Evaluation

Figure 3.3 Project and community interaction during the project cycle. Points of technical support required at different stages of a project are highlighted. *Source:* adapted from World Bank-BNWP 2002.

be involved, with a particular focus on the role of a project manager. The discussion draws heavily on Deverill et al. (2002) and the World Bank-BNWP (2002).

Before proceeding, several important points should be noted:

- Although the focus of this book is clearly on groundwater development for rural water supply, the discussion below is not specific to groundwater. This is because water supply options are not usually predetermined before project planning and strategy development has begun. So, the discussion does not prejudge decisions on options or service levels, but rather aims to show how groundwater development – along with other options – might be screened by a project and discussed with communities.
- What follows is a summary of the project process, not an in-depth manual for planning and implementation. There are comprehensive guideline documents dealing with rural water supply planning, and references to these are provided at the end of the chapter.

3.3.2 Project preparation – developing a project strategy

Why prepare a strategy?

This is one of the most important steps in the project process. Strategy development provides an opportunity to develop a dialogue with key stakeholders, such as local government or regional agencies with support or oversight responsibilities. It is also an opportunity to define and agree responsibilities within the project team (and with those outside), and to develop or adapt project objectives and rules within the wider framework of rural water supply in which the project must operate. This includes looking at the policies and institutions that guide service delivery within a country, and that define 'who does what, when and how'.

What is involved?

Developing a strategy is likely to include the following elements:

- A review of the political, institutional and legal framework for rural water supply within which the project operates.
- The development or adaptation of project rules. Project rules guide the operation of a project, and inform stakeholders of their rights and responsibilities. This should be supported by a review of the technical, management and contribution-related options that may be applicable to the local situation and which will inform rule development.
- Definition of and agreement on the roles and responsibilities of different team members, and the identification of training or additional support needs, as necessary.

Who should do it?

Strategy development is normally the responsibility of the project or programme manager. However, the project manager needs to draw on the skills of the rest of the team, perhaps delegating different elements of strategy development to those with the most appropriate skills. For example, the project technician or engineer might be responsible for looking at service targets, standards and option feasibility, in terms of the technical and environmental constraints affecting supply possibilities (groundwater versus surface water) and service levels (single point systems, standpipes and household connections). Meanwhile, the social development specialist or community facilitator might focus on procedures for communicating with and prioritising communities for project assistance. There are no hard and fast rules about who does what, however. The key is to ensure that strategy development is comprehensive, and initiates a dialogue with key stakeholders – the people and institutions that are likely to have an important bearing on the success of the project.

Is it covered in this book?

Yes. Section 3.4 discusses what is involved in more detail, and provides some suggestions on issues that need to be addressed. Chapter 4 discusses the technical process of groundwater reconnaissance: how to determine whether groundwater can provide a source of rural water supply within a project area.

3.3.3 Project promotion – engaging and selecting communities

Why is a promotion phase important?

Under a demand-responsive approach, priority is given to communities that are actively seeking improvements to their water services. A promotion phase can therefore provide a first opportunity for the project to engage communities in deciding whether or not they want a project, and in the case of multisector projects, defining their development priorities, one of which may be improved water supply.

If rural water supply is **defined by the community** as a priority, then a promotion phase can provide a window for communicating information about the project approach, including eligibility criteria, procedures for project implementation and community responsibilities.

What is involved?

A promotion phase can be used to communicate the basic approach, rules and procedures under which communities are eligible to receive support. An effective strategy generally involves the use of several communication channels, such as radio broadcasts and pamphlet distribution, supported by community visits. A degree of facilitation or capacity building may be required to move the process along, and to help poorer, more remote communities articulate their priorities in the first place. Seeking out the disadvantaged and ensuring their inclusion should be a top priority.

Various indicators or demonstrations of demand can be used to select communities, including:

- the completion of an application form, or project–community **memorandum of understanding**
- the establishment of a project fund, for example a savings account in a local bank
- a village clean-up campaign, in which people come together to achieve a shared goal, as a demonstration of demand and community motivation and organization
- the completion of a basic village map, showing the distribution of households and existing water points
- direct observation by a community facilitator (a facilitator may be

employed by the project or local government to identify priority communities as a complement to, or substitute for, other demonstrations of demand).

Of course local demand, however flexibly facilitated and interpreted, may not be the only criteria used in the selection process, even where formal policies state otherwise. In practice, selection may also be based on external priorities such as local government plans, or on coverage data held by a government department. In these circumstances, initial selection decisions may be based on an external determination of need. At this stage, the project manager will need to ensure that community selection is not compromised by targets, or incentives, that favour the 'easy' areas where community supplies supply can be developed quickly (see Box 3.6).

BOX 3.6   Conflicting objectives and definitions of success

In a project in Ghana, many of the boreholes drilled under a donor-funded project were concentrated in a small number of villages. Yet there were many villages in the project area that had no improved water supply. Why?

One reason relates to the conflicting incentives that agencies, drilling contractors and projects may have in prioritizing areas and selecting communities for rural water supply. A private contractor, for example, may be paid according to the number of successful boreholes drilled, with 'success' defined by the number of boreholes that meet minimum yield and quality requirements. A project-implementing agency, keen to demonstrate success in terms of meeting targets within a limited period, may employ similar reasoning. The outcome in both cases can be that easier environments are chosen first, where groundwater can be easily found and success rates are higher. Wells and boreholes are developed in less vulnerable areas; more difficult, water insecure areas are ignored.

Lessons? Risks can be reduced in two main ways:

- *Firstly, by working with those involved in the oversight of projects and programmes (e.g. local and regional government) to ensure that the targets they set for investment in rural water supply do not distort or dilute their own policy objectives.*
- *Secondly, by ensuring that contracts are written in such a way that they do not make it unreasonably difficult for contractors to go to geologically difficult areas where groundwater is harder to find.*

Source: Calow et al. (2002)

Who is involved?

A number of different stakeholders may be involved in the promotion and selection process. Some projects engage promoters familiar with community facilitation, for example, to visit communities (especially those unlikely to

BOX 3.7 Monitoring demand from a community

Indicators or demonstrations of demand that can be used to monitor a project's demand orientation are listed below. They can be used by project staff to indicate how effective service options offered will be in terms of meeting community, household and individual demands. Identifying those people who are **not** demonstrating their demand, and finding out why, is also important.

Project selection

- Application form completed and signed
- Community meetings held
- Bank account opened
- Water and/or sanitation committee formed, or committee functions delegated to existing community-based organization.

Planning

- Water and/or sanitation committee formed, or committee functions delegated to existing community-based organization
- Bank account opened
- Focus groups formed and sustained (to discuss options)
- Community participation in baseline data collection
- Community action plan prepared
- Cash or other contributions made.

Appraisal

- Action plan agreed by community
- Contract signed between community, implementing agency, local government and/or private sector.

Implementation

- Contributions of cash, materials, time and labour linked to specific services and service levels
- Continuing participation of different households and wealth groups
- Operation
- Maintenance contributions collected
- Upgrading of service levels, e.g. from standpipe to household connection
- Extension of existing service to new areas/community members.

Source: based on Deverill et al. (2002)

hear about the project through other channels) to assess priorities and discuss mechanisms for project assistance. They may be team members, or contracted separately by the project to do the job. The government may also have an important role to play in making initial area/community selection decisions, and in promoting new rural water supply policies and project guidelines.

Is it covered in this book?

No. Those wishing to find out more should consult one of the manuals identified in the further reading section at the end of this chapter.

3.3.4 Developing a community plan

Why is the development of a plan important?

The planning phase is important because, through a process of project–community dialogue, it should allow communities to make informed decisions about the type of facilities they receive, and how they are going to be managed and maintained. The plan should, therefore, include a detailed technical design, with associated costs and a management-contribution systems included. In areas where water supply options are limited to a single community well or borehole, the process is likely to be relatively straightforward. In other areas (those with larger, more heterogeneous communities, and a greater number of technically feasible options and service levels) the development of a plan will be more time-consuming. Whatever the circumstances, good information and effective communication are essential: users need to be fully informed of the characteristics, costs, benefits and risks associated with a particular option.

What is involved?

Several steps are involved in developing a community plan. These are illustrated in Figure 3.4, and described briefly below.

Evaluating problems, defining objectives

The starting point for any plan is an understanding of what the current situation is regarding water availability, access and use, and why improved services are wanted in the first place. Understanding the needs and priorities of different households is essential, and the project will need experienced community facilitators to identify different groups and explore problems and priorities without pre-judging what is and isn't important for people. Useful tools include:

- **Focus group discussions**, based on locally defined wealth groups, for example, and separate discussions with men and women. Seasonal calendars of water availability, access and use, developed

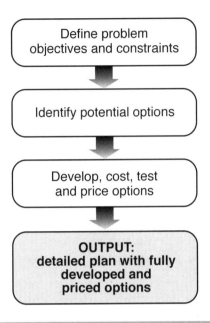

| Figure 3.4 | Developing a community plan.
Source: Deverill et al. (2002). |

separately or as part of a broader activity calendar (i.e. related to work-income calendars), provide a useful reference point for discussion, and can highlight problems some people may have contributing cash during lean periods.

- **Participatory mapping** – identifying where different groups live, for example, and the different water sources they use – and developing a community map, which can be used to focus and guide discussion.
- **Problem trees and problem ranking**, useful for prioritizing problems and identifying cause–effect relationships.
- **Water point interviews**, where project staff spend time at a village well, for example, to speak with the people queuing and collecting water.

The project engineer or technician has an important role to play here, working with a community or taking on some of the participatory exercises her/himself, as appropriate. For example, understanding why certain groundwater sources fail (or are not used) seasonally or during drought (mechanical failures and their causes; lack of water; changing taste and quality) may have an important bearing on final option selection. This kind of information can often be gathered by spending time talking to people at individual water points.

Identifying potential options

The analysis and discussions above should establish the attributes of a water supply that different people in the community think important. These attributes will be informed by men's and women's perceptions of convenience, security, privacy and other values, which may well differ. The identification of options with the **potential** to meet this demand (pre-screened according to their technical feasibility) can then take place, with the advantages and disadvantages of each discussed with the community. The discussion will focus around differences in likely water availability, reliability, quality and accessibility for different people in relation to existing and intended uses. Again, there is a real need for technical input into this dialogue. People must be fully informed of the potential benefits (and costs) of different technology types and service levels.

Developing, costing, testing and pricing options

Once one, or more, potential options have been identified, they can be developed into **real** options with management and contribution systems attached. In practice this is likely to be an extension of the option identification step above: the difference is in the level of detail involved, and the comparisons that need to be made between cost, service level and willingness to pay, amongst other things, before a final decision is reached. Useful approaches for developing options with communities through dialogue and demonstration include:

- visits to neighbouring projects where similar options have been developed
- pictures and photographs of similar options as a focus for dialogue
- physical models of the proposed facilities to help explain how they work and what is required to maintain them
- role-plays and street theatre to illustrate how a management and/or contribution system could work.

To reiterate, **informed** choice is essential. This means that, while any final decision on option selection needs to reflect users' priorities, it must also be technically feasible and environmentally sustainable. This amplifies again the need for technical input. Project technicians do not have a monopoly on technical know-how, however. It will be important also to tap into local knowledge about resource conditions and availability, recognizing the contribution that local people can make in screening options and identifying good sites for a well or borehole (see Chapter 5).

At this stage, it will also be necessary to make users aware of the risks associated with the development of options. For example, if a decision is taken to develop a borehole, it must be made clear that finding groundwater may not be a foregone conclusion. Drilling may be unsuccessful in the preferred location, and other sources may need to be discussed.

Alternatively the project technician may need to make users aware of the trade-offs between convenience and security of supply – if the most drought-resistant location for a borehole would involve a longer walk to collect water for certain households, for example. In either case, it will be important to have a clear project rule about who bears the risk, and cost, of drilling unsuccessful boreholes. If this is borne by the community, then a 10 per cent contribution towards total capital costs could turn out to be very expensive. An alternative would be for the community to meet 15 per cent (say) of capital costs **net** of siting and drilling costs, avoiding the uncertainty and risk of an open-ended cost commitment.

The project technician will also need to consider the impact of future demand in system design. Planning for future population growth and other drivers of demand can be difficult, but designing systems with upgrade **potential** – assuming water resources are available – can provide some flexibility. In this case, the project will need to think carefully about the duration of any subsidies on offer, so that people who join a scheme late are not denied the support offered during the initial project period.

The principle of user choice can also be extended to management and contribution systems, though guidance may already be provided through local and regional policies. For example, policies may outline the makeup, role and legal status of a water committee, its responsibilities in relation to local government, the expected contribution of communities towards project costs, and subsidy arrangements (usually for capital costs only). If not, or if some flexibility in interpretation is possible, then the project will need to develop its own guidance based on what works elsewhere, local politics and any existing community planning arrangements. Whatever the situation, it will be important to:

- Carry out some form of assessment that tests people's demand for an option and their willingness to pay for it. Various techniques can be used, but all are based on (a) a detailed description of the option(s), including the expected service level (for rural groundwater supply, this usually varies from a simple well with windlass, to borehole and handpump, and in some circumstances motorized pumps and a distribution system); and (b) asking people what they would be willing to pay for it. Demand assessment should combine individual interviews with focus group discussions.
- Determine the likely capital and operation and maintenance (O&M) costs of the option(s) selected, which are often location-specific. This should include projected replacement costs of parts, and any additional costs associated with the purchase and replacement of tools, for example.
- Establish a financial management and tariff plan based on outcomes from the above. This needs to be transparent, with a clear process for setting, reviewing an adjusting prices with user approval. The

potential impact on poorer users must also be assessed by the project before a pricing system is implemented, and any subsidy arrangements agreed. Flexibility is important. In contributing to capital costs, for example, poorer households could be allowed to increase their labour contribution in return for a lower cash payment.

■ Develop a facilities management plan for O&M, including arrangements for collecting and saving agreed contributions. The roles and responsibilities of the designated community organization responsible for managing the system, and of the external organizations it has to interact with (e.g. local government) must also be clear. Though policy may state that the creation of a water committee is a prerequisite for project assistance, experience suggests that communities should be allowed flexibility in deciding what kind of organization they want to operate and manage the system. This may be a new water committee, but it could also be an existing community organization (Sara and Katz 1997).

■ Consider what might happen to existing water points, the people who may continue using them and management arrangements. For example, experience in Sri Lanka suggests that those who do not sign up for new schemes (often the poorest) end up paying more for the upkeep of old ones. In other words, the burden of maintenance for an existing well or borehole falls on a smaller, impoverished section of the community (Ariyabandu and Aheeyar 2004). In these circumstances, there are arguments for bringing both old and new community water supplies under one management system.

Appraising a community plan

Drawing on these outcomes, a written plan or proposal can then be drawn up with the community. Assistance may be provided directly by the project, or recruited and paid for from among consultants and NGOs, or by hiring a qualified individual within the community.

Such a proposal can serve a number of different purposes:

■ Firstly, it can be presented in draft form to the community for explanation, discussion and approval. In UNICEF-supported rural water supply projects in Orissa (India), for example, community action plans are represented in picture form on a large wall in the centre of each participating village, providing a focal point for discussion (Deverill et al. 2002).

■ Secondly, it can be used to inform the project's funder or local government about the outcomes of the planning process following community approval, providing both a demonstration of demand and capacity, and a means of checking that important qualifying steps have been followed.

The form the proposal takes and the way it is presented will need to be tailored to the needs of the audience, but it might include:

- the alternatives considered
- the decisions which were taken and the process through which they were reached
- details of the management and contribution systems that have been worked out.

Who is involved?

The discussion above highlights the need for different skills and expertise, and the need for a mix of top-down advice (in identifying technically and environmentally feasible options, for example), and bottom-up decision-making (ensuring the views of different users are taken on board). Without this balance, there can be no informed choice. It is important to emphasize, therefore, that a demand-led approach does not mean that project staff – or those they contract – can leave all decisions to community members. Neither does it mean, however, that project technicians or community workers can impose their preferred choices, with communities agreeing to decisions made with token community participation.

Is this covered in the book?

This book does not discuss any further the process of option screening and selection discussed above, demand assessment techniques such as contingent valuation, or the development of management and cost-sharing arrangements. These issues are comprehensively dealt with in other books and reference texts (see the end of this chapter for further reading). However, Chapter 5 provides guidance on working with communities on the siting of wells and boreholes.

3.3.5 Implementation with community support

Why is it important?

Implementing a plan involves the community, the project and contractors working closely together to achieve a shared objective: to put in place firm foundations for sustainable service delivery and operations and maintenance. This requires intensive community-level assistance and training to reinforce ownership, and to formalize (and if necessary reach final agreement on) contribution and management systems set out in the community plan.

What is involved?

A number of different issues need to be considered, from agreeing a final plan (if this has not been done already) to organizing and paying for construction work. An effective communication strategy for the project is essential.

Agreeing options

Important issues to raise include:

- details of project implementation (management structure, budget, timeframe, reporting and feedback arrangements)
- what options are available (for mixed technologies and service levels)
- contribution size and method(s) of payment
- how users can apply to receive a particular service.

Confirming user commitment

The commitment of users to a project intervention can be demonstrated in a number of different ways. For example contracts, upfront cash payments, and contributions of labour and/or materials for construction can all be used to confirm demand for a system (or particular service level), and indicate to project staff, the donor and/or local government that planned improvements match user expectations.

Training for operations and maintenance

Operations and maintenance responsibility starts with the management organizations chosen by, and accountable to, the community. An individual, or individuals, should therefore receive basic training in the day-to-day maintenance of a system, organized by or through the project. A technical manual should be left with the management organization for future reference, listing both maintenance tasks and a task schedule for preventative maintenance. Backstopping services also need to be planned for major repairs.

Preparing management

Ideally, all the responsibilities of a management organization, such as a water point committee, should be practised during implementation with the assistance of the project. This is a vital area of capacity building, and can include:

- price review and the collection of contributions
- the procurement of services from local government or the private sector (e.g. for drilling and equipping the new borehole, or the projected repair or extension/upgrading of facilities using simple job cards)
- the establishment of monitoring systems (e.g. for monitoring the quality of work undertaken, recording problems and requests for assistance, and so on).

To complement this, it is recommended that the project also prepares a handbook for the management organization, explaining its responsibilities and tasks, and with suggestions on who to contact should a problem arise. This may be in addition to the traditional technical manual on operation and maintenance, or part of it. In either case, the handbook(s) can be used as both a training aid during planning and implementation, and as a reference manual in the future.

Who is involved?

As is clear from the above, the community must be involved throughout the implementation phase, from agreeing options, service levels and cost-sharing arrangements, to training in the technical and managerial aspects of system upkeep. The role of the project team may vary, however, depending on which (if any) support functions are contracted out, either by the project (on behalf of a community) or by communities themselves. For example, a project team may be directly involved in all of the activities listed above, providing training, management support and technical assistance. Alternatively, the community may manage some or all funds themselves, and hire (and supervise) qualified individuals or firms to carry out specific tasks. In the later case individuals within the community, or the water committee, would require prior training in the procurement of goods, services and works, including rules, procedures and responsibilities for letting contracts, selection and supervision.

Are these steps covered in the book?

The technical aspects of groundwater development for rural water supply are covered. The community facilitation aspects of option and service level agreement, training and capacity building for management organizations are not. However, Chapter 5 provides some guidance on locating wells and boreholes through community consultation. Tips for further reading are provided at the end of the chapter.

3.3.6 Operation and maintenance, monitoring and evaluation

Why is this important?

Lack of effective O&M is the most common problem of rural water supply projects. To address this problem, O&M training should begin during the implementation phase, focusing on the community's capacity to ensure reliable and sustainable service delivery. This issue is covered under implementation above.

Monitoring and evaluation (M&E) systems can be viewed as tools for helping stakeholders at various levels focus on achieving sustainable service delivery. Traditionally, M&E has been the responsibility of the external agency responsible for implementing the project, or the government agency responsible for ensuring rural water supply objectives have been met, and investments carried out as planned. More recently, attention has turned to community-based M&E on the basis that it can help local management sustain a project, and is not just a tool for external assessment.

What is involved?

Issues of O&M are dealt with above. Here we focus on the indicators and tools that can be used to help local management monitor the performance of rural water supply services. Indicators should ideally be tuned to the local situation, Table 3.1 provides some possible suggestions.

Tools that can be used in M&E include:

- **logbooks**, which can be used by a water committee to record problems, actions taken to address them and response times (e.g. for external contractors)
- **questionnaires**, which are more difficult to complete for some users, but can be used to uncover a wider variety of problems
- **posters**, which can help communicate messages about how to report a fault or apply for an improved service, for example, or may advertise the forthcoming meeting of the water committee.

Are these steps covered in the book?

Not specifically, though much of the guidance in this book is designed to prevent technical problems occurring with wells and boreholes.

3.4 Developing a project strategy

In this section we look at how the project manager, or team leader, can develop a project strategy – taking some of the ideas presented in section 3.3 a little further. This is one of the most important parts of the project cycle: during strategy development, key relationships are forged between team members, and between team members and other stakeholders; responsibilities are defined and agreed; project rules and objectives are defined in the wider context of rural water supply targets and policies; and sub-projects selected.

Below, we focus on four elements of strategy development:

- Rapid sector assessment: a review of the enabling environment in which the project sits, including the political, institutional and legal framework.
- Following on from this, the development or adaptation of project rules, defining who receives support and how support can be provided in a demand-responsive way.

Table 3.1 Possible indicators for monitoring the performance of a rural water supply system

Indicator	Notes
Upfront cash or other contributions	A strong indicator of demand, and can be used during project implementation
Regular payment for services provided	If users are not satisfied with the service they are receiving, they may be reluctant to pay for it. However, there may be other reasons for non-payment. In drought years, for example, users may be unable to pay. Even in normal years, some users may struggle to contribute regular cash income. It is therefore important to find out who is not paying, and why
Water availability	A properly designed, sited and constructed well or borehole should provide a reliable supply of water, even during the dry season
Water access	If water is available but some people are not using the improved supply, reasons need to uncovered. They might include factors related to discrimination (social status, gender, religion), difficulty in meeting user fees/contributions and preference for other sources
User satisfaction and complaints	It is important to measure user satisfaction that is not related to payment, particularly for women who may not control the financial resources used to pay for services, but are the ones collecting most of the water
Upgrading	Upgrading (e.g. extension of an existing system) is a good indicator that people are valuing water supply more, and there is a system in place that can respond to changes in demand
Hand washing and use of soap	An indicator of both the effectiveness of a health and sanitation programme that may be part of the rural water supply project, and an indicator that there is enough water to meet basic needs

- Simple economic assessment of groundwater exploration techniques which can be used to help (a) assess whether groundwater development is a realistic option; and (b) guide the type of groundwater exploration techniques employed in particular area.
- The roles and responsibilities of different project team members, employed directly by the project or contracted-in (with project oversight) by the community, and/or local government. In particular, we focus on the essential role of the engineer or technician.

3.4.1 Rapid sector assessment

As noted in section 3.2, the sustainability of community-based systems is heavily dependent on the technical, financial and management support networks in which they are embedded. These support networks, in turn, are shaped by the policies and institutions that set the 'rules of the game' for investment in rural water supply. Understanding this external environment in terms of the opportunities and constraints it creates (see Table 3.2) will help the project manager design and oversee interventions that have the greatest chance of providing sustainable water supplies. So what exactly is involved?

Table 3.2 Sector assessment: a data collection checklist

Key questions and information needs	Sources and Tools
1 Rural water supply objectives, targets and indicators	
What are the national, regional and local priorities and plans related to service provision and water resources management?	Policy documents
	Interviews with regional and local government staff
Do plans make any reference to wider poverty alleviation goals? If so, how?	Discussion with other programmes and projects
What targets are defined? Are basic service levels for water (& sanitation) set in terms of quantity and quality, distance to improved sources etc?	
What scope is there for flexible application, if any?	
What procedures are there for water quality testing and monitoring?	
What technical specifications, norms or standards apply to infrastructure design and construction? Who monitors them?	
2 Rural water supply policies	
What is the strategy to meet the targets and standards described above?	Policy documents
	Interviews with regional and local government staff
What are the underlying principles of the strategy? Does it include elements of a DRA? If so, which ones?	Discussions with other programmes and projects
Do selection criteria exist to prioritize communities or households? What are they, and who is involved in the selection process?	
Do policies define for what purposes water may be provided?	
Is RWS integrated with hygiene and sanitation strategies or policies, or wider poverty alleviation activities (e.g. credit schemes, food security interventions)? If so, how?	
Is RWS linked with national or regional policies on water resources management, such as integrated basin management? If so, how?	
3 Institutional roles and responsibilities	
Which institutions are responsible for policy development?	Institutional mapping

Table 3.2—*cont.*

Key Questions and Information Needs	Sources and Tools
Which institutions are responsible for policy implementation?	Stakeholder analysis, based on review of formal roles and responsibilities (from policy documents) and discussion with government, civil society and private sector agencies
How are roles and responsibilities distributed between different organizations? Are responsibilities for service provision and support defined? If so, how?	
How does RWS 'fit' within the decentralisation agenda (both political and administrative)?	
Which particular tasks, duties and responsibilities have been devolved, and which retained?	
What is the actual capacity of local government, the private sector, NGOs and CBOs to plan, implement and sustain projects?	
Do community-based organisations (e.g. water committees) for managing water points already exist in target villages (the legacy of previous RWS interventions)?	
Do policies provide any guidance on what, if anything, should happen to existing RWS systems and management arrangements?	
Is the formation of a new water committee a prerequisite for receiving project assistance, or can the community delegate management to an existing organization?	

4 Legal framework

Is local government legally mandated to support service provision?	Policy documents
	Water laws
Is the project and/or the community management organization authorized to propose, implement and operate projects, form contracts, make bye-laws, set tariffs and collect payments?	Review of customary rights and practices
	Key informant interviews
Is the local management organization obliged to register with local/regional government? How effective is this process?	
What is the legal framework regarding asset ownership?	
What is the legal framework regarding water use (e.g. registration or licensing of new boreholes; spacing requirements between boreholes, and between boreholes and latrines)?	
Have there been any serious conflicts regarding water resource use, and are there mechanisms in place for resolving such conflicts?	

Table 3.2—*cont.*

Key Questions and Information Needs	Sources and Tools
5 Technology options and standards	
Do policies allow or promote community choice in the type, level, design and siting of services and systems? Does this extend to individual households	Policy documents
	Discussion with government, civil society and private sector agencies
How are these choices framed, or screened, and by whom?	Discussions with other RWS projects and programmes
Are certain types of technology or sources favoured, or forbidden (e.g. boreholes in certain areas; surface water sources in others)?	
Are there standards and norms for RWS service levels and technical design and construction (see Q1 above)?	
Are standards monitored and enforced? If so, by whom?	
6 Finance and cost recovery	
What policies are there for the financing of service provision? (from construction and installation to operation and maintenance)?	Policy documents
	Discussion with government, civil society and private sector agencies
Are contribution levels towards capital and recurrent costs defined? If so, how?	Discussions with other RWS projects and programmes
What is the policy on subsidies? Over what period of time are communities and households eligible for subsidies?	
Are subsidy rules rigid, or is there scope for flexibility (e.g. allowing poorer households to exchange cash for labour contributions)?	
What is the policy on cost limits, if any?	
Who bears the risk and cost of unsuccessful drilling? (e.g. do communities pay only a percentage cost of a successful borehole?)	
Are funds available to start up savings and credit schemes, to make services more affordable?	
What are the sources of funds, and what procedures are in place for connecting source with recipient?	

■ Firstly, it requires a clear understanding of the **policies** that influence how projects are designed and implemented. For example, the national standards or targets that any project should support, and the approach (and its rationale) for achieving them. A review of policy documents and statements can provide this, as well as providing a route map of functional responsibilities held by government institutions – both political and administrative – at different levels.

- Secondly, and following on from the above, it requires a clear understanding of **institutional responsibilities and functions**. These may still be evolving where decentralization policies are being promoted and there is increased scope for private sector and/or NGO involvement in service delivery. In these circumstances, the nature of partnership arrangements (intended and existing) between government, private sector and civil society organizations will need to be explored, particularly in terms of the capacity of different stakeholders to undertake prescribed roles. It is also important to look at the rights and obligations of users themselves.

The institutional analysis should also include a review of **relevant legislation** affecting ownership of assets and the mandate and powers of local management committees. For example, a local management organization such as a water committee can be authorized through legislation to award contracts, to set and adjust tariffs, and to collect payments for services provided. The same mandate may also set limits to these powers requiring, for example, an annual audit of accounts (Deverill et al. 2002). Customary rules existing outside the formal legal framework should also be explored, particularly in relation to the status of local management organizations (do customary and formal powers conflict in any way?), and their potential influence on rights of access to improved water supplies (might some groups be excluded?).

How can this be carried out? A lot of information should be available in general policy documents, statements and manuals available from government departments, or indirectly through other organizations. Talking to people is also essential. Developing a dialogue with some of the key stakeholders involved can provide valuable insights into what actually happens on the ground, and not just what should happen. In particular, the following stakeholders and the fulfilment of their roles should be examined:

- **Local politicians**, for example those in local government, with respect to their mandate and capacity to support communities.
- **Civil servants** in administrative departments with responsibilities for identifying and/or supporting local communities. In many countries, for example, borehole drilling units are still in the public sector, and it will be important to find out how they operate and to whom they are accountable.
- **Private sector suppliers** of goods and services for the design, construction, procurement and sale of spare parts. In particular, the capacity of private sector operators to fulfil roles envisaged in new policies should be scrutinized.

- **Other projects and programmes in the area** with experience in following new policies, and the constraints they have faced.
- **Communities themselves** in terms of their ability to manage the procurement and oversight of equipment supply and O&M services.

3.4.2 Developing project rules

Project rules guide the operation of a project. They inform stakeholders of their rights and responsibilities, detailing basic principles and obligations. Stakeholders include potential users (communities, and the households within them) and those responsible for implementing and supporting projects. The starting point for developing rules is the sector assessment described above as rural water supply policies are likely to guide – and in some cases specify – the technical, management and contribution-related options that are available, and can therefore be offered. For the project manager, key questions relate to the degree of flexibility a project has in interpreting, adapting and implementing policies in ways suited to the local situation.

Five broad categories of project rules can be identified (after Sara and Katz 1997):

- **Eligibility criteria**. Service commitments should ideally follow, not precede, community initiative in seeking assistance. As noted previously, a basic tenet of a demand-responsive approach is that more communities should be eligible to receive services than can be served. In this way, priority for service should be given to those communities **actively** seeking improvements to their water supply system. However, communities may need assistance in registering or articulating their demand, hence the need for a project promotion phase, and the need for flexibility in agreeing which indicators of demand can be used by a project to signal 'active' community initiative (see earlier). In this respect, the project may need to move beyond recommended indicators and information pathways to ensure that poorer groups and communities are not excluded.
- **Informed requests from the community**. At the same time, a project needs to have procedures in place that ensure an adequate flow of information to communities. Communities should, for example, be able to make informed choices about whether to participate in a project, based on **prior knowledge about the terms of their participation and responsibilities for sustaining a water supply system**. Again, these issues need to be dealt with during a project promotion phase (section 3.2), paying particular attention to ensuring messages reach poorer groups in an appropriate, understandable format.

■ **Technical options and service levels**. Demand-responsive approaches emphasize the need for community engagement in selecting service options, levels and locations, with related cost and operational consideration made clear. In order for people to make informed choices, however, projects need procedures for (a) screening options before project-community dialogue over choice begins; and (b) communicating information about the advantages and disadvantages of feasible (screened) options, including the costs and complexity of O&M. In practice, rural water supply policies may favour or prescribe certain sources and technologies, reducing opportunities for local decision making and innovation. Moreover, a project's capacity to support choice, and what this implies in terms of technical, logistical and training support, may be limited. The project manager therefore needs to work within the constraints imposed by policy, and the constraints of their own organization (Box 3.8).

■ **Cost-sharing arrangements**. The basic principles of cost-sharing should be specified and made clear to all stakeholders at the outset. A basic principle of the demand-responsive approach holds that cost-sharing arrangements should be designed so that the community chooses the level of service for which it is willing to pay.

BOX 3.8   Working with constraints

The technical choices that can be offered to communities are often constrained by:

■ the policies set by government
■ the availability of water – rainwater, surface sources, groundwater resources
■ the availability of good information on water availability, especially groundwater
■ the capacity of a project to design, implement and sustain different options
■ the capacity of local government and private sector organizations to support different options and choices (e.g. for construction work and the provision of spare parts).

Constraints can be eased by building the capacity of the implementing organization, for example by ensuring project staff are familiar with a range of technical, management and financial options, and the inputs required to sustain a scheme. Where constraints cannot be easily removed, flexibility is still possible. Even where water resource constraints limit options to a single village well or borehole, for example, local people may still be able to decide on the details of design, the location of the water point, how and when contributions are to be made, and how the service is to be managed.

Again, cost-sharing arrangements and subsidy packages may be guided by government policy, and the project manager will need to investigate what scope there is for refining or adapting rules to the local situation.

- **Responsibilities for investment support**. Rules regarding asset ownership, O&M and ongoing recovery of system costs should be established and agreed upon by all stakeholders.

3.4.3 Assessing the cost-effectiveness of groundwater exploration

Here we look specifically at the issue of groundwater development for rural water supply, focusing on the cost-effectiveness of alternative exploration methods. Why is this important, and why consider it here as an element of strategy development? There are several reasons:

- Simple cost analysis can help the project team decide between different technology options and even whether groundwater development is feasible in an area. Of course other factors will influence decisions about potentially feasible options – not least the availability (and quality) of other water sources – but cost is an important consideration.
- Projects have a finite source of money, therefore higher costs of individual sources means other communities go unserved.
- Too many projects attempt to develop groundwater by drilling boreholes more-or-less randomly, with negative consequences. This often leads to large numbers of unsuccessful boreholes and therefore a higher cost per working water point, and a cost to communities, in terms of unmet expectations.

Groundwater exploration

In some areas, for example on major alluvial plains with abundant rainfall, groundwater may be widely available at relatively shallow depths. In these areas, little or no hydrogeological investigation is necessary as wells or boreholes may be successful wherever they are developed. Siting can therefore be determined by the local population alone.

In environments which are more geologically heterogeneous, however, investigations ranging from simple field observation to more costly exploratory drilling and surveying may be necessary to ensure success (see Table 3.3). Where investigations help reduce the number of unsuccessful wells drilled, cost savings may be significant, more than covering the cost of the investigation procedure (Figure 3.5). A simple methodological approach for evaluating the most appropriate approach to groundwater exploration, based on cost-effectiveness criteria, is outlined below.

One approach is to compare the costs of groundwater exploration with the costs of drilling, on the basis that hydrogeological knowledge can reduce the

Table 3.3 The costs of different exploratory techniques

	Groundwater exploration technique	Costs	Notes
One-off project cost			
Reconnaissance	Gathering background maps and information on the geology and hydrogeological conditions (see techniques in Chapter 4)	A one off cost – several weeks' time of a project member or consultant. More expensive (but not prohibitively so) if data have to be generated from satellite images etc.	Essential first step for understanding the groundwater resources. To generate new data a consultant or university would need to be involved
Costs per borehole			
Hydro-geological fieldwork	Siting by eye – examining the geomorphology and the rocks in an area Discussion with local communities	Requires a well trained and experienced engineer to visit the community	Objective is to 'ground-truth' results gathered from reconnaissance
Geophysical surveying	See Chapter 5 for the different techniques. Must be combined with reconnaissance data and hydrogeological fieldwork	Equipment varies in price but is generally <$US 20 k. A well-trained geophysics team will need at least 1 day in each community	Important to have good analysis of the data. Investment in training staff highly beneficial
Exploratory drilling	Drill exploratory boreholes in a community – often combined with hydrogeological fieldwork and geophysics	Costs equivalent to drilling a dry borehole, but considerably reduced if the team has control over their own rig. Could be a one off cost if the exploratory drilling leads to better interpretation of geophysics	The only way to 'prove' that groundwater occurs in an area. Requires careful facilitation to ensure that communities do not get frustrated by drilling of 'test' boreholes

increasing costs

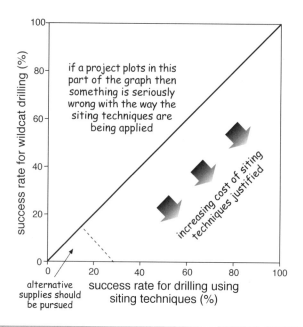

Figure 3.5 Summary of the circumstances when siting techniques can be economically justified.

number of unsuccessful wells or boreholes drilled (Reedman et al. 2002). Hence, the benefits of acquiring hydrogeological knowledge can be quantified as drilling costs saved. This type of economic approach is known as a **cost-effectiveness analysis**. As in any economic appraisal, comparisons are made between a baseline scenario (what would happen without investigation, or a certain level of investigation), and one or more alternatives (what would happen with a certain level of investigation).

Technology choice

A second important cost factor for the project is the costs of different technologies, or varying designs of technologies. Drilling rigs vary enormously in cost – from less than $100 000 for a small airflush down-the-hole hammer rig, to more than $500 000 for large truck-mounted rigs. If a project has control over buying a rig, it is important that the most appropriate rig is bought for the project (see Table 3.4). There is no point in buying a large heavy rig with a high-capacity compressor if the boreholes are to be less than 100 m into basement rocks.

Another related cost is the diameter of the borehole drilled. A 200-mm diameter borehole will remove nearly 3 times as much spoil from the ground than a 125-mm borehole. The difference in the running costs of

BOX 3.9 Investing in groundwater investigation: is it worth it?

A project manager in Nigeria was faced with the following dilemma. Information collected during the reconnaissance phase of the project suggested the project was underlain by crystalline basement. Previous projects had reported a 40 per cent success rate from drilling boreholes in the village centres using no groundwater exploration methods. The project manager has calculated that an unsuccessful borehole (unequipped) will cost the project $3000 and a successful borehole (equipped and functioning) $5000. A geophysics team is available at $500 per borehole. What success rate would they need to get to make it worthwhile?

Random drilling

For every successful borehole, 1.5 unsuccessful boreholes need to be drilled, so the project cost per successful borehole is

$$1.5 \times \$3000 + 1 \times \$5000 = \$9500$$

With groundwater exploration

With groundwater exploration, an unsuccessful borehole will cost $3500 and a successful borehole $5500.

The money that can be spent on unsuccessful boreholes is

$$\$9500 - \$5500 = \$4000$$

This is equivalent to 1.14 unsuccessful boreholes.

The breakeven success rate is 2.14 boreholes per successful borehole (47 per cent)

Therefore, any success over 47 per cent will give significant savings to the project and allow more communities to be served.

- **Drawbacks:** This method assumes prior knowledge about the success of random drilling in an area. Accurate information can be difficult to get hold of since success rates often go unreported, or different definitions of 'success' are used by different agencies.
- **Conclusion:** it is useful to find out as much as you can about the successes – and failures – of other projects and programmes so that mistakes are not repeated. If data are available, it can be useful to carry out some simple economic tests.

the compressor and wear on the rig per borehole are huge. In low-yielding rocks there is little difference in hydraulic efficiency between a 200-mm and a 125-mm borehole. The diameter should be determined by the size of the pump to fit down the casing.

Table 3.4 Summary of the costs and constraints of different drilling methods

	Hand digging	Hand drilling	Percussion rig	Small multi-purpose air flush rig	Large multi-purpose rig
Capital cost (US$ k)	1	<5	20–100	<150	>200
Running costs	Very low	Low	Low	Medium	Very high
Training requirements	Very low	Low	Low-medium	Medium	Very high
Repair skills	Very low	Low	Low-medium	Medium	Very high
Holes to 15 m in unconsolidated material	Slow	Fast	Fast	Difficult	Fast
Holes to 50 m in unconsolidated material	Generally impossible	Slow and difficult	Moderately-fast	Very difficult	Fast
Holes to 15–50 m in consolidated material	Very slow	Impossible	Very slow	Very fast	Very fast

Source: adapted from Foster et al. (2000).

3.4.4 The project team and the role of the engineer

In this final section, we look at the roles and responsibilities of different team members, focusing particularly on the role of the engineer in a more demand-led approach to service provision. For the project manager, assessing the capacity of those involved to fulfil new roles, particularly in terms of support for local decision making, is vital. This issue needs to be considered before implementation begins, hence its inclusion here under strategy development.

In section 3.2, we highlighted the need for multidisciplinary approaches, noting that sustainable rural water supply projects require both technical inputs – particularly in terms of option screening – and substantial investment in community sensitization, mobilization and participation. The shift to more demand-responsive approaches also has implications for the ways in which inputs are provided. We therefore need to look beyond the need for disciplinary balance, to consider how decisions are made with respect to service provision. Traditionally, engineers and other technical specialists have been trained to take important technical decisions on behalf of communities, or donors. With demand-responsive approaches, engineers are expected to work with communities.

The need to involve users in decision making is well rehearsed, but it can create some uncertainty for engineers and technicians. In particular, they may be uncomfortable with an approach that appears to contradict their training by giving community members decision-making powers. For government engineers, the uncertainly may be compounded by wider institutional changes, especially the change in the role of the state from direct implementation to facilitation (Gross et al. 2001; Deverill et al. 2002).

Below we highlight some key responsibilities in the project process, amplifying some of the points made above. Table 3.5 provides a checklist of skills

Table 3.5 Knowledge, skills and attitudes of project staff needed to help design and implement rural water supply projects

	Project manager	Engineer or technician	Social development
Knowledge			
Policy, legal and institutional framework	Essential	Useful	Useful
Roles and responsibilities of relevant external (to project) people	Essential	Useful	Useful
Individual and team project roles and responsibilities	Essential	Essential	Essential
Advantages and limitations of different water supply options	Essential	Essential	Essential
Wider uses and benefits of water	Essential	Essential	Essential
Household livelihood strategies	Essential	Essential	Essential
Water resource constraints	Useful	Essential	Useful
How to cost options accurately	Useful	Essential	Essential
Technical and design standards	Essential	Essential	NA
Different community management options	Useful	Useful	Essential
Different participatory techniques for assessing demand	Useful	Useful	Essential
Skills			
Ability to adapt technologies to meet demand	Devolve	Essential	Useful
Ability to cost options and recommend prices	Devolve	Essential	Essential
Ability to communicate technical concepts to people with little technical background	Devolve	Essential	Essential
Ability to communicate financial concepts to people with little experience of community financing	Devolve	Useful	Essential
Ability to adapt to resource and environmental constraints	Devolve	Essential	Useful
Ability to engage with all users, especially women and poorer households	Devolve	Essential	Essential
Attitudes			
Ability to lead, motivate and supervise	Essential	Useful	Useful
Ability to work as part of a multidisciplinary team	Essential	Essential	Essential

Table 3.5—*cont.*

	Project manager	Engineer or technician	Social development
Willingness and patience to devolve decision-making to communities and households	Essential	Essential	Essential
Willingness to work unconventional hours and to work in remote or difficult situations	Essential	Essential	Essential
Willingness to adapt standards as appropriate, assessing risk and retaining responsibility	Essential	Essential	Essential
Sensitivity to the demands, culture and circumstances of vulnerable groups	Essential	Essential	Essential
Commitment to continuous professional development	Essential	Essential	Essential

Source: adapted from Deverill et al. (2002).

required for project design and implementation. A key question the project manager needs to ask is: are these skills available or can they be developed in the team, or does specialist assistance need to be contracted-in or outsourced?

Skills for strategy development and project promotion

The project engineer or technician should be able to provide advice on rural water supply objectives, and the feasibility of meeting them through different options in the project area. This can be achieved by:

- Working with other team members to assess the political, institutional and legal framework for rural water supply from a technical perspective. This may include an assessment of targets and standards, and of the capacity of partner agencies – private contractors, local government – to provide support services, including the provision of equipment and spare parts, well or borehole siting, drilling, technical training and maintenance.
- Identifying potential water supply options from a technical perspective, based on policy guidance, the experience of other projects and programmes in the area, and the engineer's own assessment of water resource availability and quality constraints. This may include an assessment of the development potential of groundwater resources to meet rural water supply targets, and the cost-effectiveness of alternative investigation/siting techniques (3.4.3 above).
- Working with other team members to examine the potential 'fit' between the options identified above and people's likely demand and ability to pay. Messages about informed choice – and the need

to screen options according to their technical and environmental feasibility – will need to be fed into the project promotion phase.

Skills for developing and implementing a community plan

In order for consumers to be able to take decisions, they have to be informed about their options. Drawing on the initial feasibility assessment above, the project engineer will need to work with the community to develop potential options into real ones, including appropriate management and contribution systems (see section 3.3.4). At this stage the engineer will need to guard against foreclosing on alternatives, based on what s/he considers most appropriate. Particular responsibilities and skills are likely to include:

■ Assessing local water resource conditions and helping to assess demand (alongside social facilitators or community development specialists), including the attributes of an improved water supply that different people consider important, and potential changes in demand over time (between seasons, and over the longer term).

■ Discussing with communities, and different groups within them, the characteristics, benefits and limitations of different option types and service levels. This implies that the engineer will need to be familiar with a wide range of options – including the technology and materials used, and the mechanisms used to supply, operate, maintain and upgrade services (Deverill et al. 2002). A willingness and ability to adapt standard designs, based on demand and resource assessments, is also useful.

■ Based on this knowledge, the costing of different options, including capital, recurrent and replacement costs, so that affordable options can be identified with the social facilitator or community development specialist. Even where projects employ a financial adviser for this role, the engineer should be involved in the process.

Capacity building for the project team

Capacity building is not just something a project is supporting within a community; it may also be required for the project team. Relatively few engineers or technical specialists have the breadth of knowledge and experience to carry out these tasks. And not all social development specialists are used to working with, and not just alongside, engineers. What can be done?

One possibility – noted in Box 3.8 – is training and experience-building for project staff. This requires time and money, but is an investment in the sustainability of follow-on activities. Training could take several forms, including:

■ formal courses at local, regional or national resource centres
■ fact-finding visits to other projects and programmes

■ structured workshops, where staff from several projects (and government agencies and other stakeholders, as appropriate) meet to share ideas and experiences.

Another possibility is for project staff to contract in or otherwise outsource specialist assistance as and when required. For example the project might employ a financial specialist, or outsource advice on the appropriateness of wells or boreholes in a specific area. If this is the case, the manager will need to make provision for this during the initial design or strategy development phase.

Finally, the project manager may have to ask hard questions about what the project can realistically offer. After all, there are limits to the number of informed choices that can be offered, service levels arranged, training courses organized and subsidy/cost-sharing schemes developed. It may be better to stick with the 'tried-and-tested', rather than offer options and choices that are ill-informed and unfamiliar.

3.5   Summary: key messages for the project manager

■ Investment in rural water supply is about much more than achieving health goals, or coverage targets. The benefits of rural water supply extend to income generation, education and, further downstream, to improvements in food security and livelihood resilience. This has implications for the way projects are conceived, designed and implemented.

Lessons? Avoid pre-judging what is and isn't important to people. Ensure that demand assessments carried out by team members consider the wider role of water in the community and household economy, and not just water for drinking, washing and cooking. Investment in rural water supply is an investment in poverty alleviation, not just about meeting basic needs.

■ People often have entrenched opinions about what is and isn't important. For example, it is not uncommon to hear that 'technical issues are not important', or are less important than social ones in ensuring sustainability. In reality, projects require both software and hardware. Good technical design informed by an understanding of resource conditions (availability, quality, reliability) is essential. So is investment in community mobilization and participation.

Lessons? Sustainability has different dimensions. It is not just about financing and community management and ownership of assets. It is also about whether there is enough water, of a suitable quality, to support livelihoods across seasons, and between good and bad years. This element of environmental sustainability is often ignored in the literature on the demand-responsive approach. The project manager must resist the temptation to collapse sustainability into a single area and invest in this element only.

■ Many of the current shifts in rural water supply policy stem from a change in thinking about the value of water, and a recognition that centralized approaches to service delivery are unsustainable. More bottom-up, demand-responsive approaches emphasize community decision making, where communities make informed choices about: whether to participate in a project; the preferred level of service based on willingness to pay; how services are planned, implemented, operated and maintained; and how funds are managed and accounted for. Cost-sharing arrangements under which the community owns assets, and is responsible for their upkeep, are the norm. Partnership arrangements between the community and government (as facilitator-supervisor), NGOs and the private sector (as contractors and service providers) are advocated.

Lessons? The institutional and political framework for service delivery and natural resource management is changing. Roles and responsibilities may still be unclear, and partnership arrangements not yet developed. In this environment, the project manager needs to understand formal policy objectives and institutional relationships (defining how things 'should' work), and informal realities (how things actually work in practice), learning from the experience of other projects. For example, new community-based, demand-led initiatives may challenge the vested interests of old bureaucracies, including government maintenance departments and their agents. Understanding feasibility – political, institutional, logistical – is essential.

■ Community participation in the selection and siting of services, and community management and ownership of systems, has a major bearing on the sustainability of the infrastructure of rural water supply. Despite its 'feelgood' overtones, however, community decision making and management does not, by itself, ensure the interests of all households are met. Care needs to be taken to ensure that the needs of all groups – especially women, children and the poor or marginalized – are factored into decisions on service type, level, location and financing.

Lessons? Projects should take steps to ensure that the views of different people are heard and acted upon. Traditional leaders and water committees will need to be consulted, but as part of a wider consultation exercise that includes focus group discussions (based on wealth groups, for example), household and water point interviews, and (larger) village meetings. This can be time-consuming – especially in larger settlements – and demands good skills in participatory rural appraisal (PRA). However, it is time well spent. The quality of participation and the quality of information provided to users will largely determine the success of the project and the sustainability of the services provided.

■ New approaches to service provision emphasize the need for key investment decisions to be guided by consumer demand. In other words communities (and sometimes individual households) should make informed choices from a range of options, service levels and potential sites for the location of services, with opportunities for people to choose a higher level of service by paying more. In practice, choices are likely to be constrained by both the availability of water, and by the ability of service providers to support local choice. Offering different communities a range of supply options and service levels can create a heavy administrative and logistical burden for a project tasked with developing different technical, training and cost-sharing/subsidy packages on a place-by-place basis.

Lessons? In many rural areas, options are likely to be very limited. Care must therefore be taken to avoid raising unrealistic expectations about choice where local decision making may be limited to consultation on siting a single well or borehole. The project engineer, or technical contractor, has a vital role to play here in ensuring that options are screened by an understanding of technical and environmental feasibility. At the same time, the project manager must be realistic about what a project can do, given its administrative and technical capacity, and the capacity of other stakeholders (e.g. the private sector; local government) to support, or back-up, community decision-making. Knowing the difference between what should be done and what can be done – given the capacity of the project and wider support structures – is essential.

■ Good projects need to draw on a range of skills and experience. New approaches to rural water supply also imply new ways of applying skills and experience. Traditionally, the project engineer has made key technical decisions on behalf of communities. Now, the engineer is expected to provide users with informed choices, leaving them to take final decisions. Traditionally, a community development worker or social development specialist has handled the project–community dialogue. Now, they should be expected to work with engineers to screen and develop options, and develop management and cost-sharing systems.

Lessons? The project manager needs to ensure the project can draw on a mix of skills, and that there is communication and learning across the team. For example, the project engineer/technician and community development worker need to work together to ensure that the options offered to communities reflect resource constraints as well as user preferences and payment abilities. The project manager may need to invest in capacity building for the team to ensure it is familiar with a wide range of technical, management and cost-sharing possibilities, and is equipped with the necessary skills to work with, rather than in, communities.

References, further reading and resources

Ariyabandu, R.S. and Aheeyar, M.M.M. (2004) Secure water through demand-responsive approaches: the Sri Lankan experience. ODI Water Policy Report No. 3, Overseas Development Institute, London.

Calow, R.C., Robins, N.S., MacDonald, A.M., Macdonald, D.M.J., Gibbs, B.R., Orpen, W.R.G., Mtembezeka, P., Andrews, A.J. and Appiah, S.O. (1997) Groundwater management in drought-prone areas of Africa. *International Journal of Water Resources Development*, **13**, 241–61.

Calow, R., MacDonald, A., Nicol, A., Robins, N. and Kebede, S. (2002) The struggle for water: drought, water security and rural livelihoods. BGS Commissioned Report CR/02/226N.

Deverill, P., Bibby, S., Wedgewood, A. and Smout, I. (2002) Designing water and sanitation projects to meet demand in rural and peri-urban communities. Water, Engineering and Development Centre (WEDC), Loughborough, UK. Available at: http://wedc.lboro.ac.uk/publications/

DFID (2001) Sustainable Livelihoods Guidance Sheets. Department for International Development, London. Available at: http://www.livelihoods.org

Evans, P. and Appleton, B. (1993) Community management today: the role of communities in the management of improved water supply systems. Occasional Paper 20, IRC International Water and Sanitation Centre, Delft, The Netherlands. Available at: http://www.irc.nl/

Foster, S.S.D., Chilton, P.J., Moench, M., Cardy, F. and Schiffler, M. (2000) Groundwater in rural development. World Bank Technical Paper No 463. World Bank, Washington DC. Available at: http://www-wds.worldbank.org/

Gross, B., Van Wijk, C. and Mukherjee, N. (2001) Linking sustainability with demand, gender and poverty: a study in community-managed water supply projects in 15 countries. Study undertaken by WSP and IRC. Water and Sanitation Programme, Washington DC. Available at: http://www.wsp.org

Joshi, D., (2004) Secure water—whither poverty? Livelihoods in the DRA: a case study of the Water Supply Programme in India. ODI Water Policy Report No. 4, Overseas Development Institute, London.

Moriarty, P. and Butterworth, J. (2003) The productive use of domestic water supplies: how water supplies can play a wider role in livelihood improvement and poverty reduction. Thematic Overview Paper, IRC International Water and Sanitation Centre. Available at: http://www.irc.nl/

Nicol, A.L. (2000) Adopting a sustainable livelihoods approach to water projects: implications for policy and practice. Working Paper 133, Overseas Development Institute, London. Available at: http://www.odi.org.uk/publications/

Perry, C.J., Rock, M. and Seckler, D. (1997) Water as an economic good: a solution, or a problem? Research Report 14, International Irrigation Management Institute, Colombo, Sri Lanka. Available at: http://www.iwmi.cgiar.org

Reedman, A., Calow, R.C. and Bate, D. (2002) The value of geoscience information in less developed countries. BGS Commissioned Report CR/02/087N.

Sara, J. and Katz, T. (1997) Making rural water supply sustainable: report on the impact of project rules. Water and Sanitation Programme, Washington, DC. Available at: http://www.wsp.org/publications/global_ruralstudy.pdf

UNICEF (1999) Towards better programming: a water handbook. Water, Environment and

Sanitation Technical Guidelines Series No.2, United Nations Children's Fund, New York. Available at: http://www.unicef.org/wes/

WaterAid (2001) Looking back: the long term impacts of water and sanitation projects. A condensed version of the WaterAid research report, 'Looking back: participatory impact assessment of older projects'. WaterAid, London, June 2001. Available at: http://www.wateraid.org/

WaterAid (2004) Water and sanitation – the education drain. Education Media Report 3, written by Gideon Burrows, Jules Acton and Tamsin Maunder. Available at: http://www.wateraid.org/

World Bank-BNWP (2002) Rural water supply and sanitation toolkit. Bank-Netherlands-Water Partnership, World Bank, Washington, DC. Available at: http://www.worldbank.org/rwsstoolkit/

Basic principles and concepts in rural water supply

Black, M. (1998). Learning what works: a 20 year retrospective view on international water and sanitation cooperation, 1978–1998. Published by the UNDP-World Bank Water and Sanitation Programme, Washington, DC. Available at: www.wsp.org

Schouten, T. and Moriarty, P. (2003) Community water, community management: from system to service in rural areas. ITDG Publishing, London.

Useful websites

Water and Sanitation Programme: http://www.wsp.org

WaterAid: http://www.wateraid.org

The Africa Water Page: http://www.thewaterpage.com/

The Water and Environment Development Centre (WEDC): http://www.wedc.lboro.ac.uk/

IRC International Water and Sanitation Centre: http://www.irc.nl

Practical guidance – different steps of the project cycle

Brikke, F. and Bredero, M. (2003) Linking technology choice with operation and maintenance in the context of community water supply and sanitation. A reference document for planners and project staff. World Health Organization and IRC Water and Sanitation Centre. Geneva, Switzerland. Available at: http://who.int/en/

Deverill, P., Bibby, S., Wedgewood, A. and Smout, I. (2002) Designing water and sanitation projects to meet demand in rural and peri-urban communities. Water, Engineering and Development Centre (WEDC), Loughborough University, UK. Available at: http://wedc.lboro.ac.uk/

HR Wallingford Ltd (2003) Handbook for the Assessment of Catchment Water Demand and Use. Hydraulics Research Wallingford Ltd, UK. Available at: http://www.hrwallingford.co.uk/

Ockelford, J. and Reed, R. (2002) Participatory planning for integrated RWS and sanitation programmes. Guidelines for Planning and Designing Rural Water Supply and Sanitation Programmes. WEDC. Loughborough University, UK. Available at: http://wedc.lboro.ac.uk/

UNICEF (1999) Towards better programming: a water handbook. Water, Environment and Sanitation Technical Guidelines Series No.2, United Nations Children's Fund. Available at: http://www.unicef.org/publications/

WELL (1998) DFID guidance manual on water supply and sanitation programmes. Available at: http://wedc.lboro.ac.uk/publications/

4 Reconnaissance

4.1 Why is reconnaissance important?

Every good football manager and army general knows the importance of reconnaissance. Only with accurate intelligence on key parameters is it possible to plan a strategy for success. The same is true for water projects. Before a water project can be planned, key socio-economic, institutional and physical information must be gathered. There is little point in planning a groundwater project if there is no groundwater available, or buying sophisticated exploration equipment if groundwater can be found everywhere. In this chapter we describe how to carry out simple, effective reconnaissance on the groundwater resources.

The main aim of reconnaissance is to develop an initial conceptual framework of how the groundwater resources occur in the project area and therefore to guide expectations (and budgets) for the project. By the end of the reconnaissance period it should be possible to have answers to most of the following questions:

- Is groundwater easily found in the area?
- Is the hydrogeology fairly uniform across the area, or do conditions vary?
- Is groundwater best exploited through boreholes/hand-dug wells/springs, or a combination of these?
- What level of expense and expertise is required to develop groundwater supplies in the area?
- Are there any concerns over the water quality?
- What is the condition of the roads: will significant improvements be required before work can commence? Will work have to stop in the rainy season?
- Are there any special circumstances; e.g. very deep groundwater, saline water?
- Are there viable alternatives to groundwater (e.g. rainwater harvesting)?

Building a conceptual model of how groundwater exists is of course only one aspect of planning a rural water supply and sanitation project (as discussed in detail in Chapter 3). Consultation with local communities and institutions is fundamental to building a successful project. Other information, such as the water requirements of the area, the socio-economic conditions, health, legal aspects, population etc. are also required. Other manuals, such as Ockleford and Reed (2002), give valuable guidance on where to gather such information and how to integrate all stakeholders into the planning phase of water programmes.

4.2 Checklist for useful information

Below is a description of the different types of data to be collected during the reconnaissance phase of a groundwater project. Gathering this information should give sufficient knowledge to build a first conceptual model of the groundwater resources.

4.2.1 Topographic maps

Fundamental to any water supply project is knowing the size and shape of the project area. Topographic maps come in many different scales, from very detailed (1:10 000) to general (1:1 000 000). Throughout much of the world topographic maps are available at scales of 1:250 000 or less. Many of these maps were made after 1950, when aerial photographs began to be used widely for surveying. The location and names of communities may be out of date or inaccurate, but the topography and rivers are usually correct and form a useful base for reconnaissance.

Often, topographic maps are difficult to get hold of. If none are available locally in local or regional government offices, then the national survey department should be visited. If no maps are available in country then US and Soviet military maps at 1:250 000 and 1:200 000 scale respectively are available for much of the world. The Soviet maps have the best coverage, but are in Russian. These, and other maps, can be purchased online (see the 'Further resources' section at the end of the chapter).

4.2.2 Geological maps

Geological maps are the basis of any hydrogeological understanding of an area. Without a geological map, it is very difficult to build a conceptual mode of the hydrogeology of an area, particularly if the geology is diverse or complex. Fortunately, geological maps exist at some scale across the world. Most countries have at least a national geological map which can give an idea of what geology is likely to be present in a project area. For Africa, maps at 1:5 000 000 scale have been produced across the whole continent and can be bought as a six-map set.

In many countries maps are available at a more useable scale of 1:250 000 or 1:500 000. The availability of these maps can be checked at the offices of the national Geological Survey. If available, these maps can usually be bought, or at least copied or traced. Some maps are also held in international libraries (e.g. the British Geological Survey or the Geological Society of London) or available to buy from international retailers (see the 'Further resources' section at the end of the chapter).

BOX 4.1 Geological maps

Geological maps show the nature, extent and relative age of the different rocks in an area. The maps are based mainly on surface information, but may also include information from boreholes and aspects of geochemistry, geophysics, mineralogy and sedimentology.

A geological map is usually printed on top of a regular topographic base map, to help with locating features. The base map is printed in light colours, with the geology represented by colours, lines, and special symbols unique to geological maps. Each colour on a geological map represents a different geological unit where it appears at the surface.

On geological maps the rock units are generally divided up according to age into different rock **formations**. These formations may be made up of one rock type or consist of a number of different types of rocks arranged in a recognizable sequence. Formations are often aggregated to form **groups** that have broadly similar characteristics. Since on geology maps rocks are mainly divided on the basis of age, two sandstones of different ages would appear as different colours. The location of major faults, and the direction that different rocks are dipping, are also recorded on geological maps.

The map key shows all the units represented on the map and indicates their relative age. Usually there is a description of the different geological units on the map, which gives information about the character of the rock. Sometimes there is a generalized cross-section across the area. Maps can also be accompanied by a written description (often called memoirs).

Further resources describing geological maps are given at the end of the chapter.

4.2.3 Hydrogeological and geophysical maps

Hydrogeological maps are interpretations of geological maps which give information about the likely groundwater conditions. If available, they are a very useful resource, effectively carrying out much of the reconnaissance work for you. Unfortunately, it is rare to find a hydrogeological map at a scale useful for using on a project. Many countries, however, will have at least a national hydrogeological map, which can give an approximate indication of the likely conditions that the project will meet. The availability of hydrogeological maps can usually be checked at the national Geological Survey office. If no national map exists, then regional maps, such as the 1:5 000 000 hydrogeological map of Africa can be used (see websites in the 'Further resources' section at the end of the chapter).

Geophysical maps (also to be found in the national Geological Survey, or mining office) can also be useful. Maps of variations in the earth's gravity or magnetic field are available for many parts of the world. Of particular help in some areas are the magnetic maps (sometimes known as **aeromagnetic** maps since they have been created by towing scientific instruments behind aeroplanes). These can help identify variations in geology – particularly igneous rocks, which are often more magnetic than sedimentary rocks.

4.2.4 Borehole data

Information from any boreholes or wells already drilled in the area is fundamental to reconnaissance to the area. Many places will have had some attempt at borehole drilling or well construction. However finding records of this is often very difficult. Data that should be (but generally aren't) recorded from an existing borehole are listed below. (Later on in the book we describe in detail how to leave good records from a drilled borehole):

- borehole location
- borehole construction (e.g. depth, diameter, screen depth and size)
- the geology or a driller's log
- borehole yields
- drilling methods
- water strike; water levels.
- aquifer properties, such as transmissivity or specific capacity.

Borehole records may be lodged with the local or regional government or the organization for which the boreholes were drilled. In some countries a national agency will hold records, and every new borehole must be lodged with them. It is worthwhile searching in offices and filing cabinets and getting in touch with anybody who worked in earlier projects, not just to get the records, but to get inside knowledge of the area. Few people make adequate records of abandoned boreholes, so it is important to remember that any borehole records found for an area may give an optimistic view of the likely success rate.

Borehole information is only useful if you know where the boreholes are located on the ground. Some boreholes records may have accurate co-ordinates, particularly recent records since the widespread use of GPS (see Box 4.2). More often the record will just contain a village name, and even then it can sometimes be difficult to match up this name to any villages that local residents have heard of! However, with a little time and consultation it may be possible to plot many of the villages on a map.

4.2.5 Technical reports and scientific papers

Reconnaissance becomes a whole lot easier if someone else has done some of the work for you. For some parts of the world technical reports on the hydrogeology may already have been written: maybe as part of a previous water project or a student's thesis. Getting to know of the existence of these reports may be difficult, but it is always worth trying. They are unlikely to be in libraries, or widely distributed, but will be in a filing cabinet, or in a pile beside someone's desk. The best way to locate this sort of information is to find a hydrogeologist or water engineer who has worked in the area before. If there is no one available locally then it is worth getting in touch with a national resource centre, such as a university, a national water institute or geological survey. There are several international resource centres (see web links in the 'Further resources' section at the end of the chapter) that can provide access to a hydrogeologist and large libraries of reports and scientific papers free of charge to users in developing countries.

Several thousand scientific papers have been written about various aspects of the hydrogeology of Africa, Asia and South America. Increasingly, papers are indexed and available on the World Wide Web. It is possible that someone has carried out a scientific study of an area close to where you are working. It is a specialist skill to sift through all the literature to find something appropriate, so it may be more useful to link up with a local university or national resource centre.

4.2.6 Aerial photographs

Aerial photographs can be an excellent reconnaissance tool. They allow you to see what the ground is like around a community and map out the landforms, rivers, geological structures (such as faults and fractures), land use and vegetation. Aerial photographs are usually found in the same places that you find topographic and geology maps – survey departments or the national Geological Survey. In some countries access to them is restricted for security reasons and permission from a state official is required. Available aerial photographs are often more than 30 years old and some as much as 50 years, so the land use and roads may now be different.

When buying aerial photographs it is important to buy overlapping photos – usually with an overlap of at least 60 per cent to ensure that a 3D picture can be built up. The photographs should include information about the camera lens to allow corrections to be made for variations in the lens surface (Avery and Berlin 1992).

A **stereoscope** is required to interpret aerial photographs. This allows two overlapping photographs to be viewed at the same time giving a 3D picture of the ground surface. It takes a little bit of practice to be able to see the 3D image, but once the technique is mastered, the photographs come to life and much more detail becomes available. To record the interpretation, a clear plastic sheet is overlaid on one of the photos and the information drawn on top. Geologists often mark on **photolineaments** – straight lines on the photos which may be faults (and in some environments good targets for wells and boreholes).

4.2.7 Meteorological and hydrological data

Rainfall and evaporation are used to find information about the length of the dry season, the potential for groundwater recharge and the feasibility of using other sources of water, such as rainwater harvesting. Data from stream gauging can be interpreted to give useful information on the importance of groundwater in a catchment, by giving a measure of contribution of groundwater to streams. However, in many parts of the world stream gauges are not available.

Rainfall gauges are often located at schools, clinics, hospitals, churches and government departments, and there is likely to be a local enthusiast who has kept records for many years. Evaporation pans are more difficult to maintain and are, therefore, usually only found at airfields or large irrigation schemes. If no raingauge is available in the area, it is worth setting one up. The most important consideration is to find someone with an interest (maybe at a hospital, school or local government department) who will keep the measurements year after year. Gunston (1998) has written an excellent practical manual for setting up realistic monitoring networks across the world.

However, for reconnaissance purposes the information is required straight away – the project cannot wait 5 years until representative data have been collected. A rough idea of climate can be obtained from national rainfall charts or a map of rainfall across the country. Some international datasets are available, for example from the World Meteorological Organization (WMO) and the Intergovernmental Panel on Climate Change (IPCC); see the links in the 'Further resources' section at the end of the chapter.

4.3 Tapping into existing knowledge

It is always helpful to find someone who has worked in the area before. Not only can they give their own opinion of the area, but also they can help point in the direction of other projects in the area or maps and reports that might have been written. The local hydrogeological expert, however, can be elusive. S/he may be in the local or regional government, attached to a drilling company or in a local or international consultancy. Many of these places will be visited anyway, to try and gather some of the data and information required for reconnaissance (see Table 4.1), so it shouldn't add too much time to search out a valuable 'key informant'.

Once one has been found, it is important to ask the right questions and if possible to keep the lines of communication open. Here are some examples of questions to ask:

- What was their involvement in the area?
- How easy is it to find groundwater – what was their success rate?
- What do they know about the geology?

Table 4.1 Information available from different organisations

Institution	Data and information
Mapping or Survey Institute	Topographic maps, aerial photographs
Geological Survey	Geological maps, aerial photographs, hydrogeological maps, aeromagnetic maps
Rural Water Department	Databases of boreholes, reports of previous projects or district-wide surveys
Universities	Geological maps, local research in the area, student theses, academic literature
Agricultural/irrigation programmes	Borehole databases and reports. Possibly some maps
Local consultancies	Databases of boreholes, reports of previous projects, files on geophysical surveys
Drilling company	Local knowledge, databases of existing (and abandoned) boreholes
Local NGOs, local government	Databases of boreholes, consultants' reports, records of those who have worked in the area, local hydrogeological knowledge
International geological organisations	Geological maps, consultants, reports, academic literature

- Do they have records or reports of borehole drilling, or the project in general?
- Is there any poor water quality in the area?
- What techniques would they consider for finding groundwater?
- What knowledge do they have of other projects, or of people knowledgeable about the area?

Most engineers or geologists think best when they are drawing. It can often be highly instructive to get them to draw the following:

- a map of the area, showing geology and easy/difficult areas to find water
- a conceptual diagram of how they believe groundwater exists in the area.

However, all advice and information given should be treated cautiously and always checked in the field: people can often give misleading information in their enthusiasm to be helpful.

4.4 A reconnaissance site visit

The first visit to a project area is very important. It is at this time that lasting impressions are made. The project is also at its most fluid in the early stages, so design alterations are much easier. If possible, a visit should be made when the water problems are likely to be at their worst – during the height of the dry season. Several days should be spent visiting different parts of the area, trying to get a balanced overview of the water situation in an area. This will be helped if some of the other reconnaissance information (particularly maps) has already been gathered. It is better to cover more ground and make a rapid assessment, rather than making a detailed assessment in only one or two areas.

The main aims of a reconnaissance hydrogeological visit are:

- to triangulate information already collected
- to meet and discuss issues with the local engineers (note that within the project there will have been much contact with local partners in preparation for the project – so it is important to work within this framework)
- to make rapid assessments of geology, hydrogeology and existing water points
- to get an impression of road access and other practical difficulties in the area
- to get an early impression of the population distribution and settlement types (for example, are they clustered or scattered) as this will have an impact on the type and location of new water sources.

4.4.1 Equipment

Below is a list of equipment that it would be useful to take.

- Field notebook: obvious – but make sure it is a good notebook (not scraps of paper) and that all observations are written carefully.
- Camera: a photograph is an excellent way of recording information – make sure you record the location of the photograph and try to match up photos to locations soon after the visit.
- Magnifying glass: for examining rocks in more detail – Appendix 1 contains a detailed description of how to assess the geology.
- Geological hammer: for breaking rocks to get fresh unweathered samples to look at.
- GPS: this is a small, inexpensive piece of equipment about the size of a mobile phone or calculator which can accurately locate where it is on the ground (see Box 4.2).
- Water conductivity meter: this is a simple robust field instrument that can measure the salt content of water (see Chapter 8 on water quality).
- Water-level dipper: for measuring the depth of water levels in existing wells or boreholes (see Chapter 7).
- Bags and labels: for keeping samples of rocks that you are unsure of and need a second opinion on.

BOX 4.2   Using a global positioning system (GPS)

A GPS is a robust pocket-sized instrument that can accurately give the location of where it is (see Figure 4.1). It is very easy to use – when switched on it should automatically give the coordinates of its position after a few minutes. When switched on, the GPS tracks the position of satellites and from this information uses mathematics to work out where it is. It is, therefore important that the equipment has a clear view of the sky, to be able to pick up the satellites.

It is important to have the GPS set up to give the same readings as the base map being used on the project. For example, if the map is in degrees and minutes, then the GPS should give readings in degrees and minutes; if the map uses local grid coordinates (e.g. 125600, 034560) then the GPS should be set to read in these coordinates. The GPS should also be set up in the correct datum: the maps should have the datum used to make the map written on them (e.g. Transverse Mercator, etc.). If this information is not easily available then a standard datum (such as WGS84) is usually fine for accuracy up to 1 km.

Figure 4.1   A GPS being used in the field; carrying it on your head is not obligatory.
Photo: BGS; © NERC 1998.

4.4.2 A rough procedure

Meeting local officials and partners

The first thing to do when visiting the project area is to meet up with the local partners (or potential partners). By the time that a reconnaissance survey is necessary, there will have been several other meetings with partners to discuss the potential project – it is vital that the hydrogeologists and water engineers work within this framework (see Chapter 3).

Take your time in these initial discussions, and go over all the details you have written down to make sure that nothing has been missed. It is often useful to have a number of questions prepared beforehand. The following questions may be useful.

- With the partners, discuss all the reconnaissance information that has already been collected and if possible give them copies. Discuss in detail what other data may exist.
- Discuss what other projects have occurred in the area and who was involved.
- Prepare a plan (with the partners) of key informants to meet.
- With a base map for the area (even a rough sketch), ask them to draw a map of existing water points and also areas where it is easy or difficult to find groundwater.
- Prepare with them a field visit which will cut across the area to show a variety of hydrogeological environments.
- Discuss the condition of the roads and bridges for access of a drilling rig.

These discussions can then be repeated with other key informants identified by the partners.

A field visit

Plan a drive across the area which takes in the variety of geological conditions and existing water points. To get a representative sample it is useful to make two traverses across the area, perpendicular to each other (see Figure 4.2). For this rapid reconnaissance it is generally sufficient to keep to the better roads so that more ground can be covered in the time. A project partner should accompany you on a field visit, both so that s/he can learn about the geology, but also to facilitate and explain to local communities what is being done.

- Stop at rock cuttings and examine the geology: describe the rocks (see Appendix 1), take a sample, and also a GPS reading so it can be marked on the map. Check the geological maps available for the area, and try to work out how variable different rock types are.
- Stop at water sources. Make a description: pump type, whether it is working, depth (measure with dipper if it is open – a dull thud is felt

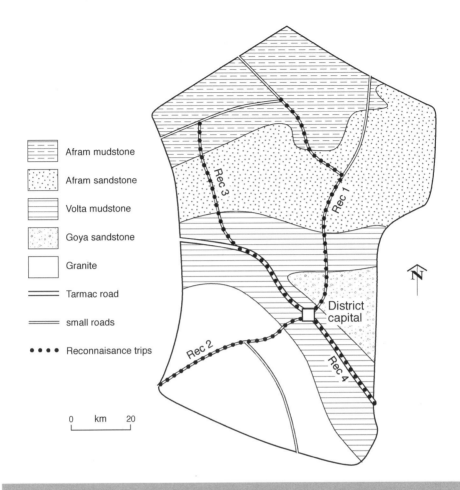

Afram mudstone

Afram sandstone

Volta mudstone

Goya sandstone

Granite

Tarmac road

small roads

Reconnaisance trips

0   km   20

Figure 4.2 How to design reconnaissance field visits for understanding the geology and hydrogeology. Each of the geological units should be visited – preferably using good roads.

when the dipper touches the bottom), water level and electrical conductivity (SEC) of the water. Discuss with the community how well the source works at different times of year (how many basins or jerrycans can be collected? does a queue form? does the colour or taste change during the day or year? does it frequently break down? does the yield decline over the year? etc.). Ensure that the community know exactly why you are there; it is often useful to discuss with the project partner beforehand a strategy for approaching communities so that hopes are not raised or a false impression given.

- With local partners, visit one or two villages in different hydrogeological areas to discuss the water supply problems in more detail. Walk to the dry season water sources to try to work out why water occurs there: maybe a river, a small pond, or groundwater seepage. Note any successful or dry wells and boreholes and work out the geology for the village from the material excavated from hand dug wells, or nearby river valleys. (More information on how to carry out a community reconnaissance visit is given in Chapter 5.)

■ Make a rough assessment of the quality of the roads – particularly noting the quality of road bridges and culverts and areas that are inaccessible to drilling rigs, or accessible only at certain times of year.

4.5 Filling in the gaps

In most areas there will be some information that is not available: no list of existing water points, or – more seriously – no available geological or topographic map at a useful scale. However, all information can be generated from scratch, given the right expertise; and this is often fairly inexpensive compared to the overall cost of a water supply project.

4.5.1 Locating villages and existing water points

A GPS can be used to locate villages, water sources and past borehole drilling sites quickly and cheaply (see Box 4.2). Anyone can be trained to use a GPS in a few hours, and provided it has been set up correctly it will provide an accurate location (within about 100 m). Arrange for someone to visit all the villages to take and record GPS readings for village centres and existing improved water points. The water points can be described briefly: type (e.g. borehole or hand-dug well), depth, condition (i.e. working or not), type of pump, etc.

4.5.2 Creating a topographic map

In the absence of topographic maps, information from satellites can be used to help create a base map for the area. Satellite images are now widely available and relatively inexpensive (several hundred dollars); however, interpreting them correctly is a specialized technique and will require input from a good consultant or university. Rivers and roads can be easily interpreted from satellite images, and sometimes land use or geology (see below). With the increasing availability of Soviet military maps over the past few years, however (see above), it should be possible and cheaper to purchase the 1:200 000 scale map rather than create a new one from satellite imagery. The map could be traced and the Russian translated to a more useful language for the project.

4.5.3 Creating a geological map

If there is no geological map for the area apart from a small scale (1:1 000 000) national map it may be useful to have a new geological map made of the area. A university, consultant or Geological Survey is best placed to carry out this work – a map at 1:250 000 scale could be made in a matter of months. More detailed maps can also be made for selected areas. Reconnaissance geological maps are made using satellite images along with aerial photographs. The geologist will then visit the area to 'ground truth' the map and take samples of the rocks for further analysis.

4.5.4 Hydrogeological understanding

If during the reconnaissance phase there is little or no information about how groundwater occurs, it may be necessary to carry out a more detailed hydrogeological survey. Again, this is something that a good consultant would be best placed to carry out. A detailed hydrogeological investigation generally involves testing the different rocks units on a geological map. If no boreholes are available, test boreholes are drilled and the aquifer properties estimated using pumping tests (see Chapter 7). Several boreholes are required in each rock unit to try to give a more representative impression.

In areas where little is know about the water quality, it can be useful to take water samples from existing sources to map out variations. There are certain procedures for taking samples (see Chapter 8) and samples need to be sent to a reliable laboratory. Again a good consultant or university should be able to carry out the work and interpret the data.

4.6 Making use of the information: creating a conceptual model

4.6.1 Getting it all together

The aim of reconnaissance is to create a conceptual model for how groundwater exists in an area. If, for example, the geological maps indicate that the project area is underlain by granite and the field visit confirms that the granite is weathered and that there are some sustainable water supplies present in the area, then a programme can be developed based on finding groundwater in weathered granite.

To interpret all the data and information collected during reconnaissance it should be first brought together. There are two main ways of doing this: spreading out all the data collected on a large table, or putting all the data on a geographical information system (GIS) – both are equally valid. A GIS is essentially a computer method of overlaying and arranging maps (see Box 4.3).

1 First, the geological map should be reviewed with the geological data collected on the field visit and any other geological information collected from reports or interviews.

■ The location of each of the rock samples collected should be plotted on the map, and also the interpretations from reports and interviews (see Figure 4.3).

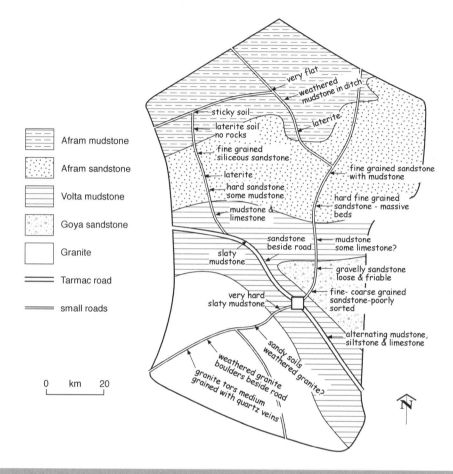

Afram mudstone

Afram sandstone

Volta mudstone

Goya sandstone

Granite

Tarmac road

small roads

0   km   20

Figure 4.3 Confirming the geology – field notes are plotted on the geological base map to help interpret the geology map, and in some cases to update it.

- Ask the following questions: are the different sources of information consistent? If not, how serious are the inconsistencies? If serious then it is best to get a second opinion from a geologist at a university, consultancy or Geological Survey.
- Write a summary of the geology of each of the units: e.g. 'sandstone and mudstone layers – more sandstone in the south'; or 'granite – deep pockets of weathering throughout the area'.

2 A preliminary hydrogeological interpretation for the different geological units can then be given (see Figure 4.4).

- The location of all known existing water points are plotted on the geological map and descriptions added about depth, yield and water quality.

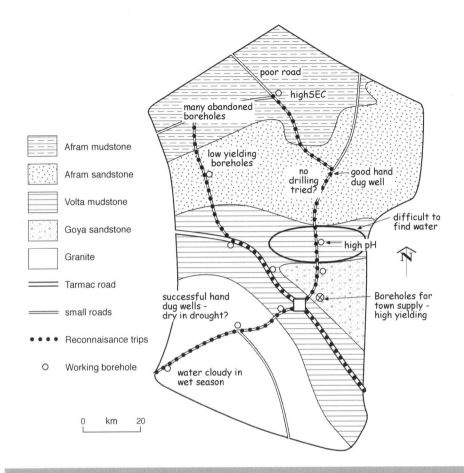

Afram mudstone

Afram sandstone

Volta mudstone

Goya sandstone

Granite

Tarmac road

small roads

• • • • Reconnaisance trips

○ Working borehole

0   km   20

Figure 4.4 Hydrogeological field notes plotted on the base geological map.

- Information from key informants, reports and interviews is then noted on the map.
- First look for consistencies across the map – for example areas where there are many successful boreholes and the geology is marked as a sandstone, or an area where many boreholes have been drilled, but most are unsuccessful and the geology is unweathered granite.
- As a first attempt at a hydrogeological interpretation extrapolate information across the different geological units.
- Mark down areas of uncertainty and complexity – for example, a sandy area where the boreholes are unsuccessful, or geological units with no hydrogeological data.
- If there are no existing boreholes or wells in an area then a judgement has to be made from the initial geological descriptions alone. The tables and conceptual diagrams in Chapter 2 should then be used as a first guess.

This map then forms the basis for a preliminary groundwater potential map. It should be considered a dynamic map and will have to be refined several times once the project has started and information is gathered from new wells and boreholes.

4.6.2 Producing a groundwater development plan

The preliminary groundwater potential map can now be used to discuss options with other team members and project partners to form a groundwater development plan. The map should enable a judgement to be made on the expertise and equipment required to find sustainable groundwater supplies in different areas – and the likely success rates. Figure 4.5 shows a rough groundwater potential map, drawn up from the reconnaissance visit.

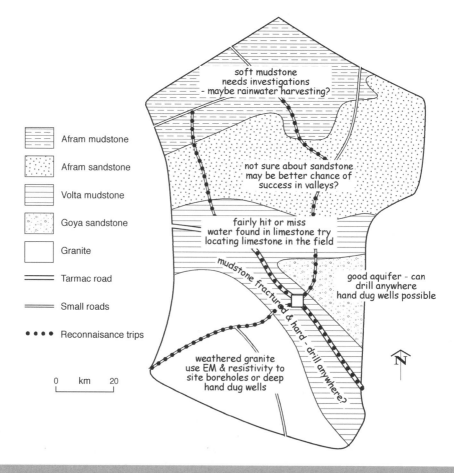

Afram mudstone

Afram sandstone

Volta mudstone

Goya sandstone

Granite

Tarmac road

Small roads

Reconnaisance trips

0   km   20

soft mudstone
needs investigations
- maybe rainwater harvesting?

not sure about sandstone
may be better chance of
success in valleys?

fairly hit or miss
water found in limestone try
locating limestone in the field

mudstone fractured & hard - drill anywhere?

good aquifer - can
drill anywhere
hand dug wells possible

weathered granite
use EM & resistivity to
site boreholes or deep
hand dug wells

N

Figure 4.5 A preliminary groundwater development plan developed from the reconnaissance information.

BOX 4.3 Geographical information systems (GIS)

A GIS is an excellent tool for water supply projects. It allows digital map information to be combined, analysed and presented in many different ways. Topographic maps, geology maps and hydrogeological maps can be overlain with point data, such as the location of villages and water points (Figure 4.6). All the different types of data can be combined to produce new maps – tailor made for the project and easy to update. This means that different maps can be easily created for different project stakeholders. Once map data is in a GIS it can be rapidly analysed, e.g. to find the average rainfall over a selected area, or finding how many wells are lying on a certain rock type

To set up a GIS demands specific expertise and considerable effort to get all the data in the appropriate format. Universities and consultants should, however, be able to carry out this work. To create a GIS for an area, the available data are first put into digital form and georeferenced. That means digitizing topographic and geological maps and making sure they are in the same map registration. Once this is done, other information, such as databases of village location or water points can be added and plotted on top.

Once a GIS is set up, it is easy to manipulate and change, unlike a printed map. Therefore, when new data is available and the hydrogeology is known in more detail a new map can printed for use in the field. The main GIS programmes used around the world are Arc® and MapInfo®. Like all computer software, however, it must be remembered that GIS is just a tool to help the project and not an end in itself.

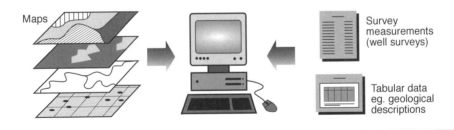

Maps

Survey measurements (well surveys)

Tabular data eg. geological descriptions

Figure 4.6 Summary of a geographical information system.

For one area, hand dug wells may be able to be constructed anywhere with no hydrogeological constraints. Another area may require boreholes to be drilled to a depth of 100 m for the best chance of success. In some places there may be little chance of success for groundwater, so another supply option may need to be considered. Such a map can be useful for assessing whether targets set by a project (such as a certain amount of water per person within a certain distance) are likely to be met over the whole project area, or whether they are unrealistic.

It is a valid (but often unpopular) approach to say that after the reconnaissance we do not know the best way to proceed and further investigations are required. However, it is much better to highlight uncertainty now, than build up expectations and waste time and resources developing a plan based on uncertain groundwater resources.

As Chapter 3 describes, the hydrogeology is only one part of the story for rural water supply. Deciding which communities to start work in is a complex process and will also depend on other factors, such as community demand, community poverty or vulnerability or where partners already have strong links. Plotting the communities onto the preliminary groundwater development map allows the hydrogeology to be factored into these decisions.

- The location of communities can be plotted on the groundwater development map.
- From reading the map, each community can then be ascribed a groundwater unit and added to the project database on communities.
- When a community is prioritized for whatever reason, the likely potential for groundwater can be quickly assessed from the map to help inform the decision as to whether to proceed or not.

To take it further (and some projects have done this successfully) it is possible to use several criteria (e.g. groundwater potential, community vulnerability and road access) to rank communities. This information can then be used to help prioritize project promotion to generate demand in the poorer areas where groundwater may be easily found.

References, further reading and resources

Avery, T.E. and Berlin, G.L. (1992) *Fundamentals of remote sensing and airphoto interpretation.* Prentice Hall, Englewood Cliffs, NJ.

Gunston, H. (1998) *Field hydrology in tropical countries. A practical introduction.* Intermediate Technology Publications, London.

Ockleford, J. and Reed, R.A. (2002) Participatory planning for integrated rural water supply and sanitation programmes. WEDC, Loughborough University, UK. Available at: http://wedc.lboro.ac.uk/publications/

Manuals to help with non-hydrogeological reconnaissance

Howard, G. (2001) Water supply surveillance. WEDC, Loughborough University, UK. Available at: http://wedc.lboro.ac.uk/publications/

Kuar S. (2002) *Methods for community participation – a complete guide for practitioners.* ITDG Publishing, London. Available at: http://www.developmentbookshop.com/

Online map shops and libraries

http://www.maplink.com/q

http://www.omnimap.com/

http://www.cartographic.com/

http://www.bgs.ac.uk/

http://www.geolsoc.org.uk/

More information on geological maps

http://www2.nature.nps.gov/geology/usgsnps/gmap/gmap1.html

http://www.bgs.ac.uk/education

Barnes, J.W. and Lisle, R.J. (2004) *Basic geological mapping* (4th edition). Geological Field Guide Series. John Wiley & Sons, Chichester, UK.

Information and data on world rainfall

http://ipcc-ddc.cru.uea.ac.uk

5 Finding groundwater

5.1 Introduction

Finding sites for wells and boreholes can be a stressful business. If the borehole or well is dry, there is usually one person blamed – the person who stuck the peg in the ground for the drilling team to drill, or the well diggers to dig. Sometimes projects try to get around this problem by asking the community to choose a site – then if the borehole is dry the community have only themselves to blame! Community involvement in siting wells and boreholes is essential (see Chapter 3); however, it should not be used as a substitute for the technical people on a water supply project doing their work properly.

An informed approach to siting wells and boreholes can have many benefits for projects: increased drilling success rates, higher borehole yields, and shallower (less expensive) boreholes (see Figure 5.1). There are many

Figure 5.1   Poorly sited boreholes can result in long queues for collecting water.
Photo: BGS, © NERC 1998.

examples throughout Africa of the economic benefits, in terms of costs saved, of appropriate well siting (van Dongen and Woodhouse 1994). Less well documented are the other benefits of improved success rates and higher yielding boreholes: handpumps fitted on higher-yielding boreholes are less likely to break down and the pumping lift is smaller, making them easier to operate. Also, the investment a community has made in time, resources and trust is much less likely to be jeopardized (on current and future projects) if drilling is successful.

There are many different methods used around the world for finding good sites for wells and boreholes. These can range from choosing random sites or water divining to highly complex geophysics, satellite interpretation or geobotany (recognizing different plants as being associated with different rocks types or the occurrence of shallow groundwater). The success or failure of all these techniques depends on their being used in the appropriate rock type or environment. A technique that may give 90 per cent success in one geological environment may be worse than useless in another. No technique or piece of equipment is consistently useful in all environments.

It is the aim of this chapter to help indicate which techniques are most suited to different hydrogeological environments and how to carry out the most common surveys. We also discuss how to involve communities in the siting process. Much of this chapter will focus on geophysical methods since they are the most widely used (and misused) method for siting wells and boreholes.

5.2 Choosing a siting technique

5.2.1 The level of sophistication required

The reconnaissance techniques of Chapter 4 should have helped identify the hydrogeological environment of the project area. Knowledge about the hydrogeological environment is vital before making any decisions on the methods for siting wells and boreholes. Depending on the results of the reconnaissance, three broad approaches can be taken (Figure 5.2):

- Where groundwater is easily found, complex siting techniques are rarely cost-effective. For example, if satisfactory yielding boreholes can be successfully located 80 per cent of the time without the use of geophysics or other techniques, then the benefits of introducing siting techniques will be unlikely to outweigh the costs. In these areas there can be a high degree of flexibility over the location of the boreholes or wells. Water points can be sited primarily on factors such as community access or the potential for contamination. Other hydrogeological issues may be important, however, such as the quality of the water, or the potential for overexploitation or silting up of boreholes.

Easy to find groundwater:
boreholes and wells can be sited anywhere

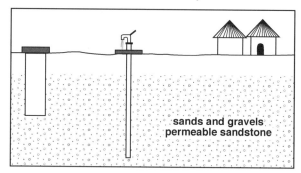

Hydrogeology generally understood:
geophysics interpreted using simple rules can be used
to site boreholes

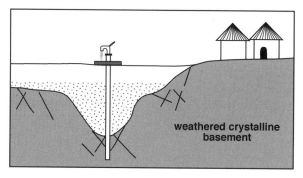

Hydrogeology complex:
successful boreholes and wells difficult to locate using
simple rules. Detailed investigations required.

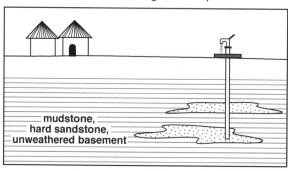

Figure 5.2	Borehole and well siting in different hydrogeological environments.
	Source: MacDonald 2001.

- In many areas groundwater resources are not ubiquitous but can be found using well-established techniques. It is in these areas that siting techniques are most cost-effective (see Chapter 3). Aerial photos, local geomorphological knowledge or geophysical techniques can be used to locate several areas where there is a greater likelihood of finding groundwater. The final choice of location can be made after taking into consideration other, nonhydrogeological, issues.
- However, there are many areas where the hydrogeological environment is complex and there are no tried and tested techniques for siting wells and boreholes. In these areas, geophysical and other techniques must first be systematically tested to provide methods for using and interpreting them that are appropriate for that environment. To be able to site boreholes and wells successfully, the hydrogeological environment must first be understood.

5.2.2 The most widely used techniques

So what techniques are available for siting wells and boreholes where fresh groundwater cannot be found everywhere? The most widely used techniques (apart from drilling exploratory boreholes) give only indirect information on the presence of groundwater.

Geophysical techniques are by far the most common methods for siting wells and boreholes for rural water supply. They measure physical properties of rocks (hence the name **geophysics**), but most cannot directly detect the presence of water – they can only help interpret the geology of an area. There are many different geophysical techniques available and countless pieces of equipment. Many require sophisticated equipment or complex analysis and are, therefore, not appropriate for use in rural water supply programmes. A summary of different geophysical techniques that have been used for rural water supply throughout the world is given in Table 5.1. A brief description of what they measure and the survey methodology is also given. More detail on the techniques can be found in standard geophysical textbooks (see the 'Further resources' section at the end of this chapter).

Aerial photographs are also sometimes used to site boreholes, but generally they are used for reconnaissance and geophysical methods are used to check the interpretation on the ground. Note that satellite images should not be used directly to site boreholes, but to help with reconnaissance: experience from many projects has shown that features identified on satellite images must always be ground-truthed using geophysics. Geomorphological surveys can also be used in some areas, where the hydrogeology is well known. Siting boreholes using local experience of certain plants, for example, can work in certain specified areas although there is little documented evidence of the success of such methods. Another siting method (not used as often as it could be) is drilling small exploratory boreholes.

Table 5.1 A summary of common geophysical techniques used in groundwater investigations

Geophysical technique	What it measures	Output	Approximate maximum depth of penetration (m)	Comments
Resistivity	Apparent electrical resistivity of ground	1D vertical geoelectric section; more complex equipment gives 2D or even 3D geoelectric sections	100	Can locate changes in the weathered zone and differences in geology. Also useful for identifying thickness of sand or gravel within superficial deposits. Often used to calibrate FEM surveys (see below). Slow survey method and requires careful interpretation
Frequency domain Electro-magnetic methods (FEM)	Apparent terrain electrical conductivity (calculated from the ratio of secondary to primary electromagnetic fields)	Single traverse lines or 2D contoured surfaces of bulk ground conductivity	50	Quick and easy method for determining changes in thickness of weathered zones or alluvium. Interpretation is non-unique and requires careful geological control. Can also be used in basement rocks to help identify fracture zones
Transient Electro-magnetic methods (TEM)	Apparent electrical resistance of ground (calculated from the transient decay of induced secondary electromagnetic fields)	Output generally interpreted to give 1D resistivity sounding	150	Better at locating targets through conductive overburden than FEM, also better depth of penetration. Expensive and difficult to operate
Very low frequency (VLF)	Secondary magnetic fields induced in the ground by military communi-cations transmitters	Single traverse lines, or 2D contoured surfaces	40	Can locate vertical fracture zones and dykes within basement rocks or major aquifers

Table 5.1 contd.

Ground penetrating radar (GPR)	Reflections from boundaries between bodies of different dielectric constant	2D section showing time for EM waves to reach reflectors	10	Accurate method for determining thickness of sand and gravel. The technique will not penetrate clay, however, and has a depth of penetration of about 10 m in saturated sand or gravel
Seismic refraction	P-wave velocity through the ground	2D vertical section of P-wave velocity	30	Can locate fracture zones in basement rock and also thickness of drift deposits. Not particularly suited to measuring variations in composition of drift. Fairly slow and difficult to interpret
Magnetic	Intensity (and sometimes direction) of earth's magnetic field	Variations in the earth's magnetic field either along a traverse or on a contoured grid	100	Can locate magnetic bodies such as dykes or sills. Susceptible to noise from any metallic objects or power cables

Resistivity

The resistivity technique is the longest established geophysical method used to site wells and boreholes throughout the world. It is a relatively simple technique: an electric current is passed through the ground and the potential difference measured using two electrodes. The use of Ohm's law allows the resistance of the ground to be calculated, which in turn can be changed to the fundamental property **resistivity** by making a few assumptions. There are two main survey techniques: profiling (measuring changes of resistivity along a traverse) and depth sounding (measuring changes of resistivity with depth at a certain point). Profiling has largely been superseded by EM or VLF surveys, or, where more detail is required, 2D electrical imaging. Therefore, resistivity is now generally used for vertical electrical sounding (VES).

Since resistivity is such an important technique it is described in much more detail later in this chapter.

Electromagnetic (EM) techniques

Many geophysical techniques rely on electromagnetic induction – e.g. VLF and GPR described below. However, in surveying for groundwater, EM usually refers to one of two methods: **frequency domain EM** (FEM) or **time domain EM** (TEM). FEM has become popular due to the ease with which surveys can be carried out, and equipment, particularly Geonics EM34, is found in many parts of the world. This method is described in detail later in the chapter. However, TEM is not used routinely to survey for rural water supplies in Africa and India although it has a number of advantages: it generally has a better depth penetration and can 'see' through clays much better than FEM. The main problem with TEM, which holds it back from widespread use, is that it is expensive and still fairly complex to use and interpret.

VLF

The 15–25 kHz frequency band is used by the military for communication with their submarines. These signals can also be used by geophysicists for examining the geology. Electrical eddy currents induced in the ground by very low frequency (VLF) magnetic fields produce secondary magnetic fields with the same frequency as the primary field but different phase. VLF instruments have been designed to compare the vertical and horizontal magnetic fields and find anomalies induced by strong secondary fields.

Steeply dipping sheet-like conductors, or steeply dipping geological contacts, can be detected using VLF. This makes the method useful for identifying dykes and fracture zones. VLF is generally more sensitive than EM to conductors, including artificial noise (Milsom 2003), so it is often used as a precursor to more conventional detailed EM surveys. VLF measurements can be made quickly and require only one operator.

Ground-penetrating radar

Ground-penetrating radar (GPR) works on a similar principle to echo sounding. Short pulses of electromagnetic radiation are propagated into the ground and reflections are recorded on a receiver. Reflections are produced where there are changes in the ground conditions, e.g. a change from sand to clay or sometimes the water table. The larger the contrast in properties, the stronger the signal reflected back to the surface. A subsurface profile is built up by moving the antennae over the ground surface keeping a fixed distance between the transmitter and receiver. Data are then collated to give a graphical plot of reflectors against depth (the depth being determined from the two-way travel times). A typical GPR section and interpretation is shown in Figure 5.3.

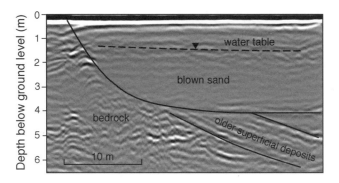

Figure 5.3	Interpretation of a GPR profile through superficial deposits in Scotland.
	Source: MacDonald et al. 2000

GPR is widely used in Europe and North America to study very shallow targets. The depth of penetration of radar is low, generally a few metres, and depends on the electrical conductivity of the rocks. For example, in clay the depth of penetration may be less than 0.5 m, whereas in dry gravels it could be more than 10 m. The depth of penetration also depends on the frequency of the signal used – lower frequencies have deeper penetrations. For the hydrogeologist, this technique is most useful for examining superficial deposits. GPR should be able to identify the thickness of superficial cover, the depth to water table and sometimes the structure of superficial cover. However, if the shallow layers have much clay, GPR will not be able to penetrate far. GPR data require extensively processing, but this can generally be done in the field using a laptop computer.

Seismic refraction

Seismic refraction is widely used for engineering purposes and for studying the water table. It should not be confused with **seismic reflection**, which is used in the oil industry to find oil and gas reserves. Seismic refraction relies on low-energy pressure waves, P-waves, which transmit energy through the ground by a series of compressions and rarefaction. The seismic waves are usually generated by sledgehammer or a small explosive and detected by geophones (see the 'Further resources' section at the end of the chapter for more details).

Seismic refraction is best used where layers are shallow (<20 m) and approximately horizontal. Interpreting seismic refraction data should give the thickness of each layer and also the P-wave velocity. Seismic waves travel at different speeds depending on the rock characteristics and also the pore fluid. P-waves travel much faster in water than in air, so this is a useful technique for finding the water table. Wave velocities are also much faster in bedrock than superficial deposits, so seismic refraction is often used to detect the thickness of the weathering zone or superficial deposits.

Undertaking a seismic survey generally takes about the same amount of time as a resistivity survey. The geophones need to be positioned and then sufficient readings taken to give a time–distance plot from both ends of the geophone string. The equipment is heavy and requires a two-person team to carry out a survey. A series of five surveys could be undertaken in a day.

Magnetic methods

Magnetic techniques are used to measure small changes in the earth's magnetic field. Local variations in the magnetic field are usually due to the presence of magnetic material. The most highly magnetic materials are manufactured – steel and iron. However, some rock minerals are also magnetic – e.g. magnetite, maghemite and pyrrhotite. Basic igneous rocks, such as basaltic lavas or dolerite dykes, contain a large proportion of these minerals and can therefore be identified using magnetic surveys. However, surveys can be difficult to carry out, because of the daily changes in the magnetic field and also the large anomalies caused by iron and steel. Magnetic survey techniques are discussed in more detail later in the chapter.

Electrical imaging

Two-dimensional (2D) electrical imaging surveys are becoming popular for mapping areas of complex geology or the flow of contaminants through aquifers. Essentially they are an evolution of the resistivity survey and measure the electrical resistivity of a 2D section of the ground. To carry out a survey, a long line of electrodes is set out and connected via a multicore cable to a console. Then the electrodes are used to carry out a series of VES readings with different midpoints and at various separations. Usually a computer controls the operation. The results from such surveys are plotted in the form of a pseudo-section which gives an approximate but distorted picture of the subsurface geology. This can then be processed using software to give an undistorted view of the subsurface. The technique gives excellent detail, and has been used to site boreholes in both India and Africa (see Figure 5.4). However, because of the complexity and requirement for highly

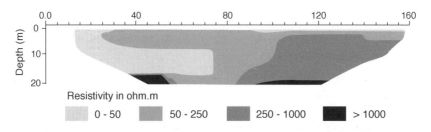

Resistivity in ohm.m

0 - 50   50 - 250   250 - 1000   > 1000

Figure 5.4 An example of 2D electrical imaging from India. A large fracture zone can easily be seen at 80 m – a borehole drilled here was successful.
Source: Ron Barker, University of Birmingham.

technical staff to carry out the surveys, it is generally economical only for large supplies, or in areas where it is very difficult to find groundwater.

Dowsers

Water dowsers are sometimes used to site wells and boreholes. Often they use forked twigs or bent welding rods; others prefer to use maps and crystals (see Figure 5.5). Banks and Robins (2002) give us several reasons why diviners are used: they are cheaper than hydrogeologists; groundwater is often thought of as magical or mysterious; in areas of great uncertainty people are generally drawn to mysterious and religious methods rather then science.

Despite water divining not being rooted in any science, it appears to work in some places. There can be several reasons for this:

- The amount of water being looked for is very small, so random drilling will still produce good results
- If the dowser is local, s/he may have a good eye for the hydrogeology. For example, in Scotland water dowers contact trained hydrogeologists to help them know what targets they are looking for.

It can be useful to make a distinction between 'practical dowsers', who have an understanding of the local hydrogeology through many years of

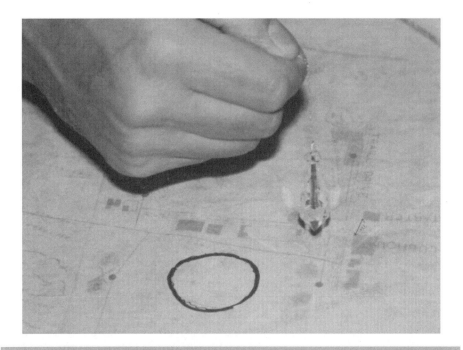

Figure 5.5   Crystal pendulum being used by a dowser to find sites for boreholes.
Photo: BGS, © NERC 1997.

experience siting wells and boreholes in an area, and 'magical dowsers' who swing pendulums over maps. Practical diviners may be of some help, but magical dowsers should be avoided. There is no magical way to site wells and boreholes, and no substitute for hard work and experience.

Geomorphological studies

In certain areas, studying the geomorphology can be an excellent way of siting wells and boreholes. For example, in some areas valleys follow the lines of major faults, so the valleys may be a good place to site boreholes. In some basement areas where the topography is undulating good borehole sites have been found halfway down the slope towards the valley bottoms; the valley bottoms are too clayey, and the tops of the interfluves too unweathered, to support good boreholes.

Other good examples are inselbergs (also known as bornhardts, tors, whale-backs or kopjes) in basement areas. Good borehole or well sites can often be found in the gravels found around the base of these large, rounded hills (see Figure 5.6). In sedimentary areas, where sandstones and mudstone are interbedded, sandstone can often be identified by slight ridges or high ground. Geomorphological studies can also be linked with general geological and hydrogeological observation and fieldwork, with good success.

Figure 5.6 Boreholes or wells can be often be successfully sited at the edge of inselbergs.
Photo: BSG, © NERC 2000.

Drilling exploratory boreholes

Another way of choosing sites for wells and boreholes is to drill narrow-diameter trial boreholes. Trial boreholes are often used to find good sites for high-yielding boreholes, such as a town supply, where the high cost can be justified; but they are rarely used for siting community water supplies.

There are different ways of siting trial boreholes: they can be drilled at several sites that have been identified using another siting technique; drilled at preferred sites selected by the community; or drilled randomly within the community. Drilling exploratory boreholes is of most use in areas of complex hydrogeology, where other siting methods are difficult to interpret. With time, as your conceptual understanding of the hydrogeology of the area becomes clearer, it may be possible to dispense with trial boreholes and rely solely on other methods.

Drilling exploratory boreholes is most cost-effective where the project has control of a drilling rig. Lightweight, relatively inexpensive rigs are now available which can drill shallow narrow-diameter boreholes (see Chapter 6). Although these may not always be suitable for drilling a production borehole they can be excellent for drilling trial boreholes – particularly as they are easy to operate and could be used by the project engineer. For finding sites for hand-dug wells, a power auger rather than a drilling rig could be used.

In practice, many projects drill trial boreholes – but usually in an informal manner. The siting team will often identify two or three sites; if the drilling team drill the first and it is dry, they will move to the second site and so on. This can be misleading, however. If the siting team keep getting the interpretation of the geophysics wrong, they may consistently be identifying the wrong sites. In areas where success is low it would be worthwhile carrying out a detailed geophysical survey and asking the drillers to drill trial boreholes along it, even in areas you think should be dry – you may surprise yourself.

Past experience

Past experience is a common method of siting boreholes. After several years experience of rural water supply in different areas, you will notice that boreholes often occur in clusters. This is a great way of increase a project's success rate – put in new water points close to existing successful water points. Although this approach may be of benefit if the new water points are much safer than the existing ones, it does little to benefit water coverage as a whole in the area. It is the communities with no improved water supplies, where previous interventions have failed, that are often the most needy. In these communities, where there is little past experience, most effort has to be made to try to understand the hydrogeology and site successful water points.

Random drilling

Random drilling of production boreholes is sometimes known as wildcat drilling. As discussed above, and in Chapter 3, this method can work well in areas where groundwater can be found easily. However, the method is of little benefit elsewhere unless accompanied by other siting methods to help understand how groundwater occurs; when wildcat drilling is accompanied by this sort of analysis it becomes trial drilling (see above).

5.2.3 Appropriate siting methods in different hydrogeological environments

In Chapter 3, four main hydrogeological environments are described: crystalline basement, consolidated sediments, volcanic rocks and unconsolidated sediments. In this section the main methods for finding groundwater in these environments is described. Much more detail and some examples for EM, resistivity and magnetic methods are given later in the chapter.

Crystalline basement rocks

There are usually two main targets for groundwater in crystalline basement rocks: areas of deep weathering and vertical fracture zones (see Chapter 2). EM techniques, resistivity and seismic refraction can all give information on the degree of weathering in the basement. Which techniques are preferred depends on how weathered the basement is:

- If the basement is deeply weathered, as in parts of Uganda, little or no technique may be required to find sufficient groundwater resources to sustain the supply of a handpump.
- If weathering is generally, but not uniformly deep, using resistivity or seismic refraction at several locations around the village may be sufficient find an area of deep weathering.
- If the weathering is poorly developed, techniques that can survey a large area quickly, such as EM, are more effective.

An approach that is widely used to good effect is to combine EM and resistivity (Beeson and Jones 1988; Barker et al. 1992). EM surveys can cover large areas rapidly (up to 1 km in an hour). Deep weathering will usually show itself as higher conductivity in EM surveys (see more detailed descriptions later). Promising areas can then be resurveyed using resistivity soundings which give detailed information at one point about resistivity (the inverse of electrical conductivity) and depth. Seismic refraction can also be useful at detecting the degree and depth of weathering, but like resistivity soundings large areas cannot be surveyed quickly.

To locate fractures in crystalline basement rocks, profiling techniques such as horizontal loop EM (generally using Geonics EM34 equipment or sometimes Apex MaxMin equipment) or VLF can be used (e.g. Carruthers and Smith 1992). These techniques are used to find geophysical anomalies caused by vertical fractures. Magnetic profiling can also sometimes be used to detect fracture zones. However, this is only useful if the fractures have certain magnetic properties; for example, if they are associated with igneous intrusions such as dykes, or with faults between rocks with different magnetic properties.

Consolidated sedimentary rocks

In consolidated sedimentary rocks there are many different targets for finding groundwater. Groundwater can be found in sandstones, limestones and mudstones. How variable the sediments are may determine the complexity of techniques and interpretation required to find groundwater: where the rocks are fairly uniform, one or two techniques can be used across large areas. However, where the rocks are complex and variable, techniques are required to first help unravel the geology, before choosing the most appropriate method for siting within that particular geology type.

In porous or highly fractured sandstones, groundwater will occur in most locations. If the sandstones form part of a layered sequence of mudstones and limestones, geophysics (EM or resistivity) can be used to distinguish sandstone. However, geophysics is often not required and boreholes can be sited anywhere with good success. In areas where the sandstones are highly cemented and porosity is low, fracture zones or zones of deep weathering may need to be identified. The same techniques as for crystalline basement can be used: EM or VLF to identify fracture zones, EM and resistivity to identify areas of deeper weathering.

In karstic limestones, water flows though individual fractures, which can be widely spaced. These fractures are generally too small to be identified using the most common geophysical techniques, although some methods have proved useful. Microgravity methods, which measure small changes in the earth's gravitational field, have been used to identify large fractures or caves; GPR has also been used to identify shallow fractures. One of the main characteristic of karstic terrains is the large, number of sustainable springs. The most certain method for having a successful water point is to tap water from the springs. If this is not possible, then boreholes drilled near springs, or in dry valleys, have the highest chance of success. However, any groundwater abstracted through boreholes will reduce the flow from the springs.

Recent coastal limestones have high permeability, and groundwater can easily be found. However, water in these aquifers can be saline and pumping can induce saline water to flow in from the coast. EM surveys can be useful in mapping the extent of saline intrusion – saline water has high conductivity – or if the aquifers are layered, resistivity can show the variation of conductivity with depth.

Mudstones are the most difficult sedimentary rock in which to find usable groundwater. The main targets for groundwater are fractures within more consolidated mudstones, interbedded sandstones or limestones, or igneous intrusions in softer mudstones. Electromagnetic methods have been found the most useful at locating areas where mudstone are more consolidated, or sandstones within mudstones (MacDonald et al. 2001). Magnetic methods will be required to find igneous intrusions. In some mudstone areas, particularly where the mudstones are soft, there may be no usable groundwater.

Volcanic terrains

Groundwater is found within fractures in volcanic rocks. Often the best targets for groundwater are the top and bottom of lava flows, which can be highly fractured. Vertical fracture zones can also be highly productive. Siting wells and boreholes can be difficult and relies on a good understanding of the geology of an area. In highland areas (e.g. parts of Ethiopia and Eritrea) springs are common and can be developed for water supplies. Mapping of the location of these springs in relation to the geology can help identify the major fracture zones. Resistivity techniques are sometimes used to identify lower resistivity (higher conductivity) at depth, which may indicate a zone of high fracturing. However, often the fractures are too small to detect from the surface. Knowledge of the geology, combined with trial drilling, may be the best way of identifying horizontal fracture zones.

Vertical fracture zones can be identified using a combination of EM methods, VLF or magnetic profiling (e.g. Drury et al. 2001). Electromagnetic anomalies are often associated with fractures; however, experience and knowledge of the geology is required to know how to accurately interpret the anomalies. Magnetic profiling has been used in some cases, where intrusions have been associated with large fault zones and also to detect the different magnetic properties of rocks on either side of a fault.

Buried river channels can also be important in volcanic terrains. Magnetic techniques combined with electrical techniques (either resistivity or EM) can usefully locate buried channels. The electrical conductivity of the channel is likely to be higher than the surrounding volcanic rocks, and magnetic anomalies may be found at the edge of the channel.

Unconsolidated aquifers

Significant volumes of groundwater are found within unconsolidated sedimentary aquifers. Often such basins comprise complex layers of sands, gravels and clays. In large sedimentary basins groundwater is easily found in sand or gravel layers. Resistivity methods can be used to distinguish clays from sands or gravels – sands and gravels have higher resistivity (lower conductivity) than clay. In most areas, no siting techniques are required to find sufficient groundwater to sustain a handpump – boreholes can be sited according to other priorities.

Alluvium is also present along many river valleys. Sustainable wells or bore-holes are best sited where the alluvium is thick and is made up of mostly sand or gravel. Drilling shallow boreholes in unconsolidated sediments is straightforward, and there are many examples around the world where they can be drilled by hand. Therefore, exploratory boreholes can often be cost-effective. Resistivity soundings are particularly useful in helping to interpret the geology where the sediments are layered. Clay layers can be identified by their lower resistivity; sands and gravel by higher resistivity and the bedrock beneath (if crystalline basement) generally as much higher resistiv-ity. EM methods can also be used to infer lithological changes (from clay to sand/gravel) or changes in thickness where the lithology is fairly uniform. The problem of non-uniqueness in interpreting EM data means that a high level of geological control is required before making any interpretation. Otherwise the presence of a thin clay layer in the alluvium may be wrongly interpreted as an area of thicker alluvium.

One of the most effective techniques for identifying the nature of unconsolidated sediments is using electrical imaging. This can give excel-lent resolution of the nature of the sediments, but is complex to carry out, requiring computers and sophisticated equipment. It is cost-effective only where other techniques have failed.

5.3 Village observations and discussions

5.3.1 Overview

As discussed in Chapter 3, choosing a location for a new water source is not simply a technical matter, to be determined by the driller or hydrogeologist alone. Decisions should also reflect community needs and preferences, and be informed by local knowledge and experience of what 'works' and 'doesn't work'. Making the right choice (often by reaching some form of negotiated consensus) can take place only with good communication and consultation between implementing agency, project staff and the community, and with good information about the consequences of certain choices.

In this section, we begin by looking at the general advantages and disadvan-tages of user participation in site selection. We then examine three specific elements of project/community decision making in site selection. These focus on groundwater availability – finding out about resource potential and reliability by tapping local knowledge; groundwater access – ensuring the source is accessible to the community, and the different households within it; and ensuring the source fits the intended uses (see Figure 5.7).

In Figure 5.7, the assessment of groundwater availability is highlighted. For a project hydrogeologist, this is the traditional entry point for technical advice, based on an assessment of environmentally feasible supply options. In terms of source access and use, we move beyond the technical to look at

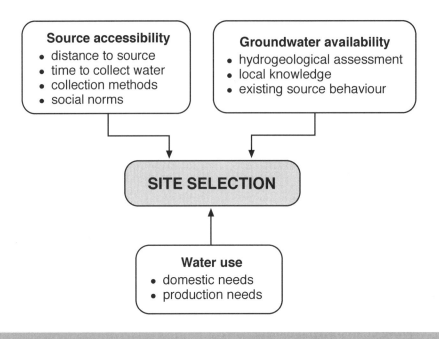

Figure 5.7 Factors to consider when siting wells and boreholes.

the socio-economic aspects of site selection. In practice, an assessment of community demand for water and option identification and design should already have been undertaken with the community. This would normally include a wider assessment of water access and use considerations (see Chapter 3), emphasizing the needs of poorer, more vulnerable groups (e.g. households headed by women) who generally make up the majority of those lacking access to improved services.

The aim here is not to provide detailed guidance for technical specialists on how to carry out water use and livelihood surveys, though tips on further reading are listed at the end of the chapter. Rather, the aim is to highlight other (non-technical) considerations in site selection, and to provide check-lists that the technical specialist could expect to see factored into decisions that, traditionally, may have been theirs alone.

5.3.2 Working with communities in site selection: pros and cons

Traditionally, engineers and other technical specialists have been trained to take important technical decisions **on behalf** of communities, or a project's donors. However, with more demand responsive approaches to project implementation, this situation is changing (Chapter 3). The need to involve users in decision-making is now well established, but it can create some uncertainty for engineers and technicians used to taking decisions by themselves.

Table 5.2 summarizes some of the advantages, and disadvantages, of involving users in decision making. One of the most important points to note is that user involvement can benefit both users **and** project technicians. This is because communities can contribute local knowledge about groundwater occurrence that can usefully supplement data provided by the formal assessment techniques discussed elsewhere in this chapter. More generally, seeking the views of users in site selection, as in other aspects of option design and implementation, helps ensure the following:

■ Site selection decisions reflect, and benefit, different groups within the community. Communities are not homogeneous, and making sure that the voices of poorer, less articulate households are factored into the decision-making process is one of the key challenges of project design and implementation.
■ The sustainability of water supply infrastructure, as users who have been involved in making decisions about the services they want are often prepared to invest in their provision and maintenance.

Despite its obvious advantages, however, a participatory approach to decision making has its drawbacks. These should not be underestimated. For the busy project technician trying to meet tight deadlines within budget, involving users presents some major challenges:

■ Consulting different users within a community does not necessarily lead to consensus. It is often difficult or impossible to satisfy every need and preference, and a degree of compromise is inevitable.
■ Although some technicians are familiar with the tools of livelihoods analysis, demand assessment and community negotiation, many are

Table 5.2 Involving users in site selection: some advantages and disadvantages

Advantages	Potential problems
More opportunity to identify, assess, use or adapt local knowledge, e.g. in understanding user preferences, and local indicators of water availability (vegetation, topography, etc.).	More time consuming for the engineer/ technician than unilateral decision-making, and more demanding in terms of consultation-negotiation skills (though others can assist).
Involving users in decision-making helps build community ownership of infrastructure and acceptance of follow-on responsibilities (e.g. cost recovery and maintenance).	More time consuming for potential beneficiaries: users may not be willing, or able, to contribute as required.
Understanding the views of different households within a community helps ensure site(s) selected meet broad needs, and not just the needs of the most powerful or articulate.	Ensuring the voice of marginal groups is factored into decision-making is challenging, in terms of the time and skills of the project team. The preferences of different groups may vary, calling for delicate negotiation and compromise.

not. For this reason teamwork is essential, with the technician working closely with team members who are trained in participatory methods to understand user needs and preferences, and to explain technically feasible siting options in this context, so that users can make an **informed** choice. See Kuar (2002) for information on participatory techniques.

■ Consulting users takes time if it is done properly. Explaining how a decision was reached is not the same as consulting people about what they want. And holding a village meeting to reach a decision will, almost certainly, mean that the views of poorer households, and women in particular, are not heard.

■ At the same time, **being** consulted is also time consuming! Users may not be able to spend hours in discussion at busy periods of the year. Users may also regard participation as unnecessary, or unwarranted, especially where there is a continuing expectation that others (the government, the project, the experts) should take decisions and provide services.

5.3.3 Groundwater availability – tapping local knowledge

Tapping into the experience and knowledge of communities can provide valuable insights into the hydrogeology, supplementing information provided through more formal investigative techniques. So how can a community assist, and become involved in, the assessment process?

■ Firstly, local people are likely to know their environment well, and can provide the history of water development within the village – successes, failures, and the reasons behind them. Of course not all villagers have the same insights and experience, and most villages are far from static. However, older members of the community – particularly women – can be a rich source of information, not least because the burden of water collection typically falls on them.

■ Secondly, community members can assist with the formal hydrogeological assessment by contributing local knowledge on rocks and topography, and by discussing local indicators of water availability (e.g. vegetation type) with project staff. Getting community members involved in this assessment is important. For example, people could be encouraged to investigate potential sites themselves, organizing their own investigation with the assistance of the project technician.

Box 5.1 summarizes some of the key groundwater availability questions that can be discussed with the community, and suggests actions that the project technician can take (perhaps with a social scientist or facilitator) to address them. Figure 5.8 shows some of the important locations to visit in a community.

BOX 5.1 Working with communities to assess groundwater availability

Assessing the geology of the community and triangulating map information:

Key questions

- What is the geology of the area?
- How does geology vary within the village boundary?
- What information or evidence (if any) did previous project teams leave?

How to get answers

- Prepare by consulting a geological map of the area. What sort of rocks are **likely** to be present?
- Visit places where rocks are exposed. River valleys and hills are often good locations, but ask the community members (children often know these places) – see Figure 5.8.
- Observe boulders in the village used for seats, grinding stones, etc., and find out where they have come from.
- Visit any wells that have been dug and examine soil-rock profiles.
- Visit any borehole sites (failed or working) and look for rock chippings from drilling.
- Encourage people to investigate potential sites themselves, e.g. by digging trial pits or using a shallow auger. In some cases, people may be able to plan their own investigation, with project staff help.

Evidence of groundwater: assessing the behaviour of existing sources:

Key questions

- What are the main water sources available for use by the community (e.g. springs/seeps, wells, boreholes)? What sources no longer provide water, and why?
- How does availability vary between sources? Which are the most reliable, and why?
- How does availability change over time, e.g. across seasons and between 'good' and 'bad' (e.g. drought) years?
- Does availability (generally, or seasonally) affect the quantity of water used by households, or the uses to which it is put? How?
- Does water quality (taste, colour, smell, preferences) vary between sources and/or over time? How? What explanations, if any, are offered? Reports of ill-health/disease related to water?

How to get answers

- Key informant interviews, focus group discussion, direct observation – develop inventory and map of water sources used by community members (maps can be drawn and annotated by community members).

BOX 5.1 – *cont.*

■ Use map to discuss characteristics of different sources, focusing on reliability and quality of supply. Supplement with more detailed water point histories (discussion is best held at the source itself with women), and ask about changes in water levels and yields, recovery and queuing times.

■ Explore links between availability and use (domestic and productive) with different households (e.g. by locally-defined wealth group). Drawing up a seasonal calendar of water availability and use from different sources, for good and bad years, can be very useful.

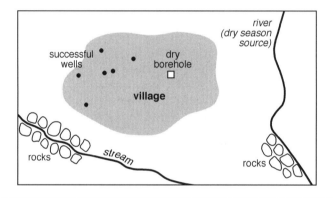

| Figure 5.8 | Places to visit on a reconnaissance visit to a community. |

5.3.4 Source access, use and siting: translating potential options into real ones

Finding a location where groundwater is available is, by itself, not sufficient. Water must also be accessible to the community, and to the different households within it, and be of sufficient quantity and quality to meet community and households needs, both now and in the future. How is this related to site selection?

Firstly, the needs of users in terms of water use should inform site selection. For example, although many water projects make the assumption (or are forced to assume) that domestic water points are used for domestic uses only, in practice the situation is often quite different (see Chapter 3). For many, water is also a productive asset, used for a wide range of uses to secure food and non-food income. These uses may not be anticipated by project teams, but are vital for supporting and strengthening livelihoods. Assessments must therefore uncover, and factor in, multiple uses of water into siting decisions, for example by examining the peak domestic and productive water demands, and ensuring that demand can be met from a particular source. A range of potential access issues must also be factored into decision making. The obvious one is time needed to collect water from different locations. Less obvious could be social-cultural barriers to access that exist in certain areas, precluding free access by some members of the community. Box 5.2 summarizes some of the key source access and use questions that should be addressed with the community.

BOX 5.2   Working with the community on access and use issues

Water use considerations:

Key questions

- What are the principal uses of water in the community?
- What uses, if any, would be specific to the new source, and why?
- What is community demand for, and how are the different components of demand prioritized or ranked by different groups (e.g. demand for more reliable, better quality water? Water for productive, income generating uses? Water that is more accessible to larger numbers of people in the required quantity)?
- How would use vary over time – across seasons, between good and bad years, over the longer term?
- Which of the potential sites/areas identified in the groundwater availability assessment are most likely to meet the needs identified above, paying particular attention to the needs of poorer groups?

How to get answers

- Key informant interviews, focus group discussion, direct observation – to develop water use calendars. Note: do not assume water use is static, or used only for domestic activities.
- Various tools can be used to evaluate community demand, e.g. development of objective trees and ranking exercises, conducted with small groups (e.g. different wealth groups). It is important that siting considerations are included (they are often left out). See 'Further resources' at the end of the chapter for more information on these tools.

Water access issues:

Key questions

- What are the key factors affecting the use and quantities of water accessed by different households (e.g. labour availability, water transport, water storage, distance, topography, etc.)?
- Which factors are linked, directly or indirectly, with source location?

BOX 5.2 – *cont.*

- Are there any social-cultural factors that might limit access to sources at certain locations (e.g. customary rules/norms affecting where women and children from certain groups can go)?

How to get answers

- Key informant interviews, focus group discussion, direct observation – as above, development of water use calendars can provide a hook to hang discussions on, especially when combined with seasonal activity calendars showing work and labour demands.
- It should not be assumed that all sites will be equally accessible to community members of different age, gender, caste and social standing. An understanding of social-cultural barriers to access can only be gained by discussing source preferences with small groups of similar status/standing.

5.4   General principles for surveys

Regardless of what methods are being used to help site wells and boreholes, there are some general principles that can be applied to help good practice:

- Use more than one technique and 'triangulate' your results.
- Keep good records and a detailed notebook.
- Look after the equipment, whether it is a geological hammer or sophisticated geophysical instrumentation.

5.4.1 Geological triangulation

For an accurate assessment of the potential for groundwater at a village, it is important not to rely on just one technique or approach. Maps can often be wrong, community discussions can be misleading and more technical surveys, such as geophysics, cannot be interpreted correctly unless the geological environment is known first. An approach that has been used successfully in many groundwater projects is to use a combination of maps, observation and geophysics. In a workshop in Nigeria a few years ago a participant suggested it be called **geological triangulation**. A summary is given in Figure 5.9.

Maps and reconnaissance data

Villages should be located accurately on available geological and topographic maps collected during the reconnaissance phase of the project (see Chapter 4). The community can be accurately located by using a GPS. The maps can then be used to give an indication of what geology should be

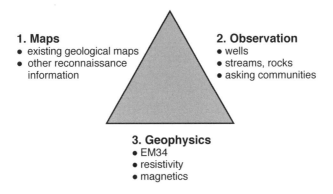

1. Maps
- existing geological maps
- other reconnaissance information

2. Observation
- wells
- streams, rocks
- asking communities

3. Geophysics
- EM34
- resistivity
- magnetics

| **Figure 5.9** | Geological triangulation method for siting boreholes and wells. |

expected in a village and where the nearest rivers are. Other information collected during reconnaissance can also be used, such as information on drilled boreholes or perhaps nearby magnetic anomalies which may indicate igneous rocks.

Observation

Before carrying out any survey, the local geology must be examined with care and discussed with the local community (see above). The nature of the rocks should be noted. Local wet and dry season sources of water should be visited, as should any locations that the community considers as possible groundwater sources. Rock samples need to be collected from local rock exposures; and rock spoil from shallow wells examined. This geological information can then be compared to the map information. In most cases they should agree, but in some places, particularly where the geology is complicated or the maps poor, they may disagree. In such cases, more emphasis should be placed on the observation data.

Geophysics

Geophysical surveys can be carried out more effectively once the geological environment has been identified from maps and confirmed by observation. The type and extent of any technical survey will depend on the nature of the geology. In same cases it may be concluded that there is no need for geophysics, in others that exploratory drilling is required. In many cases geophysics will be of some help, either in confirming the geology, if there is doubt from the maps and observation, or more usually in identifying good places to drill (or dig) within the community.

After working in this way for a while, geological triangulation becomes second nature. If the geology across the project area is fairly uniform, steps one and two (Figure 5.9) become condensed as the borehole siting teams become familiar with the terrain.

5.4.2 Keeping a notebook

Keeping a detailed notebook is fundamental to good interpretation of information from a survey. Anything of interest should be written down: the weather, changes in terrain, obvious landmarks so that the survey can be relocated, the coordinates of landmarks (using a GPS), and of course the survey data. The results of community discussions, village observation and geophysical surveys should also be faithfully recorded. Sometimes prepared sheets, indicating what information should be recorded, can help (see Appendix 2).

At the start of a geophysical survey, several pieces of information must be recorded in the notebook (an example of a page from a notebook recording an EM34 survey is shown in Figure 5.10):

```
Date       : 12 Feb 2001, 9.30
Village    : Egori Ukpute 34° 321'N 12° 012'E
Surveyors  : Bitrus Goyal, Alan MacDonald

EM34-20m coil separation      starting at the large
        receiver trailing     mango tree, roughly 1km
                              to the north of the
Sunny and dry                 villlage at the edge of
                              the river

S    D      V      H          C
                              Bearing 210°
1    0 m    31.2   33.4       large mango tree
2    20 m   32.1   35.3
3    40 m   34.3   32.2       ant hill left
4    60 m   34.1   34.6       H-coils uneven
5    80 m   32.2   32.2       dry borehole right
6    100 m  32.3   32.2
            31.1
7    120 m  29.2   31.1       Bearing 260°
8    140 m  26.1   24.2       path left @ 145 m
9    160 m  23.2   22.1
10   180 m  23.8   26.1       dry tree right
11   200 m  19.2   20.2
12   210 m  19.3   18.2       small kitchen left
```

Figure 5.10 Typical notebook for an EM34 survey.

- name of the community and survey number
- coordinates (from GPS) of the start of the survey and the landmark at which the survey starts
- the direction and route of the survey (e.g. from large mango tree SE through village)
- date and time (particularly important for magnetic surveys)
- weather conditions (rain can affect most techniques)
- the names of the people carrying out the survey
- type of survey
- other information relevant to the particular survey (e.g. station separation for magnetic profiling).

The data can then be recorded. For a profiling survey (such as EM, VLF or magnetics), the distance along the profile must be measured and recorded. Some equipment (such as EM34) will approximately measure the distance, but most wont. At least every 100 m, and preferably more often, notable (and immovable!) objects should be recorded (e.g. large anthill 5 m ahead on the right). If a number is written down wrongly, don't try to erase or alter it; cross it out and write in the correct number – this reduces the chances of confusion later. Keep the notebook safe, and photocopy the pages when back in the office as a back up. Always make sure that there is a complete back-up in files in the office in case the notebook is mislaid.

The best notebooks are made with waterproof paper. These can be written on if the paper becomes damp, and will not disintegrate or lose the ink if the notebook is soaked. However, such notebooks are expensive and can be difficult to source in some parts of the world. If normal, non-waterproof paper is used, extra care has to be taken to keep it dry – keep drinks away from notebook or sheets, and keep them in a plastic bag if it's raining. Another problem is perspiration, which can be high if you are carrying heavy equipment in the heat of the day. If this is a problem, keep a small towel with the notebook or, if there are spare people, dictate the readings and comments to someone with drier hands.

5.4.3 Looking after equipment

Geophysical equipment is expensive, sometimes delicate, and often difficult to repair. It must therefore be well looked after. Invariably, the equipment has to be transported across bumpy roads in the back of a pick-up or Land Rover. It is important that the equipment is kept secure in a strong padded box. Most manufacturers supply a good box with the equipment, but if not, get one made as soon as possible. The equipment must always be handled carefully – apart from the cost of repairing damage, it can often mean delays of months while the equipment is sent back to the manufacturers. In projects where drilling can only occur within a short allocated time, this can mean disaster.

There are four simple rules for looking after equipment:

- **Keep it calibrated**. Geophysical equipment will only work if it is well calibrated. Even if calibration is not required, most equipment needs regular checks. The manufacturer's instructions should give detailed information about carrying out equipment tests or calibration. Keep one copy of the instructions on file in the project office and take a copy (preferably laminated) out with the equipment.
- **Store it properly**. When not in use for several weeks, the equipment must be stored properly. If possible, the batteries should be removed and regularly recharged (every month or so). Certain types of batteries can be ruined if they are completely discharged. Some equipment needs to be powered down using a special sequence to stop internal batteries discharging.
- **Protect connectors**. The connectors are often the weakest link in a geophysical field system. They can become damaged, oxidized or filled with dirt. Multi-connectors are the most vulnerable and should never by dragged along the ground. If they are at the end of a long cable (as in EM34 or multicore resistivity cables) two people should wind up the cable to make sure the connector does not touch the ground. Single connectors (such as in many resistivity sets) can become oxidized, which reduces the connection and may need to be periodically scraped.
- **Look after cables**. Long cables can become stretched, broken, eaten and tangled. Looking after cables is not difficult, but makes fieldwork much simpler and less frustrating. Try always to have long cables wound around a drum. Many cables now come supplied with a drum, but if not it is straightforward to have them made. Winding them by hand usually leads to kinks or tangles. Even with drums, cables can become hopelessly tangled, especially if they are left to run freely. It is best always to have trained staff to wind the cables, although children are often willing to help. Cables can electromagnetically couple or interfere with each other – therefore, keep the cables neat and separated, particularly around the console. Drums of wound cable can also produce electromagnetic fields, so keep them several metres away from electrodes and instruments. If there are animals around, ask some community members to keep the animals away from the cables – sheep or goats will nibble at them given half a chance.

5.4.4 A simple toolkit

Keeping a simple toolkit is essential for good fieldwork. Detailed electronics is not required, since it is generally not the electronics within the equipment that is at fault (unless it is submerged in water or dropped), but other issues which are more easily fixed. The following toolkit has been adapted from Milsom (2003).

- spare fully-charged batteries for the equipment
- screwdrivers – assorted sizes, and both slotted and Phillips
- Allen keys and long-nosed pliers
- a good penknife and hand lens
- wire cutters and strippers
- emery paper or electrical contact cleaner
- a multimeter, for continuity checks
- insulating tape, superglue, silicone grease
- waterproof sealing compound
- spare crocodile clips, bare wire, insulated wire and connectors
- a 12-volt soldering iron
- a comprehensive first-aid kit.

5.5 Resistivity

5.5.1 Electrical resistivity

The resistivity technique is the longest-established geophysical method used to site wells and boreholes throughout the world. The technique measures the resistance of the ground to electrical currents passing through it. Resistance, however, is not a useful parameter on its own because it depends not only on the properties of the ground, but on the length and area being measured. Hence the requirement for a more fundamental parameter, independent of the geometry of the material. This fundamental property is called **resistivity**. It is independent of geometry and measured in ohm-metres. Several geophysical techniques depend on measuring or estimating electrical resistivity, including EM (discussed later).

Most rocks are very poor conductors of electricity (apart from graphite and some metal sulphides). Electric currents are generally carried by the ions in water within the rocks. Therefore the resistivity of the ground is generally dominated by the following:

- the electrical conductivity of the actual rock minerals (usually negligible)
- the saturated porosity of the rocks (either in pore spaces, or fractures)
- the salinity of the water
- the clay content of the rocks: bound ions on the surface of clay particles are highly conductive.

Here lies the main problem with geophysics techniques – the non-uniqueness of interpretations. It is difficult to distinguish a useful fresh groundwater resource from an increase in clay content by the use of resistivity or EM techniques alone. This is why geological triangulation is so important – the geophysical data must be interpreted in the light of some geological knowledge of the area. The approximate range of electrical resistivity and conductivity for various rock types saturated with fresh groundwater is shown in Figure 5.11.

5.5.2 Overview of the resistivity survey method

There are two main survey modes for resistivity: profiling and depth sounding. Resistivity profiling measures lateral changes in resistivity and has largely been superseded by EM conductivity traversing or 2D electrical imaging (see earlier). The most common resistivity survey method used for rural water supply in Africa and India is vertical electrical depth sounding (VES for short). This gives a one-dimensional depth-profile of the resistivity beneath the midpoint of the survey.

Ground resistivity is measured by passing an electrical current through the ground and measuring the potential difference (voltage) between two points. Ohm's law can then be used to calculate the resistance. The resistance is then multiplied by a geometric factor (normally called a K factor) to calculate resistivity. Resistivity is in fact the inverse of conductivity (see Box 5.3). To carry out a depth sounding (VES), electrodes are

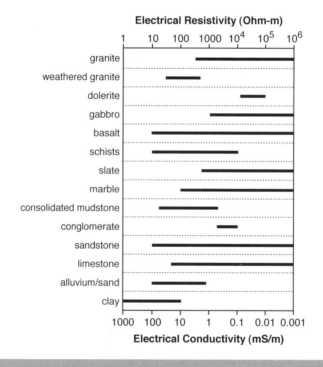

Figure 5.11	Electrical resistivity and conductivity for common rock types containing non-saline groundwater.
	Source: Telford et al. 1990; Reynolds 1997

BOX 5.3 Resistivity and conductivity

Resistivity is the inverse of conductivity – therefore high resistivity means low conductivity. Resistivity in ohm-m is related to conductivity in milliseimens per metre (mS/m) by the following formulas:

Resistivity = 1000/(conductivity)

Conductivity = 1000/(resistivity)

expanded about a single point. When the current electrode spacing is increased, there are many more paths for the current to pass and the volume of ground sampled increased. Hence, at large electrode spacings more information is given about the deeper layers. Although the technique averages the resistivity over the whole length of the survey, it is interpreted assuming the ground is homogeneous. The data are presented as a one-dimensional section beneath the mid-point of the survey. To try to minimize errors from lateral changes in the geology across the survey it is important to carry out a survey along the strike of the geology (i.e. parallel to any geological boundaries). Table 5.3 shows the advantages and disadvantages of the VES resistivity method.

There are different electrode configurations available for carrying out a VES. The three most common are Schlumberger, Wenner and offset Wenner (see Figure 5.12). In all cases the electrodes are moved to set distances on either side of a midpoint. The three arrays have similar properties: all are good at detecting changes with depth, but will not give much information about the presence of vertical features such as fractures or faults. The depth of penetration of the array is dependent on the total length of the array and also the resistivity. A rough guide is that the depth of penetration is roughly a tenth of the total length of the array.

- The **Schlumberger array** is probably the most commonly used. The potential electrodes are kept close to the centre of the array and the

Table 5.3 The advantages and disadvantages of the resistivity VES method

Advantages	Disadvantages
Can identify layers of different resistivity (in other words changes with depth)	Highly susceptible to bad electrode connections
Can penetrate deep into the ground	Difficult to interpret
Not easily affected by metal objects at the surface	Laborious and slow
Robust, easily available equipment	Can't locate vertical fracture zones
	Only takes a reading at one point
	Requires the ground to be homogeneous

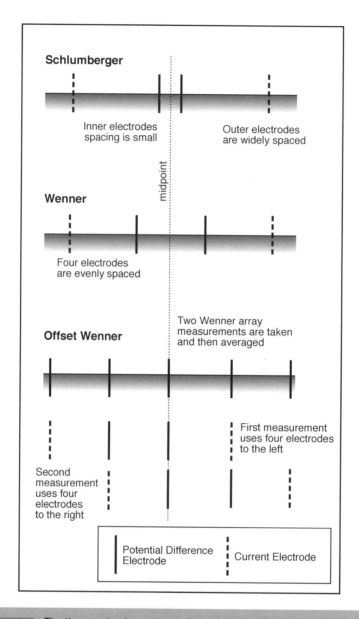

Figure 5.12   The three main electrode configurations for VES surveys.

current electrodes moved out logarithmically (usually 1, 1.5, 2, 3, 5, 7, … , 50, 70, 100 m). The results from the Schlumberger array are highly sensitive to the ground conditions around the inner potential electrodes; it is important to find a good homogeneous spot on which to centre the array. The inner potential electrodes are moved only 3 or 4 times (again logarithmically – 0.2, 1.5, 5, 10). One of the benefits of the Schlumberger array is that it is rapid to carry out since there are fewer electrodes to move for each reading.

■ The **Wenner array** is also commonly used. For this array the four electrodes are evenly spaced. The electrodes are expanded logarithmically around the midpoint (spacings are often, 1, 2, 4, 8, 26, 32, 64, 128). It is easy to get confused between electrode spacings and the distance away from the centre. Since all four electrodes must be moved for each reading, the Wenner array can be slower and more susceptible to poor readings due to electrode contacts.

■ The **offset Wenner** array addresses the problem of heterogeneity in the ground around electrodes and also the problem of having to move so many electrodes. The array is best carried out with a multicore cable and switchbox, which allow the readings to be taken rapidly (Barker 1981). Five evenly spaced electrodes are used at each spacing (1, 2, 4, 8, etc.). A reading is taken with the four electrodes to the left and average with a reading taken with the four electrodes to the right. This has been shown to be a very reliable technique for getting good quality data.

4.5.3 Carrying out a resistivity survey

Figure 5.13 shows the standard equipment required to carry out a resistivity survey. Below is a general procedure for carrying out resistivity VES.

■ Find a good location for the midpoint (ground not too hard, homogeneous, no termite mounds within a few metres).

■ Orientate the survey along the strike of the geology if possible and ensure there is enough space either side to take the electrodes out to at least 100 m.

■ Run 100-m measuring tapes out either side of the midpoint (for the further distances it can be helpful to mark the cable and tie the cables to the midpoint).

■ Hammer in electrodes at the desired locations up to about 50 m either side (see Appendix 2 for the different distances for Schlumberger, Wenner and offset Wenner). Make sure the electrodes are hammered well into the ground, and water them. At large electrode spacings an electrolyte solution (e.g. salt in water) can be used.

■ Connect up the resistivity meter and make battery checks, etc.

■ Start to take readings using the small spacings first – some (but not all) of these electrodes can then be recycled for larger spacings, if there is a shortage.

■ Take at least four readings for each spacing (most meters can do this automatically).

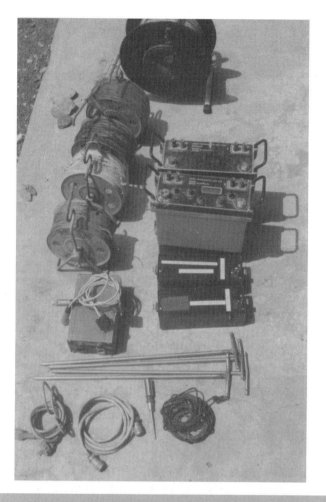

Figure 5.13 Resistivity equipment.
Photo: BGS, © NERC 2001.

- For small electrode spacings a small current should be used (<5 mA). Check that the resistivity is roughly the same at several current settings. If the current is too low, readings will vary.
- At larger electrode spacings, higher currents are required (>5 mA) since it becomes more difficult to accurately measure the potential difference at the closely spaced inner electrodes.
- Plotting the data as you go along allows you to see if any readings are anomalous. A resistivity curve should always look smooth. Resistivity is calculated by multiplying the measured resistance by the appropriate K-factor (see Appendix 2).
- If some readings appear anomalous then check the electrode spacings, the connections, and the electrode connection with the ground – add

water, or salt solution if required (see Figure 5.14). The offset Wenner system has an internal check that can be done (see Appendix 2), which should indicate if the electrodes and connections are fine.

■ For Schlumberger arrays, ensure that there are at least two crossover points when moving to larger potential electrode separations.

■ When the survey has been finished, carefully wind up the wires, and carry out an inventory – it is very easy to leave equipment behind, particularly electrodes.

5.5.4 Interpreting resistivity data

Resistivity VES data are interpreted by plotting apparent resistivity against electrode spacing on a log-log scale. This should produce a smooth curve,

Figure 5.14 In dry environments electrode contact can be improved by watering the electrodes.
Photo: BGS, © NERC 1998.

apart from the Schlumberger method where the curve will be in several segments. The data can be interpreted qualitatively by examining the curve shape, or quantitatively by using curve matching or computer modelling. Quantitative analysis involves identifying from the apparent resistivity curve a number of layers, their thickness and resistivity. Care must always be taken not to over-interpret resistivity curves and add in too many layers, particularly when using computers. Curve matching using master curves and auxiliary curves was the main interpretation method until computers became widely available. Now they are rarely used: only where there are no computers or for a quick interpretation in the field. Detailed interpretation is now generally carried out by computer using a variety of different packages (such as ResixPlus®). Neither curve matching or computer analysis is considered further here. They are, however, described in several geophysical textbooks (see further reading and resources listed at the end of the chapter).

Even without carrying out detailed quantitative analysis, a rough interpretation can be given by looking at the shape of the apparent resistivity curve. For Wenner and offset Wenner, the curve can be interpreted directly. For a Schlumberger array, where the curve is in several segments, these must first be combined into one smooth curve by using the crossover points (readings taken with the same outer electrode spacing but different inner electrode spacing). Starting with the right-hand segment, move it up or down to match the cross over points of the segment to the left. Repeat the process (always moving the right-hand segment to meet the left-hand one) until you have one smooth curve. Tracing paper is helpful.

Figure 5.15 shows some common curves for basement areas and a rough interpretation beside them. For basement areas, the main target is the low resistivity weathered zone. Curves are generally a rough U-shape. High resistivity in the shallow soil layers (mainly due to the lack of water in the soil), lower resistivity at moderate depths, corresponding to the weathered zone and higher resistivity at depth, where the basement is unweathered. If the U-shape is broad, and the tail does not rise steeply, then it may indicate deeper weathering (or a more conductive weathered zone). If the tail rises very steeply (up to 45°) there is likely to be little or no weathering. The resistivity of the soil zone can also significantly affect the shape of the resistivity curve (see Figure 5.15) and can make two curves look very different, even though the thickness of the weathered zone is similar. It is important to note that different types of bedrock may have different unweathered resistivity (e.g. a schist may have a lower resistivity than a granite). Therefore, more emphasis should be placed on the relative changes in resistivity than absolute numbers.

Figure 5.16 shows some common curves for sedimentary areas. In an area with sandstone and mudstone, the main target will usually be the sandstones. Sandstones (or sands and gravels) at depth will be indicated by

BOX 5.4 Summary for using resistivity to identify deep weathering

- Try to locate the survey in fairly homogeneous ground – particularly for inner electrodes.
- Plot the data as you do the survey and check the curve for anomalous readings.
- A broad U-shape usually indicates deep weathering – however, be aware that different soils may radically change the way the curve appears.
- If the curve rises steeply, it usually indicates unweathered basement.
- Be aware that the resistivity different types of unweathered basement may be different.

higher resistivity measurements at the wider electrode spacings; mudstones (or clays) will be indicated by low resistivity at large electrode spacings. Clays and mudstones tend to have fairly low resistivity, (see Figure 5.11) generally less than 30 ohm-m. This can be distinguished from water-filled sands, which have a higher resistivity.

Resistivity can also be used to try to differentiate hard mudstone from soft mudstone. Lower resistivity readings (sometimes less than 10 ohm-m) will generally indicate soft mudstones, which will not contain usable water. Higher resistivity (approximately 50 ohm-m or above) will generally indicate harder mudstones. It is very uncommon to have young and old mudstones interspersed within a single community – a single resistivity survey in the community will confirm the type of mudstone present.

BOX 5.5 Summary for using resistivity to site boreholes in sedimentary rocks

- It is important to orientate the survey along the strike of (parallel to) the geology.
- Plot the data as you do the survey and check the curve for anomalous readings.
- Sandstone or sand in a mudstone/sandstone or clay/sand sequence is identified as higher resistivity layers.
- Weathering in sandstone, or saturated sands, are identified as lower resistivity.
- In a mudstone sequence, harder mudstones have higher resistivity than soft clays and mudstones.

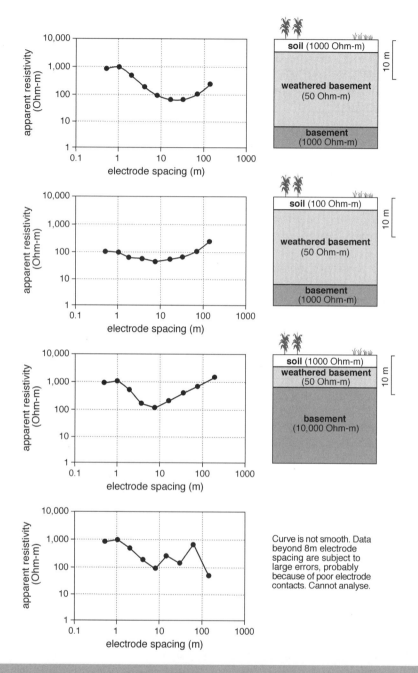

Figure 5.15 Common resistivity curves and their interpretation in crystalline basement areas. The first two curves are the most promising to drill.

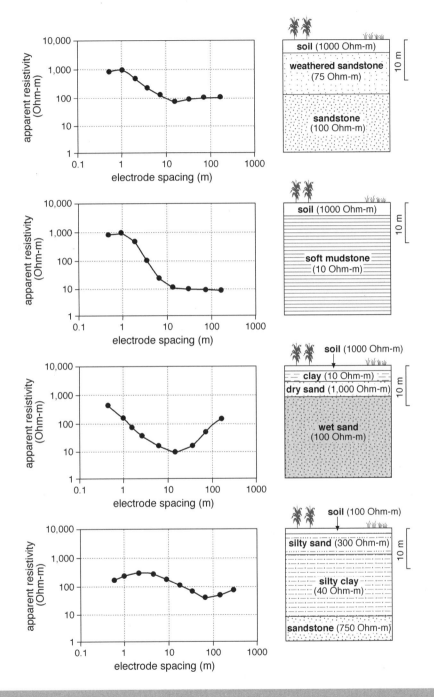

Figure 5.16 Examples of resistivity curves and interpretation for sedimentary rocks.

5.6 Electromagnetic methods – FEM

5.6.1 Overview

There are many different geophysical methods that make use of electro-magnetic (EM) induction. These include FEM, TEM and VLF. In this section we consider the most popular technique for groundwater survey throughout Africa and India – FEM using the Geonics EM34 instrument.

FEM methods measure the bulk electrical conductivity of the ground, often referred to as **ground conductivity**. (Conductivity is the inverse of resistivity; see Box 5.3.) Ground conductivity is measured by passing an alternating electromagnetic field over and through the ground and measuring the secondary electromagnetic produced. Figure 5.17 illustrates the basic principles. The time-varying electromagnetic field generated by the transmitter coil induces small currents in the earth. These currents generate a secondary electromagnetic field, which is sensed (along with the primary field) by the receiver coil. The ground conductivity (or apparent conductivity) is then calculated by assuming a linear relation between the ratio of secondary and primary fields. Over a sub-horizontally layered earth, the response will represent a weighted mean (related to depth) of the rocks within the range of investigation.

5.6.2 Coil orientation

The coils can be orientated either vertically or horizontally, as shown in Figure 5.18. Different orientation changes the direction of the inducing field:

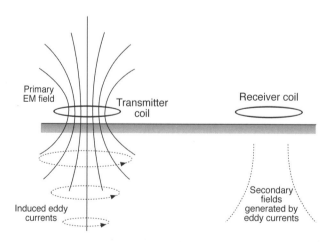

| Figure 5.17 | Basic principles of FEM geophysical surveying. |

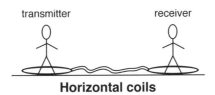

Horizontal coils

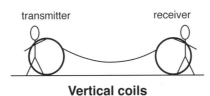

Vertical coils

| Figure 5.18 | Different coil orientations for FEM. |

- for **vertical coils** the inducing field is horizontal, so this orientation is sometimes called a **horizontal dipole**
- for **horizontal coils** the inducing field is vertical, so this orientation is sometimes called a **vertical dipole**.

The change in orientation of the inducing field significantly changes what features can be identified by the technique.

Measurements using vertical coils give a good estimate of the ground electrical conductivity. Ground conductivity is usually measured in milliseimens per metre (mS/m), sometimes quoted as mmhos/m. For vertical coils, the maximum contribution is from the ground surface, and the response reduces with depth; the average depth of penetration is about 0.5–0.7 × the coil spacing (see McNeill 1980a). For the most common instrument (the Geonics EM34), the apparent ground conductivity measured by the instrument will be roughly equivalent to the real ground conductivity (within about 10 per cent).

Measurements using horizontal coils can only give a good estimate of electrical ground conductivity where the conductivity is less than about 30 mS/m. In fact the highest reading the horizontal coils can give is 65 mS/m. Therefore, horizontal coils are generally only used to estimate conductivity in environments with low conductivity and high resistivity, such as crystalline basement areas. Horizontal coils, however, are excellent at detecting vertical conductors, such as faults, fracture zones or igneous intrusions. When passing over a vertical anomaly a negative response is given. Sometimes this can actually give readings of less than zero, which at first can be rather confusing! Care must be taken to keep the coils horizontal and in the same plane, since the readings are very sensitive to misalignment of the coils – much more so than when the coils are vertical.

5.6.3 Carrying out a survey

- Walk round the village where the survey is to be carried out and try to locate good survey lines. Bear in mind where the community may want the borehole or well sited and where field geological information is (e.g. rock exposures or existing wells, etc.). Two surveys roughly at right angles extending outside the village often provide the best information (Figure 5.19). If reconnaissance has indicated a prevailing direction for fractures in the area, then the main survey lines should run perpendicular to this direction – this will maximize the chance of finding a fracture with the survey.
- Find an area free from significant influences such as power lines or metal roofs, to set up and check the equipment.
- Choose the appropriate coil separation (and frequency) for the survey. Generally a 20-m coil separation is most useful for reconnaissance. Carry out the daily checks on the equipment, such as battery checks and nulling. Once the equipment is set up satisfactorily, the survey can start.
- Start at a noticeable feature (e.g. a large mango tree) at one end of a survey line. Always have the coils in the same order, for example with the receiver always trailing the transmitter – this avoids confusion over distances. All distance, comments and reading should be recorded from the receiver.
- Take readings using both vertical coils and horizontal coils at each location. The actual location of the reading is the midpoint between the receiver and transmitter. Therefore, if the receiver is trailing the transmitter, a reading of $50\,mS/m$ when the receiver is at $120\,m$ should be plotted at $130\,m$ for $20\,m$ coil separation, and $140\,m$ for $40\,m$ separation.

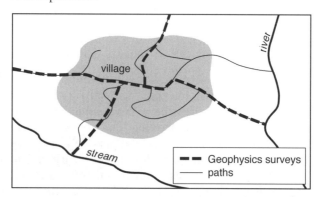

| Figure 5.19 | Choosing survey lines within a community. |

■ Roughly measure distances. The coil separation indicated by the instrument is usually a good enough measure. Make sure that noticeable features are recorded accurately at least every 40 m, so that any readings from the instrument can be pin pointed on the ground.

■ Keep a detailed notebook. Figure 5.10 shows an example of a page from a notebook for an EM survey. At the start of each survey general information should be given such as the date, location, surveyors, equipment and coil separation. The start of the survey should be carefully described. To record the readings the SDVHC system is very useful: this stands for **station, distance, vertical coil reading, horizontal coil readings** and **comments**. Make sure that any metal

Figure 5.20	Carrying out an FEM survey.
	Photo: BGS, © NERC 2001.

objects (such as tin roofs) or problems (such as misalignment of horizontal coils) are carefully recorded.

5.6.4 Interpreting EM data in crystalline basement

Crystalline basement rocks and volcanic rocks do not conduct electricity (see Figure 5.11) because they have little primary porosity. In these rocks we are generally trying to identify thick weathering or deep fracture zones. Ground conductivity has proved very useful in these environments and there are many examples of their successful use (see further reading at the end of this chapter). Before using any of these interpretative techniques, geological triangulation must have established that the community is likely to be underlain by basement or volcanic rocks.

Identifying deep weathering

Figure 5.21 illustrates a common scenario in basement rocks. The main target for a well or borehole is where the weathered zone is thickest. The response of the EM34 instrument with coil separations of 10, 20 and 40 m over this weathered pocket is shown. The response has been predicted using a 3D EM modelling package called EMIGMA (PetRos Eikon 2000). Unweathered basement rocks generally have low electrical conductivity (<1 mS/m) since they contain little water or clay.

Weathered basement often has conductivity of about 10 mS/m since it comprises decomposed basement which is often porous and contains water and also some clay. The soil zone has been modelled as 1 m thick with low

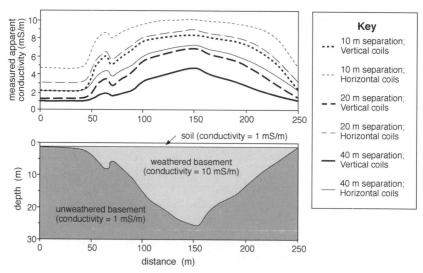

Figure 5.21 Apparent electrical conductivity measured using EM34 equipment over weathered basement.

conductivity – a common scenario. For completeness the models were rerun with a conductive soil (20 mS/m), but this did not significantly affect the results – unlike a resistivity VES, where the conductivity of the soil radically changes the shape of the curve.

Deeper weathering is clearly indicated by high conductivity measured by all coil separations and orientations. Therefore, the best target for a well or borehole in the weathered zone would be at a distance of 150 m where the weathering is thickest and the measurements highest. Some analysis methods suggest that the best target is where the horizontal coil readings become greater than the vertical coil readings. The modelling clearly shows that this does not need to be the case. In fact, readings with the horizontal coils are often uncertain because they are sensitive to errors in alignment of the coils, so more faith should be put in the vertical coil measurements.

It is not just the depth of weathering that will affect the ground conductivity measurements, but how conductive the weathered zone is. If the weathered zone is clayey, the conductivity will be greater and can be confused with deeper weathering. This problem is often less important in practice than it appears to be theoretically: clay within the weathered zone generally forms as a result of significant weathering, so the permeable basal saprolite should still be present and the locations still a good target for groundwater.

Considerably higher readings in a basement area are often associated with surface clays, such as those found in small seasonal wetlands (sometimes known as dambos). These are generally in valleys and will give rise to high

---

BOX 5.6 Summary for surveys to identify deep weathering in basement

- Carry out a survey with 20-m coil separations using both the vertical and horizontal coil configurations.
- If time permits, repeat with 40-m coil separations over areas with high readings.
- Deeper weathering and therefore good targets for wells and boreholes are indicated by high readings in vertical and horizontal coils (around 10 mS/m).
- Higher readings (20 mS/m and above) in valleys are probably due to clay development in the weathered zone in seasonal wetlands – these are not often good targets for wells and boreholes.
- Horizontal coil readings are sensitive to misalignment of coils, therefore more faith should be placed in vertical coil readings.
- If EM or resistivity are not good predictors of the presence of deep weathering; either due to the variations in the basement rock conductivity or the presence of significant clay in the weathered zone, another technique, such as seismic refraction should be used.

readings with 10- and 20-m coil separations. These are generally not great sites for wells and boreholes because of the swelling clay near to the surface. Comments in the geophysics notebook should help interpret high readings as wetlands, since they are easily identified in the field.

Some metamorphic basement rocks have a higher background conductivity (10–20 mS/m) than the 1 mS/m used in the model. It is easy to check this. Find an outcrop of the exposed rock and take some readings using vertical coils and a variety of different spacing. If the bedrock is found to have conductivity >1 mS/m, but is fairly constant across the area, then deeper weathered zone will still be indicated by an increase in conductivity. However, if the conductivity of the basement varies significantly, regardless of weathering, then conductivity or resistivity will not be much help in identifying areas of deep weathering – seismic refraction should be used.

Despite these problems of clay being confused with areas of deep weathering or variations in bedrock conductivity in metamorphic rocks, EM is generally a reliable technique in basement areas. It has been used in countless projects throughout the world with good results. McNeill (1991) gives various other examples of using EM34 in groundwater studies.

Rarely is there opportunity to carry out surveys at all coil spacings and orientations. Which configuration gives the best information for changes in weathering of interest to the hydrogeologist – 10–50 m? Figure 5.22

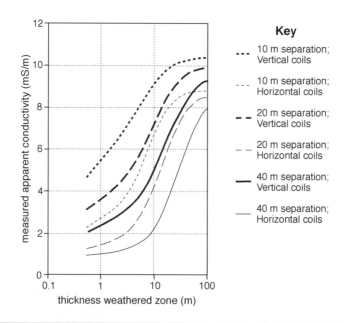

Figure 5.22 Apparent conductivity measured over increasing thicknesses of weathered basement using different coil spacings and orientations.

shows conductivity measurements from different coil orientations over different thicknesses of weathering. Although deeper weathering is indicated by higher readings in all configurations, the various coil separations and orientations have different sensitivities to changes at depth (greater sensitivity is indicated by a steeper line on the graph). The 10-m coil separation is not good at differentiating differences in the thickness of weathering below about 10 m. The 40-m coil separation is good at differentiating deep changes in weathering, but not shallow changes. Therefore, the 20-m coil separation with vertical and horizontal coils is probably the best configuration for initial surveys, repeated with 40-m separation if time allows.

Identifying fracture zones

The other main groundwater targets in basement areas are fracture zones. These are deep fractures (generally more than 20 m), often associated with faults and tectonic movement. Fracture zones tend to be more conductive to electricity than the host crystalline rock since they contain water and also the increased circulation of water has helped to weather the nearby rock to produce some clay. Fracture zones are more difficult to detect with geophysical equipment than changes in the thickness of the weathered zone. The response of fracture zones to electromagnetic methods is much more complex than the 1D response of changes in weathering. This is mainly because the width of the feature is of the same scale as the coil separation and because the fractures are often orientated horizontally.

Figure 5.23 shows modelled data for a single vertical fracture in basement rocks. This classic response is often quoted in textbooks. The vertical coils show very little response, but the horizontal coils show a marked negative anomaly centred over the fracture. This is confusing since the fracture zone actually has higher conductivity than the surrounding rocks. However, the equipment responds three-dimensionally to these complex shapes and the negative anomaly is a result of electromagnetic coupling between the inducing field and the conductive fracture.

In real life, however, single vertical fractures are very rare. Fracture zones are complex, with interactions between many different fractures at various depths and angles. With the advent of new, improved computer models it has been possible to try to model the expected EM response from more realistic fracture zones. Results from the models show much more complex anomalies than the single negative-going anomaly shown in Figure 5.23. Sometimes there are positive readings, sometimes negative. An example is shown in Figure 5.24. In our experience we have found the exact form of the anomaly unimportant for siting wells and boreholes; fractured bedrock often exists exist where the horizontal coils give a noisy profile.

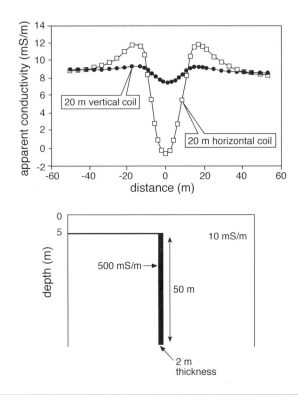

Figure 5.23 Classic response of FEM over a theoretical vertical conductor.

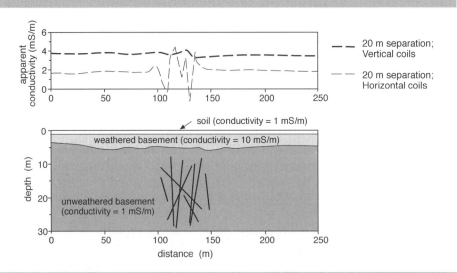

Figure 5.24 Schematic diagram showing the kind of response that is given by ground conductivity (using the EM34 instrument) over fracture zones in basement.

BOX 5.7 Summary of surveying for fracture zones in basement rocks

- Carry out a survey with 20-m coil separations using both the vertical and horizontal coil configurations.
- If time permits, repeat with 40-m coil separations over areas with noisy readings.
- Orient the survey perpendicular to any known regional fracture patterns, to maximize the chance of intersecting one.
- Keep a careful notebook and ensure that any problems with horizontal coil orientation are noted.
- Fracture zones are identified as significant noisy readings with the horizontal coils; the vertical coils are generally insensitive to fractures.
- Noisy readings can also be given by the misalignment of horizontal coils (e.g. when going up or down steep slopes) and significant metal (fences or metal roofs).

However, as discussed earlier, the horizontal coils can also give noisy profiles when misaligned. Therefore it is vital to carry out the survey carefully and record any problems in the field notebook. Then, when analysing the data you can be confident that the horizontal coils anomalies are due to fractures.

If the area is complex, or if drilling success is lower than expected, then the following tips may be helpful:

- Use aerial photographs, satellite images or topographic maps to identify the likely orientation of fractures.
- In order to confirm a linear anomaly identified in a profile, carry out additional profiles parallel to the first.
- On very narrow fracture zones it is essential to locate a fracture to within 10 m (this may mean taking readings every 2 m at potential anomalies).
- Where the fractures are not vertical (most likely in layered rocks such as gneisses, schists or metasediments, where fractures follow bedding planes), the potential drilling site should be moved down dip of where the anomaly appears at the surface – this gives a better chance of intersecting the fracture at depth.

5.6.5 Sedimentary rocks

Sedimentary rocks conduct electricity. Electricity can move through water in pore spaces in sands and sandstones, and also along the surface of clay minerals. This ambiguity makes interpreting FEM data in sedimentary areas difficult. Good ground control is required to help interpret the data so that clay can be distinguished from saturated sandstone. The geological triangulation method described earlier forms a useful strategy for gathering ground control information. The different scenarios described below can be used for either consolidated or unconsolidated sedimentary areas.

Locating sands within clay

Sands and sandstones are generally much better targets for groundwater supply than clays and mudstones. Electrical methods can easily distinguish clays and mudstones from sands and sandstones: pure clays and mudstones tend to have much higher electrical conductivity. Therefore using a rapid survey method such as EM34 can help identify areas underlain by sandstone or sands. Figure 5.25 shows how a boundary between sandstone and mud-stone can be mapped within a village. Pure sands and sandstones with little clay content and fresh water should give electrical conductivity below about 20 mS/m. Only the vertical coil reading should be compared, since horizontal coils are insensitive to changes in electrical conductivity at high conductivities.

It can be more difficult to distinguish sandstones from clays and mudstones when the sandstone layers are thin. The change can be noticeable if the sand is shallow, but may easily be missed in overall variations in ground

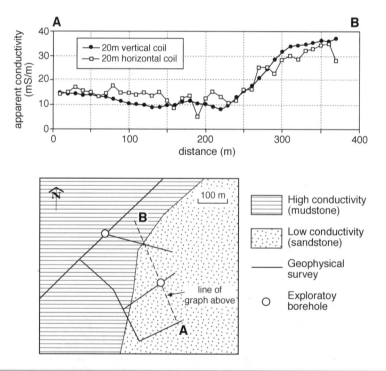

Figure 5.25   Using ground conductivity to map out the boundary between a sandstone and a mudstone in a village.

conductivity. A good practice in multilayered sedimentary environments is to carry out a resistivity survey along certain parts of the EM traverse, to help interpret it.

BOX 5.8   Summary of surveying with ground conductivity in sedimentary environments

- Carry out a survey with 20-m coil separations using both the vertical and horizontal coil configurations.
- Geological triangulation is vital to help interpret any data.
- Use the vertical coil readings for comparisons of electrical conductivity, and horizontal coil measurements to look for fractures.
- Sandstone (sand) can be distinguished from mudstone (clay) by low conductivity measurements (<20 mS/m).
- In a mudstone area, hard mudstone can be distinguished from soft mudstone by lower conductivity. If conductivity is very high (>60 mS/m) then the mudstone is likely to be soft and of no use for groundwater.
- Fractures in both sandstone and harder mudstone can be identified by noisy horizontal readings, and in particular negative anomalies. If time permits, repeat with 40-m coil separations over areas with noisy readings.

Identifying different types of mudstone

In Chapter 2 we reported the results of some recent research which indicated that groundwater may be found in certain types of mudstone. Where mudstones have been slightly metamorphosed, fractures (and therefore groundwater) are more likely. Soft mudstone contains very little usable groundwater. Soft mudstone can easily be distinguished from hard mudstone by measuring the electrical conductivity of the rocks (MacDonald et al. 2001). Soft mudstones have high conductivity (often >60 mS/m), hard mudstones have low conductivity (often <30 mS/m). The reason for these changes is the amount of smectite clay present.

Identifying fractures

Large fracture zones, similar to those targeted in basement areas, can also be useful targets in sedimentary areas, particularly if the sandstones do not have significant primary porosity and permeability. Since sandstones generally have low conductivity they can be located in a similar way to that described for basement areas.

Fracture zones in mudstones behave in a different geophysical way to basement or sandstone. Mudstones are highly conductive, therefore there is not much contrast between the conductive faults and the host rock. In fact, in soft mudstone, fracture zones may actually be less conductive to electricity than the host rock. In hard mudstones, fracture zones may be identified in the same way as for crystalline basement. In moderately hard mudstones, fractures can be identified as negative anomalies, or a generally noisy profile using horizontal coils.

5.7 Magnetic methods

5.7.1 Overview

Magnetic methods in geophysical exploration involve measuring the intensity of the earth's magnetic field. Variations in the magnetic field are complex and often highly localized, as a result of differences in the magnetic properties of rocks near to the surface. This makes the technique useful and sensitive for identifying certain types of rocks, but can also make the data quite difficult to analyse.

The earth's main magnetic field originates from electrical currents in the liquid outer core. This magnetic field can be approximated by a dipole (bar magnet) located at the earth's centre and inclined at 11° to the spin axis (see Figure 5.26). Magnetic materials can cause localized anomalies in the earth's magnetic field. There are many different forms of magnetization, but generally the most significant for geophysical surveys are ferrimagnetic and ferromagnetic. **Ferromagnetic materials** are strongly magnetic. Although they do not occur naturally, they are in use everywhere (e.g. steel in bridges, vehicles, etc.) and can give large anomalies on surveys. Some rock minerals

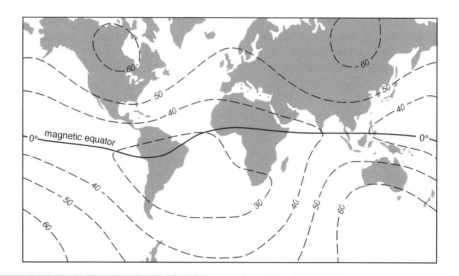

| Figure 5.26 | Intensity of the earth's magnetic field in 1000 nT. (More detailed information available from http://www.bgs.ac.uk) |

are also magnetic (known as **ferrimagnetic**), e.g. magnetite, maghaemite and pyrrhotite. When these are contained in rocks in sufficient quantities, they can cause measurable anomalies in the earth's magnetic field. Igneous rocks contain the most ferrimagnetic minerals; therefore, magnetic methods are generally only used if igneous rocks need to be identified. They can be useful for locating dykes (in some environments to avoid them and in others to target them for drilling). Other uses can be to identify the extent of lava flows in volcanic rocks (Drury et al. 2001).

Magnetic data are recorded in nanotesla (nT). The size of the earth's magnetic field depends on where you are on the earth's surface, but is generally between 30 000 and 60 000 nT. Magnetic anomalies caused by igneous intrusions such as dykes are generally less than 100 nT and most instruments are accurate to about 0.1 nT.

5.7.2 Carrying out a survey

The most common instrument used to identify magnetic anomalies is the proton precession magnetometer (PPM). This instrument makes use of the small magnetic moment of the hydrogen nucleus. A proton-rich source (usually some sort of hydrocarbon liquid) is magnetized by a strong magnetic field generated by a current passing through a copper wire passing around the source. When this current is switched off, the protons tend to realign themselves with the earth's magnetic field and precess at a frequency determined by the field strength. A secondary coil measures this frequency and displays the total field strength on the instrument console (for more information see the 'Further resources' section at the end of the chapter).

The PPM is easily portable and takes readings quickly (Figure 5.27). Most available equipment allow readings to be recorded and downloaded to a PC; however it is generally just as easy to write them into a field notebook. The equipment is generally accurate to about 0.1 nT, which is more than adequate for groundwater surveys. Surveying is simple and takes only one person (see Figure 5.27), although it can be helpful to have someone to help measure the distances. The instrument is usually carried on a long pole to keep it away from noise on the ground surface or caused by the operator and console. Modern PPMs are easy to use, and 5–10 km of survey can be carried out in one day.

Every day, the earth's magnetic field varies due to the sun. The measured field at one spot increases (roughly by 100 nT – but this varies throughout the year and from place to place) to a maximum about midday and then starts to decrease – this is called the **diurnal variation**. To carry out highly accurate magnetic surveys, a base station should be set up to record the diurnal variation of the magnetic field. At the end of the day, the diurnal variation can then be eliminated from the survey, allowing easier

Figure 5.27 The proton precessor magnetometer in use in Nigeria.
Photo: BGS, © NERC 2000.

interpretation. Also the background spatial change in magnetic field intensity should also be subtracted from the readings.

Fortunately, for groundwater surveys, this accuracy of survey is rarely required. The anomalies due to a dolerite dyke or the edge of a lava flow are normally easily distinguished from the diurnal variation, or the steady change in the earth's magnetic field across the earth's surface. A rough magnetic survey carried out by simply walking across an area recording distances and taking readings is often sufficient to identify the targets required for borehole site selection.

Very occasionally magnetic storms occur (although there is no visible sign in the weather). This is easily identified: if the magnetometer readings change significantly at the same location, with no sign of any cause, then it is likely to be a magnetic storm. The only thing to do is to go home and stop surveys for a couple of days.

Here are some tips for carrying out a survey:

- Ensure the operator is not wearing any metal (e.g. metal buckle on a belt, metal pen, etc). The sensor should be on the top of a long pole and held at arm's length.
- The sensor sometimes has to be orientated in a certain direction to get best results (often north–south).
- Several readings are taken at one location to ensure an accurate reading is taken. The instruments should be accurate to about 0.1 nT. If the readings at the same location change by more than this, it could mean that the reading is noisy. Check to see if the sensor is orientated properly and that nobody nearby is carrying metal.
- The earth's magnetic field varies naturally by about 100 nT per day. This usually causes a slow rise in the morning and a fall in the afternoon. If a survey is stopped for a few minutes, the readings will appear to jump. Therefore always mark in your notebook when you take a break.
- If readings vary by more than 5 nT within 10 m, this must be due to magnetic material – either from the rocks, or from cultural noise (metal roof, bike, etc.). Look around carefully to rule out any metal at the surface before concluding that it is the rocks that are causing the anomaly.
- It is very useful to carry out other surveys (such as EM) in conjunction with magnetics – this allows any anomalies to be cross-checked. EM surveys are not affected to the same extent by the presence of metal. If the surveys are carried out at the same time, keep the magnetometer about 30–40 m behind the EM34 to avoid the instruments affecting each other.
- Very occasionally, the earth's magnetic field varies very rapidly causing unpredictable readings. This is called a magnetic storm. They are easily detectable. Just keep the magnetometer in one place (make sure the sensor is correctly orientated), Take several readings in succession – you will find large variations which will swamp the anomalies caused by the geology.

5.7.3 Interpreting magnetic data

Magnetic data can be interpreted to a high degree of sophistication to find out the thickness, depth and orientation of igneous intrusions. However, this level of sophistication is rarely justified on rural water supply projects. Usually magnetic surveys are used to find one of the following:

- shallow igneous material below a community (e.g. a sill or small intrusion)
- contact between rocks with different magnetic susceptibilities which may indicate the presence of a fault
- a vertical intrusion, such as a dyke which may be associated with fracturing.

To give a rough interpretation of magnetic data, the readings taken in the field are plotted on a graph against the distance. Any large variations over a distance of about 100 m are likely to be due to the presence of shallow igneous rocks, or metal close by. Large smooth variations (over kilometres) will be due to the daily variations in the earth's magnetic field, or from deep igneous rocks, and can be ignored.

Once the magnetic data have been plotted, anomalies which can be justified from the notebook should be clearly marked. For example metal roofs within 50 m, a culvert or a short break in surveying (which will cause a short jump in the readings). Once these man-made anomalies have been eliminated, large anomalies that remain (>10 nT) are likely to be due to the presence of shallow igneous rocks.

Data from other surveys can then be plotted with the magnetic data to show whether there have been changes in other geophysical parameters. For example, granite may have much lower electrical conductivity than a schist or mudstone; highly conductive soils (black cotton soils) are often associated with mafic igneous rocks, such as basalt and dolerite.

Figure 5.28 shows an example of a dolerite sill being intruded into mudstones in central Nigeria. The dolerite is clearly identified by the variations in the magnetic field. Note also the large anomaly given by the steel reinforcing in the culvert. A borehole drilled within the sill had sufficient

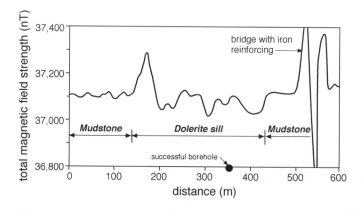

| Figure 5.28 | Magnetic survey from central Nigeria showing a dolerite sill within mudstone. |

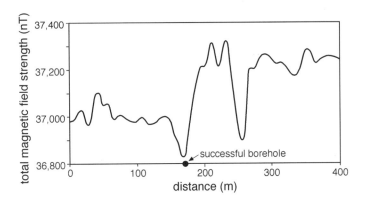

Figure 5.29 Magnetic survey from Eritrea showing a faulted boundary between rocks of different magnetic susceptibility
Source: Drury et al. 2001.

yield to be fitted with a handpump. Boreholes drilled in the mudstone were all unsuccessful. Figure 5.29 shows a magnetic survey from Eritrea. Two distinct parts to the profile can be seen: with different magnetic field strengths. This was interpreted as a fault between to different volcanic rocks. A borehole drilled into the fault was successful and gave sufficient yield for a motorized pump.

The books in the reference list give more information on detailed interpretation of magnetic data. To try to be more accurate than our rough interpretation given above, the direction of the survey needs to be known, along with the diurnal variation. This can then be modelled using a computer to give the likely size and orientation of any intrusions.

References, further reading and resources

Banks, D. and Robins, N.S. (2002) *An introduction to groundwater in crystalline bedrock.* Geological Survey of Norway, Trondheim, Norway.

Barker, R.D. (1981) The offset system of resistivity sounding and its use with a multicore cable. *Geophysical Prospecting,* **29**, 128–43.

Barker, R.D., White, C.C. and Houston, J.F.T. (1992) Borehole siting in an African accelerated drought relief project. In: Wright, E. P. and Burgess, W. G. (eds.), *The hydrogeology of crystalline basement aquifers in Africa.* Special Publication 66, Geological Society London, pp. 183–201.

Beeson, S. and Jones, C.R.C. 1988. The combined EMT/VES geophysical method for siting boreholes. *Ground Water,* **26**, 54–63.

Carruthers, R.M. and Smith, I.F. (1992) The use of ground electrical methods for siting water supply boreholes in shallow crystalline basement terrains. In: Wright, E. P. and Burgess, W.

G. (eds.), *The hydrogeology of crystalline basement aquifers in Africa*. Special Publication 66, Geological Society London, pp. 203–20.

Drury, S.A., Peart, R.J. and Andrews Deller, M.E. (2001) Hydrogeological potential of major fractures in Eritrea. *Journal of African Earth Sciences*, **32**, 163–77.

Kuar, S. (2002) *Methods for community participation – a complete guide for practitioners*. ITDG Publishing, London.

MacDonald, A.M. (2001) Geophysics – taking the magic out of black boxes. *Waterlines*, **20**(2), 12–14.

MacDonald, A.M., Ball, D.F. and McCann, D.M. (2000) Groundwater exploration in rural Scotland using geophysical techniques. In: Robins, N.S. and Misstear, B.D.R. (eds.) *Groundwater in the Celtic regions: studies in hard rock and Quaternary hydrogeology*. Special Publication 182, Geological Society, London. pp. 205–17.

MacDonald, A.M., Davies, J. and Peart, R.J. (2001) Geophysical methods for locating groundwater in low permeability sedimentary rocks: examples from southeast Nigeria. *Journal of African Earth Sciences*, **32**, 115–31.

McNeill, J.D. (1980a) Electromagnetic terrain conductivity measurement at low induction numbers. Technical Note TN-6, Geonics Limited, Mississauga, Canada. Available at http://www.geonics.com/

McNeill, J.D. (1980b) Electrical conductivity of soils and rocks. Technical Note TN-5, Geonics Limited, Mississauga, Canada. Available at http://www.geonics.com/

McNeill, J.D. (1991) Advances in electromagnetic methods for groundwater studies. *Geoexploration*, **27**, 65–80.

Milsom, J. (2003) *Field geophysics* (3rd edition). John Wiley & Sons, Chichester, UK.

PetRos Eikon Inc. (2000) EMIGMA V6: Forward 3-D Electromagnetic Simulation Platform for Comprehensive Geophysical Modelling. Petros Eikon Inc., Milton, Canada.

Reynolds, J.M. (1997) *An introduction to applied and environmental geophysics*. John Wiley & Sons, Chichester, UK.

Telford, W.M., Geldart, L.P. and Sheriff, R.E. (1990) *Applied Geophysics* (2nd edition). Cambridge University Press, Cambridge, UK.

Van Dongen, P. and Woodhouse, M. (1994) Finding groundwater: a project manager's guide to techniques and how to use them. Technical Report, UNDP-World Bank Water and Sanitation Program, Washington, DC.

6 Designing and constructing water points

6.1 Introduction

In this chapter we get to the part that most parties, particularly the communities concerned, are most interested in – the construction of the water point. This is the tangible (and expensive) part of the process of rural water supply. In this part of the project, the hydrogeologist has to work closely with drillers, civil engineers and communities to ensure that the water point is constructed properly, cost-effectively, in line with community wishes and in a manner most suitable to the hydrogeological environment. There will be many competing voices: the project accountants will be demanding value for money, and the driller may have his own preferred method of doing things and be reluctant to take instruction. Over and above this, the community must be kept involved at all times, which can be challenging with so much sophisticated equipment on site.

The technical subject of drilling boreholes, digging wells or improving springs is vast and cannot be covered in one chapter. There are several reference books which give detailed engineering information on the technical aspects of drilling and borehole design. The aims of this chapter are:

- to describe main borehole drilling methods and give some background to constructing wells and improving springs
- to give sufficient information to allow the reader to successfully supervise the construction of wells and boreholes
- to give information on the collection of relevant geological and hydrogeological data during the construction of wells and boreholes and describe how to record and report the information.

Much of the emphasis of the chapter is on boreholes, since they are the most common rural water supply intervention, but are often the least understood.

6.2 Drilling methods

6.2.1 Overview

Boreholes are the most common type of water point used in rural water supply projects. Since geological conditions are so diverse – ranging from hard rock, such as granite and gneiss, to completely unconsolidated sediments such as sand and gravel or weathered rock – various types of drilling method have had to be developed.

The choice of drilling rig for a particular job should be controlled by:

- the types of rock to be drilled
- the maximum depth of borehole to be drilled, plus an additional 25 per cent
- the types and dimensions (internal and external) of casing and screen to be used (see section 6.5)
- the depth to water table
- whether a gravel pack or formation stabilizer is required (see section 6.5)
- the accessibility of the borehole drilling sites.

Most (but not all) drilling methods require a motorized **drilling rig**. A drilling rig is a crane with a motor and a mast equipped with the necessary cables and/or slides to allow for the lift, fall and rotation of drill rods (see Figure 6.1). At the bottom of the drill rods is a bit which is designed to cut into the rock. These drilling bits come in a variety of shapes and sizes: drag bits, tricone bits, chisels and pneumatic-hammers. The combination of the drill rods and attached bit is called the **drill string**. The drilling rig must have a mechanism to remove drilled rock cuttings during and/or between periods of drilling. The **capacity** of a drilling rig depends on its lifting ability and the amount of torque that can be applied to the drilling string. The rig should have sufficient power to pull the drill string out of the borehole from its maximum depth with an additional safety factor in case the bit gets stuck, or material collapses on top of the bit. The capacity of the rig is also limited by the size of the pump or compressor which removes the cuttings from the borehole.

Drilling fluids may be used to stabilize the borehole and improve the removal of cuttings. There are two main types of drilling fluids: freshwater-based fluids and air-based fluids. Freshwater fluids include mud and polymers and are used in rotary and reverse circulation drilling. Air-based fluids, including dry air, mist or foam are used in down-the-hole hammer and rotary drilling (see later for a description of different drilling methods).

Water-based fluids are mixed and stored either in pits excavated at the site or in tanks transported to the site. When using water-based fluids, excavated pits should be lined with plastic sheeting or other material that does not allow mixing of natural materials with the drilling fluid. Non-detergent foams and water used in air-based fluids are injected into the airstream from a container mounted on the drilling rig.

Fluid additives such as bentonite and native clays can permanently damage productive aquifers, so should only be used as a last resort and with great

Figure 6.1 Typical drilling site; this example is of direct circulation rotary drilling in Fiji.
Photo: BGS, © NERC 2001.

care. To ensure that drilling fluids are fully removed from the borehole after completion of drilling, in order to avoid significant permanent damage to formation or water quality in the aquifer, it is necessary to monitor and adjust fluid density and viscosity during drilling. Standard texts (see the 'Further reading' list at the end of the chapter) give this information.

The various drilling methods used to construct water boreholes are listed in Table 6.1, along with their advantages and disadvantages. The three most common techniques are: air flush down-the-hole hammer, percussion (cable tool) and manual drilling. More information on the costs of different drilling rigs is given in Chapter 3.

Table 6.1 The advantages and disadvantages of different types of drilling

Method	Advantages	Disadvantages	Equipment
Manual	Good in shallow unconsolidated aquifers Extremely low cost and low tech Highly portable Community involvement	Cannot penetrate consolidated formations or hard rocks Small diameter of completed borehole (generally <165 mm) Limited to shallow aquifers with shallow water tables	Equipment is all available locally Slightly different methods have developed in different parts of the world
Jetting	Good in shallow unconsolidated aquifers Low cost and low tech Highly portable Rapid penetration	Cannot penetrate consolidated sediments or hard rocks Small diameter of completed borehole (generally <165 mm) Limited to shallow unconsolidated aquifers Needs source of water	Much of the equipment is available locally, and fairly low tech. A centrifugal pump is required
Cable tool	Low cost equipment Can drill in most formations, but most useful in unconsolidated sediments Easily portable equipment Low tech	Slow penetration Very slow in hard rocks Can be difficult to recognise water strikes	Specific drilling rig required, but fairly low tech and easily fixed Can range from small trailer mounted rigs, to large truck mounted drilling rigs
Air rotary and DTH Hammer	Can drill all consolidated formations Rapid penetration except in clay Good recognition of water strikes and geology Suitable for deep drilling Widely available drilling rigs	High cost of equipment Not suitable for unconsolidated aquifers Can experience problems with high yields or collapsing conditions	High tech requiring rig with hydraulics and compressor. Drilling rigs come in various sizes from small trailer rigs, to large multi-purposes truck-mounted rigs
Mud rotary	Can drill many formations Suitable for unstable, collapsible conditions Can drill through high yielding water strikes or cavities	Penetration through hard formations can be slow Expertise and equipment not readily available Difficult to recognize water strikes and poor sample recovery Can result in formation damage in some aquifers Requires source of water	High tech requiring rotary rig with hydraulics and mud pump. Rigs come in various sizes from small trailer mounted rigs to large truck-mounted multipurpose rigs

Table 6.1 contd.

| Reverse circulation rotary | Suitable for unconsolidated sedimentary formations Good for large diameter borehole drilling Good sample recovery Little or no damage to aquifer formations Less development needed after drilling | Requires large amounts of water Limited to soft and unconsolidated formations Expertise and equipment not readily available Cannot recognize water strikes | High tech, requiring large specially fitted drilling rigs. Not widely available, used for high-yielding boreholes in unconsolidated aquifers |

6.2.2 Rotary down-the-hole hammer airflush

This method is used to drill boreholes rapidly in hard rock formations and is the most widely used method for drilling community water supplies. The method uses an air-operated hammer to drill, and the cuttings are removed

Top drive motor to rotate drill string during drilling

Mast

Compressed air lines supplying air to the drill pipe from the compressor

Drill string

Levelling jack

Truck mounted compressor

Figure 6.2 Drilling in Tanzania using the down-the-hole hammer method.
Photo: BGS, © NERC 2001.

by air from a compressor. Rigs come in various shapes and sizes: from small trailer mounted rigs, capable of drilling 100–150-mm boreholes to 100 m in hard rock, to large double-axle truck-mounted rigs capable of drilling large-diameter boreholes to several hundred metres. Whatever the size of the rig, the method works in exactly the same way. Figure 6.2 shows the component parts of a down-the-hole hammer rig.

Compressed air is forced down the drill pipe to activate the hammer at the end of the drill string (see Figure 6.3). The bit is rotated slowly at 5–15 rpm. Air passes through the drill bit and flushes cuttings up the annular space to the top of the borehole, where they are collected and cleared at regular intervals. Continuous hole cleaning exposes new rock so that no energy is wasted in re-drilling old cuttings. For optimum up-hole velocity during drilling, the drill rod diameter must match the borehole diameter and air pressure/volume of flow. An injection pump can be used as necessary to inject small quantities of water or foam into the drill string during drilling to suppress dust or to improve the lifting capacity of the return air stream. At the start of borehole drilling, tricone rock-bits or drag bits are usually used to get through the soft near-surface soils and shallow weathered strata before the hammer can be fitted.

6.2.3 Cable tool percussion drilling

This is the main method used to drill boreholes into unconsolidated sediments. The operating capacity of a cable tool percussion rig is limited by the weight of tools and temporary steel casing strings that can be handled safely. The main components of the drilling system are illustrated in Figure 6.4. A full string of drill tools comprises drill bit, drill stem, drilling jars, swivel socket and cable. A bailer, strings of heavy duty temporary casing of decreasing diameter, and high-capacity jacks to retrieve temporary casing, are also needed. A rig may be truck- or trailer-mounted, with additional tools carried on a support vehicle. The rigs are relatively simple to maintain, making them popular in areas where access to spare parts and servicing facilities are lacking.

In cable tool percussion drilling there are three main operations:

- breaking of rock by the repeated lifting and dropping of the drilling bit
- removal of rock cuttings with a bailer
- driving temporary casing down the borehole as drilling proceeds to prevent borehole collapse.

The drilling bit needs to be heavy enough to break, crush and mix sediments and rocks. The drill stem provides additional weight and helps to maintain a vertical borehole alignment during drilling. Drilling jars are used to free the bit when drilling through soft and sticky sediment.

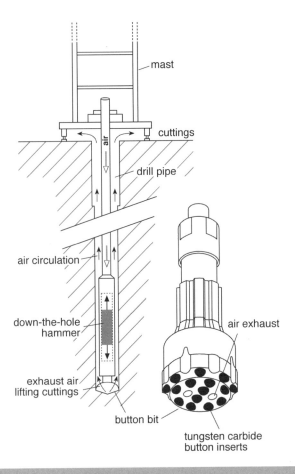

Figure 6.3	Schematic diagram of down-the-hole drilling.
	Source: Davis and Lambert 2002.

The mixture of rock fragments with water (derived from the formation or added during drilling) forms a slurry which is then be removed from the borehole using a bailer. As the borehole is deepened, temporary casing must be installed to stop the borehole collapsing. Three or four bits of different diameters may be used to drill in hard formations: the diameter is reduced in harder formations to stop the drilling grinding to a near halt. The bits need to be sharpened and redressed to the correct diameter daily. Borehole drilling can be slow, on the order of weeks (compared to days with the mud flush method); and borehole construction can take up to three days because of the time taken to remove temporary casing.

6.2.4 Manual drilling

Manual drilling, if possible, is by far the cheapest drilling method. Unfortunately it can only be used in certain specific environments: where

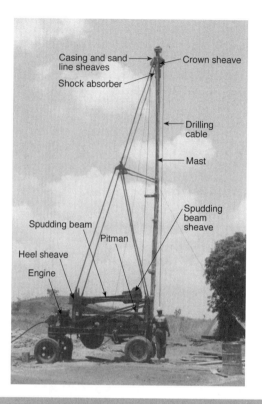

| Figure 6.4 | Large cable tool percussion rig in use in southern Africa.
Photo: BGS, © NERC 1985. |

water is easily found, the water table is shallow and in unconsolidated sediments. Often manual methods have developed gradually in an area and make use of local materials such as bamboo, so no expensive equipment is required.

The **hand flap or sludger** drilling method is a manual method commonly used for constructing boreholes in the alluvial flood plain aquifers of Bangladesh (Figures 6.5 and 6.6). Using this method 100 mm (4 inch) diameter boreholes can be drilled to depths of 50 m within sediments that are finer than gravel. Drilling will be halted by large gravel material or pebbles.

A crew of two or three is required, and the drilling equipment is made up of:

- a bamboo framework
- galvanized steel pipe in 3 m lengths with couplings to drill to 50 m
- a short length of chain
- two pipe wrenches
- a drag or wing bit and a steel catcher plate.

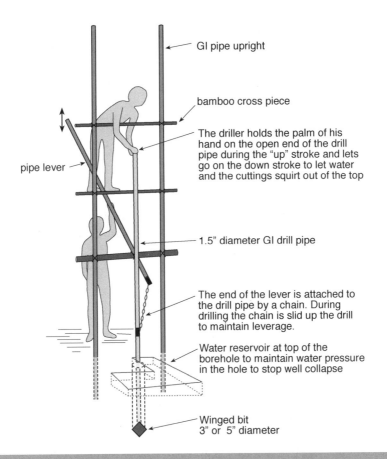

GI pipe upright

bamboo cross piece

The driller holds the palm of his hand on the open end of the drill pipe during the "up" stroke and lets go on the down stroke to let water and the cuttings squirt out of the top

pipe lever

1.5" diameter GI drill pipe

The end of the lever is attached to the drill pipe by a chain. During drilling the chain is slid up the drill to maintain leverage.

Water reservoir at top of the borehole to maintain water pressure in the hole to stop well collapse

Winged bit 3" or 5" diameter

Figure 6.5	Schematic diagram of a manual drilling method used in Bangladesh.

During the drilling procedure, the galvanized drill pipe is raised and dropped using a lever system keeping the pipe full of water. The drill cuttings are drawn out of the borehole through the steel pipe by simple suction: the driller holds the palm of his hand on the open end of the drill pipe during the 'up' stroke and lets go on the down stroke to let water and the cuttings squirt out of the top. As the drill pipe passes deeper into the formation so additional lengths of pipe are added at the surface, leverage being adjusted by sliding the chain to a better position. Truly representative samples are difficult if not impossible to obtain using this method. Once the borehole is deep enough, the drilling pipes are left in the borehole to form the casing.

| Figure 6.6 | Manual drilling using the hand flap method in Bangladesh. Photo: BGS, © NERC 1992. |

6.2.5 Mud rotary drilling

The mud-flush rotary method can be used to rapidly drill boreholes into unconsolidated sediments and can also be used for other types of rocks. Drilling rigs using this system are widely available and are typically (although not always) truck-mounted. The drill string is rotated using a top head drive. Rotary (tricone) drilling bits are generally used, although drag bits may be used in particularly soft conditions. The drill bit rotates, disaggregating, breaking and crushing the rock formation. Rock cuttings are removed by flushing the borehole with mud. Mud is pumped through the drill pipe and holes in the bit – the mud swirls in the bottom of the hole, picking up material broken by the bit before flowing upwards between the drill pipe and the wall of the borehole to carry the cuttings to the surface. The drill pipe and bit move progressively downward, deepening the hole as the operation proceeds.

At the ground surface, the mud flows into a settling pit where the cuttings settle to the bottom (it is difficult to get representative sample from the cuttings). From the settling pit the mud is recycled through the drill pipe using the mud pump. Casing is not put into the hole until drilling operations are completed, since the walls of the hole are supported by the weight of the mud. Mud cake can be difficult to remove, making the construction of the borehole difficult (see later). A biodegradable mud should be used if possible; the use of bentonite mud should be avoided as it is particularly hard to remove.

6.2.6 Rotary reverse circulation

The reverse circulation rotary drilling method is primarily used for installing large-diameter boreholes (>600 mm) within unconsolidated alluvial aquifers, so is rarely used for rural water supply boreholes. Reverse circulation drilling rigs are often mounted on 4×4 tractors to ensure access in flood plain areas. During drilling, water is channelled into the top of the borehole from a large capacity reservoir ensuring that the head of water within the borehole is always at least 3 m higher than in the aquifer to avoid borehole collapse. The circulating water passes down through the borehole annulus, to be sucked through the drill bit and up the drill pipe with the drill cuttings held in suspension, through a large-capacity centrifugal slush pump and into large-capacity settling pits. The drilling water is then recycled back down the hole. Drag bits are preferred for drilling in coarse-grained sediments. Good clean representative formation samples can be obtained using this method.

6.2.7 Water jetting

The water jetting or wash boring drilling method is used for installing shallow, low-yielding village supply boreholes in unconsolidated sands and silts. This drilling system cannot be used in highly permeable sands and gravels: gravels will stop the downward movement of the bit; and high rates of fluid loss will stop the drilled sediments being flushed to the surface.

The drilling system uses a winch, tripod, sheaves, capstan bars, drag bit and pump with hoses (see Figure 6.7). Other equipment required includes temporary casing, drill rods, suitable pipe wrenches, and catcher plate. Most importantly, the drilling system requires a reliable source of water. During drilling, sediments are loosened both by the stirring and percussive action of

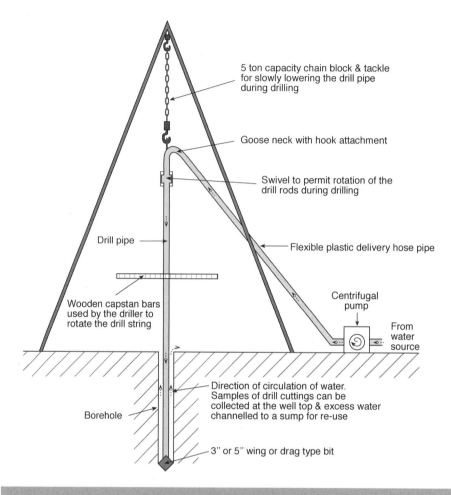

5 ton capacity chain block & tackle for slowly lowering the drill pipe during drilling

Goose neck with hook attachment

Swivel to permit rotation of the drill rods during drilling

Drill pipe

Flexible plastic delivery hose pipe

Centrifugal pump

Wooden capstan bars used by the driller to rotate the drill string

From water source

Direction of circulation of water. Samples of drill cuttings can be collected at the well top & excess water channelled to a sump for re-use

Borehole

3" or 5" wing or drag type bit

Figure 6.7 Schematic diagram of the equipment required for drilling using the jetting method.

rotating and by dropping the bit and drill string. Drill cuttings are flushed up to the surface through the annular space between drill rods and hole wall by water pumped down the hollow drill rods using a small pump. In collapsing ground, casing is driven down to support the borehole sides or drilling mud may be used to avoid borehole collapse. Sediment samples returned to the surface tend to be mixed. The borehole is completed by either incorporating screens into the drill string and then leaving the drill string to form the screen and casing; or installed within (or sometimes after the removal of) the drill pipes.

6.3 Roles and responsibilities

6.3.1 The relationship between the engineer/hydrogeologist and driller

This relationship is fundamental to a successful project. Usually drillers and hydrogeologists have had quite separate career paths. A driller might typically be a mechanical engineer with skills in the handling of machinery, and a hydrogeologist or project engineer is usually a college or university graduate with skills in managing or interpreting data and information. The role of the hydrogeologist/project engineer is described in Box 6.1.

BOX 6.1   The role of the hydrogeologist/project engineer

- Decides the detailed location of the drill site in consultation with the driller and local partners/community, thus ensuring that the drilling rig can be brought to site and can be safely operated there.
- Advises the driller where to drill and the depth and design of the borehole based on information collected during drilling.
- Should **not** attempt to tell the driller how to drill.
- Needs to have a good working knowledge of the drilling operation to understand what setting-up procedures should be followed rigorously by the driller.
- Must clearly instruct the driller about the collection of rock chip samples and how they are to be stored.
- Should be responsible for description of lithological samples.
- Needs to be able to advise the driller when core samples or other **in situ** down-the-hole measurements are to be taken, as agreed within the contract document.

6.3.2 Relationships with the community

As with all aspects of project design and implementation, it is important to work with the community during drilling operations. This involves explaining beforehand what is going to happen; keeping the community informed about developments; and ensuring that the community's questions, concerns and wishes are respected. This is not difficult, or particularly time consuming, and will reinforce the relationship of mutual understanding between project staff and community members.

Explaining what is going to happen should not be viewed as an exercise in technical translation. Instead, the aim should be to convey to the community – preferably before equipment is brought on site – what the equipment is for, what will happen, and how long it will take. Additionally, it is important that:

- health and safety concerns are raised and communicated effectively

- the community is consulted about the transport of equipment in and around the village, and the potential inconvenience – and ways of minimizing it – arising from noise, disposal of waste materials and so on
- the community has realistic expectations about the likely success of drilling operations, and the potential need to find alternative sites.

The driller/hydrogeologist should be introduced to the community head by the project partners. A follow-up 'open' meeting, organized through the head, can then be arranged if necessary. There are likely to be many questions, which should be answered with openness and patience. Identifying an ongoing point of contact to report to, and consult with, will be important as drilling gets underway.

The drilling operation itself is likely to generate considerable interest (see Figure 6.8), and keeping the community informed should be regarded as a responsibility, not a favour. At the same time, community members may have new questions or concerns about what is happening. The driller should work closely with the contact person identified, providing updates on progress, and responding to any concerns the community may have. Some compromise may be necessary, for example suspending drilling during a local funeral or religious event. When drilling is complete, the community should know what happens next, and should not be left with major clearing-up work to do, or repairs to make.

Figure 6.8   A drilling site can be a busy place.
Photo: © PAT drilling

6.3.3 Drilling contracts

If a private drilling company is used to carry out the drilling, then the specification of work for the driller is governed by a contract. Borehole drilling contracts are in essence the same as most other forms of contract in civil engineering; however, there are three main differences:

- Each borehole will be different, even although the conditions at each location appear to be similar.
- Much of the borehole construction is not visible and cannot be inspected.
- The borehole owner is unlikely to know the specialist skills required to drill and construct a successful borehole – it appears to be a black art.

It is beyond the scope of this manual to provide detailed information on developing a contract or to provide a template. Examples often exist within a country, but where absent an excellent guide has already been given by the US Environmental Protection Agency's Office of Water Supply (US EPA 1976). Although dated, this guide is still seen as a benchmark for contracts. Only an outline of what should be considered within a contract is given here, based on information from Brandon (1986).

A contract is a signed agreement between two parties, the employer and contractor, which is designed to protect both parties and agree the scope and price of work to be carried out. There are two main parts to any drilling contract: the 'General Conditions' and the 'Design Specifications'.

The 'General Conditions' govern the rights and responsibilities of each party entering into the contract. There are several published standard conditions of contracts for civil engineering work. For example in the UK, the ICE Conditions of Contract are widely used. There can be up to 70 clauses in these general conditions. Several of these general conditions need to be modified for drilling contracts:

- The site is not always clearly defined at the beginning, so flexibility must be retained in the contract.
- The engineer or representative may need to make urgent minor alterations, without having to get written permission from employer.
- The site and aquifer conditions are not always known in detail at the time of tendering,
- The accuracy of the estimated quantities may be less than for other contracts since the thickness of aquifers and the grain sizes are not always known.
- The period of maintenance (i.e. the time in which the contractor can be asked to come back and fix any problems) should be short enough so that problems can be fixed while the equipment is in the area.
- Responsibility for health and safety aspects of the drilling site must rest with the contractor.

■ Provision should be made for the contractor to work during the night without written permission.

The second part of the contract is the 'Design Specifications'. These specify the detailed work to be carried out and the specifications of the boreholes. Again, since the exact design is not known, flexibility must be retained so that the exact borehole design is finalized at the site by the project engineer or hydrogeologist. There are several parts to the design specification.

■ **General:** description, purpose and location of works, expectant drilling conditions; health and safety, units of measurement (one NASA contract got confused between millimetres and inches, resulting in an unmanned space probe spectacularly missing Mars!).
■ **Borehole drilling:** often the contracts leave the drilling method to the contractor to best define. However, special conditions should be stated (e.g. no mud – only water circulation).
■ **Borehole construction:** typical design of boreholes; schedule of construction, gravel pack, grouting, finishing at the top, role of the project engineer or representative in finalizing design.
■ **Materials:** casing, screen, reducers, gravel pack, cement, etc.
■ **Borehole development:** how long the boreholes should be developed for, acidification or hydraulic fracturing (if required).
■ **Tests:** pumping tests (and recovery), quality of the water, etc.
■ **Sampling:** what rock samples are to be taken from the borehole; frequency; how and for how long they are to be kept; responsibility for analyzing them.
■ **Recording:** drillers log; construction, material used in each borehole; final depth and diameter, etc.
■ **Site restoration:** how the site is to be left (e.g. all material to be cleared away and casing to be left sticking 0.5 m out of the ground), the filling in of abandoned boreholes.

It is helpful to have a **bill of quantities** along with a contract. The bill of quantities consists of a list of items or activities with a brief description. The contractor then puts in a provisional sum for each item or activity. It is a very useful method for comparing different quotes, and also helps the contactor give a reasonable price for the job. A bill of quantities might include the following:

■ mobilization and demobilization of equipment and personnel
■ set up rig, move between different borehole sites
■ clear and reinstate sites at end of drilling
■ drill borehole at certain diameter (per metre) through soft material
■ drill borehole at certain diameter (per metre) through hard material
■ supply, install and withdraw temporary casing (per metre)
■ supply and install casing as specified (per metre)

- supply and install screen (per metre) casing shoes, plugs reducers etc (per number)
- supply and install gravel pack (of certain grade) as specified (per m^3 of gravel, normally)
- supply and emplace cement grout
- develop borehole (sometimes specify technique – e.g. surging, airlifting, jetting, etc.)
- carry out tests (e.g. pumping tests, geophysical logs, etc.)
- provide headworks if required – e.g. lockable cap
- take and store geological samples at specified interval
- prepare and deliver full report (specify what is expected in it)
- standing time (usually per hour) must be specified in the contract and if the standing time is the responsibility of employer or contractor.

6.4 Collecting data during drilling

The main aim of data collection during borehole drilling is to identify water production zones in the geological sequence – this requires more information than is normally recorded by a driller. The project engineer or hydrogeologist must collect and analyse these data and should be onsite if at all possible. The collection of information during drilling is the only way to find out what is beneath the ground surface. The following section describes a list of useful equipment, which information should be collected and techniques for data collection and analysis.

6.4.1 Equipment required

Some basic equipment is useful for collecting and analysing data from drilling (Figure 6.9). The combined list costs much less than drilling one borehole (roughly one fifth) and much of it will last for many years.

- water level recorder (dipper), as described in Chapter 7
- GPS to accurately locate boreholes
- colour charts to accurately record colour
- stop watch
- penknife
- geological hammer
- dilute hydrochloric acid (if possible) to identify calcareous material
- hand lens with a magnification of ×8 or ×10
- permanent markers
- waterproof notebook
- plastic bags to store samples
- camera – photographs of chip samples, or even the drilling process can be a useful record and help to jog memories about various sites
- bucket for cleaning samples.

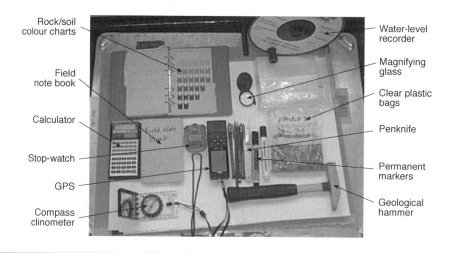

Rock/soil colour charts

Field note book

Calculator

Stop-watch

GPS

Compass clinometer

Water-level recorder

Magnifying glass

Clear plastic bags

Penknife

Permanent markers

Geological hammer

Figure 6.9 Most of the equipment required for collecting data during drilling. Photo: BGS. © NERC 2000.

6.4.2 Techniques for collecting data from the drilling process

Various data should be collected during the actual drilling process. Ideally this should be collected by on onsite hydrogeologist and recorded into a field notebook (Figure 6.10).

Drilling and construction parameters

The following information should be recorded for each borehole:

- the main drilling rig type and drill bit
- the name of the driller
- the flushing medium (air, mud or foam)
- details of additional equipment used (e.g. air compressor)
- the borehole dimensions (drilled depth and diameter, and completed depth after construction)
- the type and details (lengths and depths) of casing and screen installed.

Water strikes

One of the most important measurements to make during drilling is the depth of water strikes. This gives direct evidence of the locations of water-flow zones. In addition to obvious water strikes, the presence of zones where the rock chippings are damp should also be recorded. This is possible for airflush methods, but difficult for percussion drilling, hand drilling, jetting or drilling with mud. Figure 6.11 shows a water strike during drilling.

Date   : 11 NOV 2001, 9.30
Village   : Egori Ukpute 34° 321'N 12° 012'E
Field workers : Jeff Davies
Driller   : Peter Rastell

8 inch rock rollar
6 inch hammer
DTH - Dando Geoteck 5

Depth	Time	Comments
Rod 1		
0 - 0.5 m	35 s	
0.5 - 1 m	49s	
1 - 1.5 m	56s	jerky
1.5 - 2 m	35s	
2 - 2.5 m	1 min 20 s	
2.5 - 3 m	4 min 34 s	
Rod 2		
3 - 3.5 m	1 min 10 s	change to DTH
3.5 - 4 m	1 min 30 s	
4 - 4.5 m	50 s	dusty
4.5 - 5 m	1 min 40 s	
5 - 5.5 m	1 min 12 s	
5.5 - 6 m	3 min 4 s	damp

Figure 6.10 Example of a field notebook recording the progress of drilling.

After the first water strike, it is sometimes difficult to accurately record further strikes. For example, when each new drill pipe is put on there will be a great flush of water when the air is switched on. Also, because of changes in the airflow as the borehole deepens, the discharge can appear to change.

Water flow rates

The water blown out of the borehole during airflush drilling can give an indication of borehole yield. A basic measurement of water flow rate can be made by channelling the water away from the borehole though a pipe into a bucket of known volume and measuring the time taken to fill the bucket, giving a result in litres per second (see Chapter 7). It is more difficult to assess yield when using percussion, but a rough idea can be given by the number of bails of water taken out in a set period of time.

Figure 6.11   Striking water while drilling with down-the-hole hammer.
Photo: BGS, © NERC 2001.

Water-levels

Once the borehole is drilled, the water level in the borehole should be measured using a dipper. This should be done immediately after drilling, and also once water levels in the borehole have recovered.

Other useful information that can be collected

The drilling rate can be monitored by recording the time taken to drill a specified interval, usually every 1.0 m. Measurements are made using a stopwatch, and plotted on a graph. An example of a notebook for gathering data during drilling is shown in Figure 6.10. The speed of drilling reflects the relative hardness of the rock horizons penetrated, and can be an important indicator of water-bearing horizons. Weathered zones, which often contain groundwater, are generally soft, while the boundary between the weathered zone and harder bedrock, also a potentially water-bearing zone, may be marked by a change to a slower penetration rate. Notes on whether the drilling is jerky, or there is a sudden fall of the drill string can also indicate fracture zones.

When using down-the-hole hammer drilling, the amount of dust produced at each depth interval can also be recorded. This is a subjective measurement (it is impossible to measure the amount of dust produced accurately) but it is a good basic indicator of whether water is present. In zones of water flow, very little or no dust is produced during drilling, while in dry zones there is usually plenty of dust.

Water quality

Depending on drilling type, water quality can be monitored during drilling after groundwater has been encountered. Measurements of temperature, pH and SEC (conductivity) of borehole water during drilling will indicate basic water quality, showing immediately if the water is too saline to be drinkable. Chapter 8 gives much more detail on water quality.

In some environments, e.g. where concentrations of fluoride or arsenic are high, field measurements can be taken at different drilling depths. This can be particularly useful if there is an increase in these elements with depth. Drilling is therefore stopped when the yield is sufficient, and the arsenic or fluoride levels still low. This practice is rare, however, because of the time delays in taking samples, analysing them and getting the results in time to inform the drilling.

6.4.3 Techniques for collecting and analysing chip and core samples

Rock chip samples

A sample of fresh rock chips can be taken from the borehole at regular intervals throughout drilling (Table 6.2). The sampling intervals should be such that narrow water-bearing zones are not missed, but not so frequent that too many samples are taken. It is usually good practice to take samples more often where the geology is very changeable – such as in the shallow weathered zone. For a shallow borehole, samples can be taken every 0.5 m, but for a deep borehole this will produce too many samples to be analysed, and a sampling interval of 1.0 m is more practical. The sample must be large enough to allow a good description of the geology to be made – about 300 g is usually enough.

For airflush, the sample can be taken by placing a bucket or spade next to the top of the borehole so that the some of the chippings will captured. Figure 6.12 shows a driller collecting chip samples during drilling – it is

Table 6.2 Collecting chip samples for different drilling methods

Drilling method	Sample collection and handling
Air down the hole hammer or rotary	Container placed next to the borehole such that cuttings are collected; a representative sample from this container should then be taken; cuttings from consolidated formations can be washed as required; cuttings from unconsolidated formation should not be washed
Cable tool percussion	A representative sample of the cuttings recovered from the bailer can be collected over each metre of drilling; cuttings from consolidated formations may be washed if required, cuttings from unconsolidated formation should not be washed
Mud rotary, jetting, reverse circulation	Samples collected in a bucket from the borehole (mud rotary, jetting) or from the discharge pipe (reverse circulation); a representative sample from the interval should be taken and excess drilling fluid squeezed out. The sample should not be washed
Manual	Samples can be collected from the top of the drill pipe at regular intervals

Figure 6.12 Collecting chip samples with a bucket during drilling.
Photo: BGS, © NERC 2000.

essential to have a good working relationship with the driller. Where possible the borehole should be flushed clean before each sample interval to ensure that samples are representative of the labelled depth.

The samples can be stored in clear plastic bags, labelled with the date, the borehole name and/or number and the depth interval (e.g. 21/7/05, Borehole 5, 10.5–11.0 m). If this is not possible, they should at least be stored separately and in order of collection on a cleared area close to the drilling rig. To avoid inadvertent mixing, samples can be stored in a sample box with separate compartments for each sample. The specific interval represented by the sample (i.e. 30–31 m) should be clearly marked.

Analysis of rock chip samples

The basic tools required to analyse rock chip samples in the field are described earlier: a magnifying glass or hand lens, a penknife, a field notebook, pencils, and a core box (or a plastic pipe split in half and divided into different intervals). It is also useful to take colour photographs of the geological samples as a permanent record. Dilute hydrochloric acid can be useful to indicate calcareous rocks, including calcite veins.

For each sample in turn, hard rock chips should be washed so that they can be properly examined. Soft rock fragments from weathered horizons should not be washed as they may disintegrate. The samples are then described lithologically, creating a log of the changes in colour, lithology, weathering or fracturing, which will show the depths of permeable, potentially water-bearing horizons. The following parameters should be noted. How to measure these different parameter is described in more detail in Appendix 1.

- **Sample colour:** colour helps indicate weathered zones: red colours often indicate oxidation and therefore weathering. Colour can be described using standard colour charts such as those produced by Munsel®. This avoids confusion over what is orangey-brown or brownish-orange!
- **Grain size:** the size of grains or particles in the rock can be examined using a magnifying glass or hand lens and described using standard charts.
- **Relative hardness:** weathered rock, in which groundwater is often found, is usually softer.
- The presence of **vein material**, such as calcite or quartz veins can be indicators of fracture zones which may be water-bearing.
- The presence of **limestone**. If the rocks react to hydrochloric acid, then calcium carbonate is present.

The above information can be used to estimate the lithology: e.g. granite, limestone, sandstone, etc.

Representative chip samples can then be placed in sequence within a core box or sectioned pipe to show changes in texture and colour with depth. A standard scale should be used (e.g. 50 mm in the sectioned pipe equates to 0.5 m in the borehole). They can then be photographed to provide a permanent record.

Figure 6.13 shows an example of a notebook describing chip samples from a borehole. A Munsel® colour chart was used to describe the colours. These descriptions have then been combined to produce the log as shown in Figure 6.14. The log should not be drawn up directly from the samples: it is important always to have the detailed descriptions of each 1-m interval to refer back to. This means that important horizons will not be missed. When trying to understand what makes a borehole successful in an area, it is often the small things that are important: a calcite vein associated with fractures; orange or purple staining on chip samples in sandstones indicating flowing fractures; or slicken-sides on some samples indicating a fault zone, etc.

More information on how all the information from drilling should be reported and put together is given later in this chapter.

5.6 - 6.1   Light yellowish brown
2.5Y6/4 fine to medium grained sand with some
coarse grains . Occasional piece of
unconsolidated sandstone.

6.1 - 6.6   Light yellowish brown
2.5y6/4 fine to medium grained sand with some
coarse grains. Occasional piece of consolidated
sandstone. Some chips of dark grey mudstone
with light grey clay and reddish yellow staining.

6.6 - 7.1   Light yellowish brown
2.5y6/4 fine to medium grained sand with some
coarse grains. Occasional piece of consolidated
sandstone. Some chips of dark grey mudstone
with light grey clay and reddish yellow clay.

7.1 - 7.6   Light yellowish brown
2.5y6/4 fine to medium grained sand with some
coarse grains. Occasional piece of consolidated
sandstone. Some chips of dark grey mudstone
with light grey clay and reddish yellow clay
staining.

Figure 6.13 Example of lithological descriptions of chip samples for a borehole in Nigeria. Figure 6.14 shows the interpreted log from these descriptions.

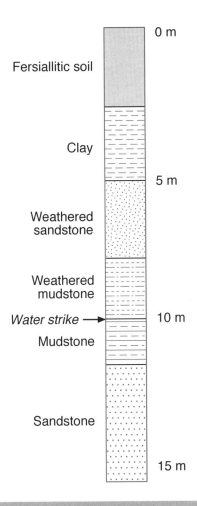

Fersiallitic soil

Clay

Weathered sandstone

Weathered mudstone

Water strike ➔

Mudstone

Sandstone

0 m

5 m

10 m

15 m

Figure 6.14 Lithological log made from chip samples as described in Figure 6.13.

Cored rock samples

Although chip samples give some idea of lithology, they are no substitute for a cored section of rock. A core can be taken relatively simply in soft formation such as such as mudstones, siltstones and sandstones. A specialized core barrel is required, but this can be used with most rigs that can operate down-the-hole hammer. The cost of such a core barrel, with bits, is less than the price of drilling one borehole.

Core samples give a true, undisturbed sample of the rock at a given depth (see Figure 6.15). Lithological logging of these samples gives a much better idea of the geology than rock chip samples. They can also be used for laboratory analysis of aquifer parameters such as primary permeability and porosity.

A technique that has been used successfully on some rural water supply projects is to take a core from the bottom of each production borehole. This gives invaluable information for only one extra hour's work. Even if a hydrogeologist is not on site, the core can be labelled and stored for someone to describe later.

Cores should be washed so that they can be properly examined, and then described geologically in the same way as for rock chip samples. More information can be gathered on how the rocks are bedded (if sedimentary). Also a cored sample can give information on fracturing in the rock. The techniques and descriptions of different rocks in Appendix 1 can be used as a guide.

Cores should be photographed, after which samples at known depths can be taken for porosity and/or permeability analysis, macro- and micro-palaeontological investigation, or petrographic and clay analysis. Cores can be useful aids for discussing geology with communities. However some sensitivity must be shown when taking samples away from the site, particularly if pyrite or chalocpyrite (fool's gold) is present!

6.5 Borehole design and construction

The first use for the data collected during drilling is to help construct the borehole. Every borehole drilled is to a degree exploratory, i.e. the geology cannot be predicted with certainty. For this reason the design must be adapted to the particular geology found at the drilling site. Under no circumstances should a standard design be adhered to rigorously at the expense of information gained during drilling.

Ideally a borehole should be designed to fulfil the following conditions:

- borehole efficiency is maximized (high pumping from small boreholes can lead to friction losses and deep drawdowns)
- sand inflow to the borehole is kept to a minimum
- materials are of sufficient quality to last at least 25 years
- any contaminated sources or aquifers, or zones of undesirable water quality, should be sealed off from the borehole.

Obviously these factors have to be balanced with the cost of the borehole. Drilling a large-diameter borehole to 100 m and lining it with expensive stainless steel screen could cost as much as 10 narrow-diameter boreholes drilled to 50 m and completed with uPVC screen and casing. Also, it is important to know whether the borehole is likely to be successful before installing expensive screen and casing. If the borehole is low yielding, but not totally dry, a simple bailer test (see Chapter 7) could be carried out to give more information on likely yield.

6.5.1 Typical borehole designs

Although a borehole design is usually site-specific, general designs can be applied to specific hydrogeological environments. These are summarized

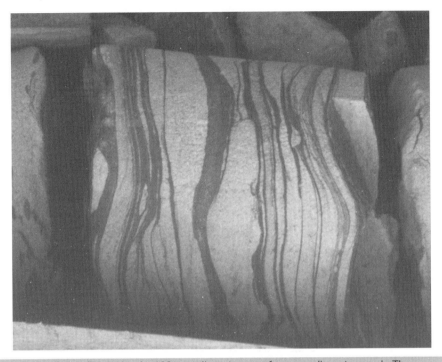

Figure 6.15	Example of a 100-mm diameter core from a sedimentary rock. The interbedded mudstone and sandstone are clearly visible. Photo: BGS, © NERC 1999.

below as a guide. Although the examples with screens depict a single aquifer zone, additional screened intervals can be included within a similar design. The first two designs are the most common for handpump boreholes.

Fundamental to all the designs shown here is that the soft weathered zone is sealed off from the rest of the borehole. This is because in joint rural water supply and sanitation projects, groundwater in the shallow weathered zone, or laterite soil, is often highly contaminated by pit latrines within the community. All the designs here are shown with surface casing pressure-grouted through this shallow zone. This is generally the simplest and most effective way of sealing out the contaminated shallow groundwater. However, it is not always carried out, particularly where there is a high borehole failure rate, since the surface casing is effectively 'lost' if the borehole is dry. A description of how to install and grout surface casing is given later in the chapter.

Open hole in consolidated formation (Figure 6.16)

This design applies to consolidated formations where both the aquifer and bedrock are stable and show no evidence of collapse. After surface casing is

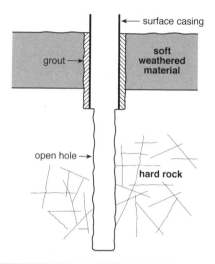

Figure 6.16 Open hole construction in a consolidated formation.

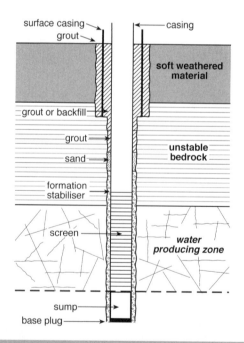

Figure 6.17 Borehole design in a consolidated formation at risk of collapse.

set through the overburden and sealed by pressure grouting, the remainder of the hole is left open. This design is low cost and efficient, but cannot be used in collapsing formations.

Cased borehole in consolidated formation with risk of collapse (Figure 6.17)

This borehole design is used where the bedrock or aquifer formations are unstable. After surface casing is set through the overburden and sealed by pressure grouting, a screened section is placed adjacent to the aquifer horizon(s) in the borehole. Formation stabilizer is place adjacent to the screens. A little sand is poured on top of the stabilizer before sealing with grout or bentonite. The remaining annular space is backfilled or grouted.

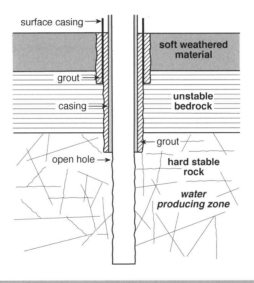

| Figure 6.18 | Borehole design in a consolidated formation with an unstable zone above the aquifer. |

Multiple casing borehole in an unstable formation above a stable aquifer zone (Figure 6.18)

This design is used to case off an unstable zone met above the aquifer. After surface casing is set through the overburden and sealed by pressure grouting, drilling is continued at a reduced diameter through the unstable zone. An inner casing is installed through the unstable zone and drilling continued at a reduced diameter. Further reductions in drilled hole and casing size may be required to case off several unstable zones above the aquifer. The rest of the borehole (including the aquifer horizon) is completed as an open hole. The final lengths of casing remain in the borehole and all larger diameter casings are recovered (apart from the grouted surface casing). The annular space between the completion casing and the borehole wall is then backfilled and grouted at the surface.

*Borehole in unconsolidated formation with formation stabilizer
(Figure 6.19)*

Boreholes drilled into unconsolidated sediments such as river alluvium must be screened. The grain size of the alluvial formation is assessed to help choose the slot size of screen and size of formation stabilizer (see below).

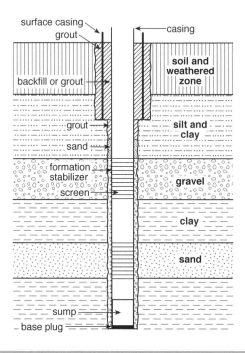

Figure 6.19	Borehole design in an unconsolidated formation, using a formation stabilizer.

After surface casing is installed, the borehole is drilled through the aquifer. Screens and casings are positioned in the borehole and formation stabilizer installed around the screens. A little sand is poured on top of the stabilizer before sealing with grout or bentonite. The remaining annular space is backfilled or grouted.

*Naturally developed borehole in unconsolidated formation
(Figure 6.20)*

A screened borehole installed in an unconsolidated sedimentary aquifer composed of well-graded coarse-grained sands and gravels can be developed without installing formation stabilizer. Temporary casing may be required to help drill the borehole. The casing and screen is positioned in the open hole and the aquifer sediments allowed to fill the annular space. A natural filter pack is developed during extensive borehole development.

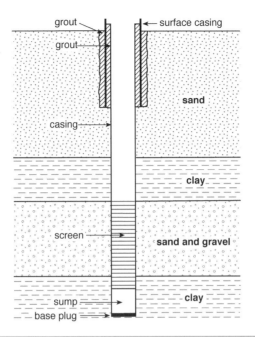

grout — surface casing

grout

casing

sand

clay

screen

sand and gravel

sump

clay

base plug

Figure 6.20 Naturally developed borehole in an unconsolidated formation.

The size of the slots should be chosen to allow about 50 per cent of the unconsolidated material through the slots during development.

Jetted or hand-flap drilled borehole (Figure 6.21)

A well point with 3 m of screen is normally installed into unconsolidated sediments by jetting water through the well-point head and screen – forcing water and cuttings to the surface. This means that the screening and casing are actually directly installed during the drilling process. A similar borehole design is used for screens and casings installed by the hand flap drilling method. The borehole is cut using a drag bit at the end of narrow-diameter drill pipe. The pipes and bit are withdrawn when the borehole has reached the required depth. Narrow-diameter casing with 3 m of screen at the bottom is then installed in the open hole, kept open by maintaining a positive head in the hole. The aquifer material is allowed to collapse back onto the screen which is then developed using a hand pump.

Borehole constructed without surface casing (Figure 6.22)

All the designs above have include surface casing which has been pressure grouted for an effective seal against contamination. This is the best way of ensuring that the borehole is not contaminated from the surface. However, other practices are also used to seal the borehole. The borehole is drilled at a single diameter from the surface to the bottom. One diameter of screen and

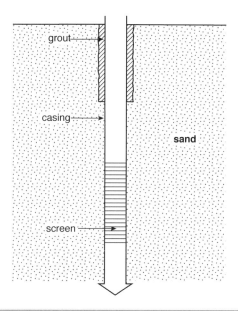

| Figure 6.21 | A jetted or hand-flapped drilled borehole. |

casing is then installed throughout the length of the borehole. Formation stabilizer is then added to a few metres above the top of the screen. Some sand is then placed on top of the formation stabilizer to stop grout from penetrating into the aquifer. The grout is then added on top of the sand to form the seal.

6.5.2 Choosing screen and casing

Casing types

The selection of a particular casing depends not only on the geological conditions, but more often on the costs, the available of materials and the equipment on the drilling rig. Casing is generally available in four different materials: steel, uPVC, stainless steel and glass-reinforced plastic (GRP). It generally come in 3-m or 6-m lengths and is coupled together using screw or sprocket fittings with plastic cement.

The choice of material depends on the conditions in the aquifer. If the borehole is deep, then the casing can come under considerable stress, both from the pressure of the water and from the formation (if unconsolidated). If the pressures are high, steel casing should be considered. Another issue is the water quality: if the water is slightly acidic then mild steel could corrode and uPVC or GRP should be considered. uPVC is the material of choice for most rural water supply boreholes.

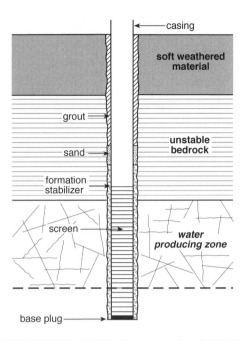

Figure 6.22 A borehole constructed without using surface casing.

Casing diameter

The diameter of casing is critical for boreholes fitted with high-yielding motorized pumps: the diameter must be large enough so that turbulent flow cannot occur. For boreholes fitted with handpumps the yields are so low that this is not a concern. The borehole diameter is therefore determined as the minimum required to safely house the pump barrel and rising main. A diameter of 100–150 mm is generally adequate for a rural water supply borehole.

Screens

Borehole screens should be installed next to the water-producing horizons. It is vital to get the calculations right, as it is all too easy to miscalculate and put blank casing instead of screen next to the only water-producing horizon. If in doubt, put enough screen into the well design (even though it is much more expensive than casing) so that no water-producing horizons are sealed off. If the aquifer is consolidated, then screen may not be required and the borehole can be left open. Table 6.3 describes the different types of screen available; some of them are shown in Figure 6.23.

Slotted uPVC screen

Continuous slot uPVC screen

Geotextile wrapped slotted uPVC screen

Stainless steel continuous slot screen

Mild steel louvre slot screen

Slotted glass reinforced plastic screen

Mild steel casing with a reducer

Glass Reinforced plastic joint

Figure 6.23 Examples of different types of screen and casing.
Photos: BGS, © NERC 1985–95.

Methods of producing screens include cutting holes with a cutting torch (steel casing) or a saw (steel and uPVC casing). Where possible, the slots or holes should be uniformly cut by machine in a workshop, and designed to block the passage of fine material into the borehole during pumping but not to reduce the strength of the screened casing such that collapse may occur. Slots in uPVC are accurately machined when manufactured which has contributed to the change of most drilling programmes to uPVC.

For very high-yielding boreholes the total area of open screen is also important. A large-diameter screen may be required to ensure that there is enough open area to let the water flow into the borehole unhindered. The velocity through the screen should be less than 0.03 m/s. Therefore the minimum open area in the screen can then be calculated using the formula:

$$A = Q/30$$

where A is the open area in m^2 and Q is the water flow in litres/s. For boreholes equipped with handpumps, the size of the open area of the screen is rarely, if ever, an issue.

Table 6.3 Common types of borehole screen

Screen type	Design	Applications
Slotted	Slots cut horizontally or vertically in steel, glass reinforced plastic, or uPVC casing	Consolidated or unconsolidated formations
Louvered and bridge slot	Openings are mechanically punched into steel which forces a lip of steel outwards – rarely used now	Mainly consolidated formations
Continuous slot screen (wedge section)	Wedge shaped wire or uPVC strip wrapped around longitudinal supports – stainless steel or plastic uPVC	Primarily unconsolidated formations
Composite	Screens with filter packing material Integrated, e.g. geotextile wrap over slotted uPVC	Primarily unconsolidated formations

Steel casing and screens should be joined by threaded joints that are watertight, maintain the straightness of the assembly and are a minimum of 50 per cent of the strength of the casing or screen. Joints should be strong enough to support the entire weight of the casing string during installation. Welds should be fully penetrating and continuous. If bell and socket couplings are used in uPVC casing, the joints need to be glued together with sufficient adhesive to bond the ends as a watertight seal and allowed to set. Casing and screen assemblies are lowered into the open borehole under the force of gravity and should under no circumstances be pushed or driven downwards.

As discussed earlier, the upper section of borehole, at least the top 5–6 m, should be cased, not screened, and grouted. This is to stop shallow contaminated water from entering the borehole. The casing should extend a minimum of 250 mm above ground level, or above the cement pad if one is installed (for all handpump boreholes).

The size of the slot is important in unconsolidated material. Where there is a choice, a slot size should be chosen that retains about 50 per cent of the aquifer material – during development (see later) the fine material passes through the screen and is pumped out. (Where a gravel pack has been installed, the slot size should be chosen to retain about 90 per cent of the gravel pack material.) This has the effect of increasing the effective radius of the borehole and increasing its performance. So if the aquifer material varies from 0.5 mm to 2 mm, a slot size of 1 mm should be sufficient: the material less than 1 mm in size in the immediate vicinity of the borehole will be pumped out during development. However, generally there is little choice over slot sizes and it can be a major problem to find a slot size small enough to keep 50 per cent of the material in the aquifer! In these cases the slot size can be reduced by wrapping geotextile netting around the screen – or, if nothing else is available, mosquito netting.

To make these calculations, the grain size of the aquifer material and gravel pack needs to be known. There are well-established techniques for measuring grain sizes which involve sieving the material through various sizes of sieve and plotting up a grain size distribution curve. If your project is primarily in unconsolidated material, and there is a problem with either silting up of boreholes or low yields, it would be very useful to carry out a detailed assessment of the grain size in the aquifer (see further reading and resources listed at the end of the chapter).

Sealing of the bottom of the casing assembly

When casings with screens are installed in a production borehole, a short section of plain casing is installed at the base of the lowest screened interval to form a sump. This section should be at least 2 m in length, to allow the collection of any formation material that may enter the borehole and settle beneath the screened section. The base of the sump should be sealed such that no material can enter the casing from beneath. This seal normally consists of a plate welded to the base of the steel casing, a threaded cap, or a bonded cap (uPVC casing). If further deepening of the borehole is anticipated in the future, it may consist of a drillable cement plug.

6.5.3 Gravel pack

Gravel pack can be installed in the annular space between the borehole casing/screen and the borehole wall. It can serve to stabilize formations and/or filter fine-grained material from entering the borehole.

Formation stabilizer

Formation stabilizer is used for screened boreholes installed in unstable consolidated formations to keep the borehole open and prevent caving from loose material into the screened portion of the borehole. Formation stabilizer material should be washed, of uniform grade and rounded to subangular in form. The quality must be checked before it is put down the borehole. It is useful to discuss the needs with a local supplier of aggregates before the start of a contract, and impress on them the quality that is required. The size of material should be chosen so that none of the gravel pack will pass through the screen slots. The formation stabilizer should not reduce the hydraulic efficiency of the borehole. Sufficient formation stabilizer material should be installed to extend several metres above the screened interval but stop about 5 or 6 m below the ground surface, to allow the emplacement of a grout seal.

Filter pack

Filter pack material is usually installed around screened sections of high-yielding boreholes – it is rarely required for low-yielding boreholes equipped with handpumps. Usually a natural gravel pack is sufficient (see above). However, if the aquifer material is fine grained and uniform, and a slot size cannot be found which can keep the sand out and still give a sufficiently high yield, then a filter pack can be used. To chose a filter pack correctly, the grain size of the aquifer material has to be assessed from sieving the material (see further reading and resources listed at the end of the chapter). The thickness of filter pack is usually about 70 mm. Where possible, filter pack materials should be composed of rounded quartz grains and graded to have a uniformity coefficient of less than 2.5. The material should be free from shale, mica, clay, dirt or organic impurities of any kind. The filter pack should be carefully installed to avoid bridging.

6.5.4 Grouting and sealing

All borehole designs should include a sanitary seal about 3–6 m below the ground surface. This is to stop poor-quality water in the soil, shallow weathered zone or laterite from flowing down the annular space between the outmost casing and the borehole wall and contaminating the borehole. A sanitary seal is a barrier between the casing and the borehole wall, usually made of bentonite clay or cement.

The following materials are often used for the sanitary seal:

- neat cement consisting of a mixture of ordinary cement and clean water in a ratio of 22 litres of water to 50 kg of cement
- bentonite clay pellets or a premixed bentonite slurry
- sand–cement grout consisting of ordinary cement, clean sand and water in a weight proportion of no more than 2 parts sand to 1 part cement.

One of the most effective and simplest methods is to place surface casing through the overburden zone, pour cement down the hole and force it up the outside of the casing using compressed air (see Figure 6.24). Best results are gained if the space is at least 40 mm. When cement-based grouts are used, the borehole should be left for a minimum of 24 hours before continuing work on the borehole. When it is dry, drilling restarts at a smaller diameter inside the surface casing; the excess hardened cement at the bottom of the hole is drilled through.

Alternatively, where a gravel pack has been used, a seal can be placed on top of the formation stabilizer (see Figure 6.22). This method involves a lot of guesswork and does not ensure that the grout reaches the specified depth, or is completely effective. Before grouting, the casing should be well seated on the bottom of the borehole, and it is recommended that the casing be filled with water or drilling fluid to avoid grout filling the casing. Several metres of sand are poured on top of the formation stabilizer to stop the grout or clay from clogging up the water-producing zone. Bentonite slurry, pellets or grout is then poured down the outside of the casing to try to get an effective seal. Once the seal is in place, the rest of the annular space can be backfilled with borehole rock chippings.

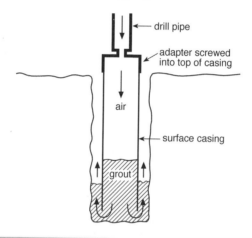

Figure 6.24   Pressure grouting in surface casing.

6.5.5 Borehole development procedures

The final operation to be undertaken before borehole test pumping is that of borehole development. During this operation various methods are applied to remove muck from the borehole and the aquifer adjacent to the borehole that may affect the operating efficiency of the borehole and the quality of water produced. The 'muck' usually includes:

■ crushed rock, mud and sand, some of which will have been forced into the aquifer or has accumulated in the borehole sump

- remaining drilling fluid such as muddy water, broken mud, unbroken bentonite mud, mud cake on the borehole wall if the borehole was drilled using mud
- fine-grained material held within the gravel pack
- fine-grained material and injected drilling mud held within the aquifer formation adjacent to the borehole wall.

A borehole must be developed before assessing whether it is successful or not. Many successful boreholes appear to be low yielding before development, but the yield improves after the muck has been removed from the sides of the borehole and the water-bearing fractures.

Various methods of borehole development have been devised. These methods are dependent on the drilling equipment available, the design of borehole and the nature of the aquifer material. Full development of a borehole to its optimum capacity may take several weeks and require the use of several of the methods described below. However, this time is rarely or ever spent developing rural water supply boreholes: usually the borehole is considered developed when the pumped water is clean and sand free. The major development methods are summarized in Table 6.4. Brief descriptions of the main methods used during rural water supply borehole drilling and their equipment requirements are presented below.

Pumping methods

- **Blowing:** This simple first method is used when drilling with compressed air. The drill pipe or an adductor pipe is run in to the bottom of the borehole and compressed air injected to force water and detrital material out of the borehole. This usually forms the first part

Table 6.4 The most common borehole development methods

Method	Rig or equipment required	Comments
Blowing	Rig with air compressor	Common first method on borehole completion
Bailing	Cable tool rig bailer	Common first method on borehole completion
Air lift pumping	Rig with air compressor and adductor pipe	Used in porous aquifers and large diameter boreholes
Over-pumping	Rig with pump	Incremental increase in step test pumping mode
Backwashing by air lift pumping/Surging	Rig with air compressor, air lift piping	Used in sandstone aquifers and in screened boreholes in unconsolidated aquifers
Surging	Cable tool rig or rotary rig, surge block	Not for use in aquifers with clay layers
Jetting (air/water)	Rotary rig, air compressor or mud pump, jetting tool	Use in screened boreholes

of the borehole cleaning procedure. Care must be taken not to bring the drill pipe in contact with any screen in the borehole, especially in boreholes that have not been constructed vertically, as any dragging of the pipe along the borehole side may cause the screen to split. During this procedure the drill pipe can be lifted progressively up the borehole and worked up and down along specific screened sections. The airflow can be used to control the rate of water flow from the borehole. This method should be regarded as a crude initial method of borehole development and will probably have little effect on gravel pack installations.

■ **Bailing:** During drilling with a cable tool rig, water and debris are removed from the borehole using a large-volume dart or flat valve bailer. This procedure is used after borehole construction to further develop the borehole. The borehole can be emptied by repeatedly bailing the well. This is in essence a simple bail test that should be repeated until the borehole is cleaned of sand and the rate of water level recovery is maximized. Water quality can also be determined with each cycle of bailing.

■ **Airlift pumping:** Airlift pumping uses an adductor pipe with an airline that reaches to 1 m above the base of the adductor pipe. Compressed air is injected via the airline to drive water upwards within the adductor pipe, with no water being forced back into the formation. The length of adductor pipe can be varied and worked up

Figure 6.25 Developing a borehole by airlifting.
Photo: BGS, © NERC 1992.

and down along the screened borehole sections. The flow of water can also be controlled by varying the rate of airflow. Water levels can be measured during this type of development to assess borehole specific capacity.

■ **Overpumping:** This method is used for development of jetted or manually drilled boreholes. The borehole is pumped at a higher than expected rate, i.e. overpumped, using a powered or a manually operated pump. Water quality and sediment content can be measured periodically to check for improvements. Yield is measured with a bucket of known volume and stopwatch. Usually drawdown cannot be measured.

Surging methods

Following initial borehole cleaning using airlift/blowing or bailing methods, more surging methods can be used to further develop the borehole; this is particularly important in boreholes with gravel packs. Water is surged into and out of the gravel pack and aquifer removing fine-grained material and drill cuttings. Methods of surging are discussed below.

■ **Airlift pumping/surging:** This method of surging involves the intermittent pumping of a borehole so that the column of water is allowed to fall back down the adductor pipe by cutting off the airflow immediately the water arrives at the ground surface. The water falls down through the screen and/or aquifer pores and fissures. This process is repeated periodically during any period of airlift development. The borehole should then be cleaned using a pumping method.

■ **Surging (surge block):** This method of borehole surging is achieved using a surge block with rotary and cable tool rigs. The tool is set about 5 m below the static water level. A surging action is created in the water column by moving the surging tool up and down, initially gently, then increasing the length and speed of the stroke. After a period of surging, the tool is removed and the borehole cleaned out, then the process repeated. The tool is incrementally moved down the borehole to the top of the borehole screen or base of the cased section (open borehole design). This method should not be applied to aquifers with thin clay layers as the method may result in clogging of the aquifer.

■ **Jetting methods:** Jetting involves directing a high-pressure stream of compressed air (supplied from a compressor) or water (pumped using a mud pump) at the borehole screen through a series of perforations or nozzles. The jetting tool consists of a tool with four nozzles; the tool diameter should be large enough for the nozzles to be within 25 mm of the screen. Jetting is started at the base of the screen and the tool is rotated slowly while moving it slowly upwards. Freed fine-grained material entering the borehole collects in the sump below the screen and should be cleaned periodically. This method is effective for cleaning the borehole screen and possibly the gravel pack.

■ **Chemicals:** A variety of chemicals can be used with the development methods described above to improve the results. The most common additive is polyphosphate. Although less common, some limestone and calcareous sandstone aquifers may respond well to certain acid treatments, which may open up fractures or dissolve cements. Acid treatment can also be important in rehabilitation of existing boreholes. These methods are rarely cost-effective when applied to low-yielding boreholes equipped with handpumps.

6.5.6 Site completion

Tidying the site

When drilling and construction is completed, the site should be restored as far as possible to the condition found on the team's arrival. Settling pits, trenches, etc. should be backfilled with clean material, and rubbish collected and disposed of properly. The borehole should be securely capped by fixing a welded or lockable cover to the borehole; access will be required to carry out the pumping test and to test the water quality.

Completing a successful borehole

A separate technical team usually will follow after the drilling and pumping tests to put in a concrete drainage apron and install the borehole. The drainage apron is relatively straightforward and is designed to meet two objectives: (1) to stop the excess water and contamination from flowing down the sides of the borehole; and (2) to provide a solid clean base for collecting water. The usual features are:

■ The apron is generally 2–3 m in diameter with a lip around the outside.
■ The apron slopes slightly to an outlet channel which takes the water several metres away to a soakaway: in some places this excess water has been used to irrigate small gardens.
■ A fence can be erected to keep animals away from the collection point – and in some places to control entry.
■ It is useful to mark the borehole number and date of completion on the concrete apron.

The choice of handpumps is an emotive subject on which many people have strong opinions. There are other manuals and resources that deal comprehensively with the subject, so handpumps are not discussed here. One of the most comprehensive resources are provided by the Rural Water Supply Network (which used to be called the Handpump Technology Network). The choice of handpump should be guided by the following factors:

- national standards
- availability of spare parts
- ease of maintenance and local expertise
- the depth of lift required
- the chemistry of the water (mild steel can corrode)
- cost.

Borehole disinfection

A water supply borehole should be disinfected on completion to kill bacteria that have entered the borehole during drilling. This is done by adding chlorine, usually in the form of chlorine-yielding compounds such as calcium hypochlorite, sodium hypochlorite and chlorinated lime into the borehole. Sufficient disinfectant needs to added to produce a concentration of about 200 mg/litre of active chlorine within the borehole. Therefore, the volume of the borehole needs to be taken into consideration when adding the disinfectant. The following formula can be useful:

$$V_s = V_w \, (C_d/C_s)$$

where V_s is the amount of disinfectant required (in litres), V_w is the volume of water in the borehole (in litres), C_d is the desired concentration of available chorine (in mg/litre) and C_s is the concentration of available chlorine in the disinfectant (mg/litre)

After addition of the disinfectant the borehole should stand for at least 4 hours, and preferably longer. A surging action can be used within the borehole to help the movement of chlorine, and ensure that the entire length of the borehole is disinfected.

Abandonment of boreholes

If a borehole is unsuccessful (dry or insufficient yield, poor quality, etc.), careful thought should be given to how it is abandoned. There are three main aims to achieve:

- eliminate physical hazards
- prevent contamination of groundwater
- prevent mixing of groundwater between different aquifer horizons.

Before sealing is undertaken, the borehole is checked to ensure that there are no obstructions down the borehole that may interfere with sealing by lowering of a suitable dummy to the borehole bottom. The borehole should be backfilled with drill cuttings to completely fill the borehole. To avoid bridging, pour clean water periodically into the borehole during backfilling. The material should be compacted manually and additional backfill poured on top. This process is repeated until there is no further subsidence. A concrete slab should be installed over the filled borehole.

It is important to keep records of abandoned boreholes. Although useless to the community, they are as valuable in understanding the groundwater resources of an area as a successful borehole. There are two main ways in which unsuccessful boreholes can be helpful.

- They can help tell us the secrets of successful boreholes. By carefully examining the lithological logs of unsuccessful boreholes and comparing to successful boreholes, the critical features needed for a successful borehole in an area can be realized. For example, an unsuccessful borehole may show a high amount of clay, or no quartz or calcite veins associated with water-bearing fractures.
- They can help us calibrate geophysical surveys. It is very useful to compare the geological logs of unsuccessful boreholes to the analyses of geophysical surveys of the site. Over time, lessons can be learned about the good and bad targets for boreholes and geophysical surveys can be interpreted with a higher degree of success. For example, higher conductivity in some areas can be associated with unsuccessful boreholes because of the high clay content.

It must be acknowledged, however, that dry boreholes happen – even when you are highly confident of the geophysical interpretation, and there is another high-yielding borehole close by. You may never know the reason why there was no water in it. We should always admit that hydrogeology is inherently uncertain.

6.6 Reporting

The information gathered during drilling boreholes or constructing wells or spring boxes is valuable and should be written up and several copies made. Often it can be difficult to find the time to write a proper report: there are always pressures to go to the next borehole or carry out a geophysical survey. However, writing up a quick report should not take much time (only one or two hours) and does not have to be done at the drilling site – so long as all the important information is recorded in your field notebook. The driller is also responsible for reporting some aspects of the work: for example the construction of the borehole, the materials used and the driller's log.

Before you leave the borehole site make sure you have the following technical information in your notebook:

- name of the village and location of borehole with GPS coordinates
- location of the borehole or well, matched to the initial geophysical surveys
- a sketch map of where the borehole/well is located in relation to prominent features
- dates of construction: names and roles of all those involved

- The depths and types of drilling or digging methods used. For example: 8-inch drag bit to 15 m; 6-inch d-t-h-hammer from 15 to 37 m; or for a well – hand-dug to 10 m, pneumatic hammers from 10 to 15 m
- main water strikes and rest water level (at least 12 hours after pumping or drilling has stopped
- the drilled diameters, position of screen and casing
- position and size of gravel pack, depth of seal
- length and type of development: if appropriate, results of bailer tests before and after development
- lithological descriptions of chip samples.

As described earlier, photographs are an excellent addition to information about a site, and can help to jog memories. Photographs of the chip samples are a useful way of summarizing information from a borehole, but cannot be a substitute for a lithological description of each sample.

This information can then be used to produce a short report on the borehole with all the necessary summary information. This can be written out by hand or on computer; often a good paper record is sufficient and sometimes standard forms can be used and filled in for each borehole. Reports usually contain the following information:

- a summary of the borehole/well/spring location details
- a summary of the drilling information
- a diagram showing the construction of the borehole
- a diagram showing the lithology of the borehole with water strikes, etc.

This drilling report is usually added to the village file along with other technical information, such as the geophysical and village surveys, and the results of pumping tests. For little extra cost or work this permanent record of the geology and hydrogeology at the site forms the building blocks for understanding how groundwater resources occur in an area. An example of a drilling report is given in Figure 6.26.

6.7 Springs

Ancient peoples had great respect for springs and often gave them religious significance. In many ways springs appear mystical: water bubbling up from the deep in places which are otherwise dry. Technically, springs are over-flows of the groundwater system – groundwater will discharge where the water table intersects the ground surface. Where the flow forms a small stream, it is called a **spring**; if it is just a damp patch, it is called a **seepage**. Springs and seepages are often marked by thick vegetation. They form important sources of water: the costs of development are low and little expertise is required to make improvements.

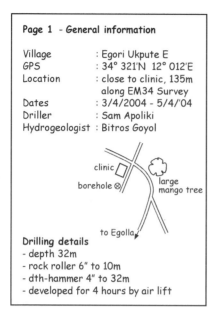

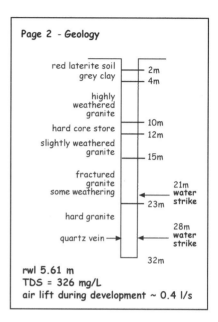

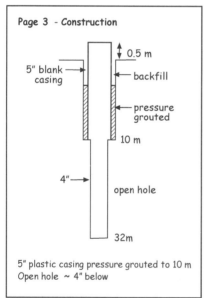

Figure 6.26 Example of a borehole drilling report. This should be added to reports on geophysics, pumping tests and water quality.

There are several books which describe in more detail the engineering aspects of springbox construction (see 'Further reading and resources' at the end of the chapter). This small section gives a flavour of the hydrogeological context for springs and what parameters should be considered before developing a spring source.

6.7.1 Hydrogeological context

Before developing a spring as a water supply, it is important to understand its hydrogeological context. There is little point in improving a spring, only to find that it dries up during a prolonged drought. Some of the main types of spring are described below (see Figure 6.27).

- Spring zones at the junction of permeable and impermeable rocks or sediments. These springs are common and found in many areas. The location of this type of spring does not often move since it is constrained by the geology.
- Valley side springs in mountainous areas where the water table meets the ground surface at a steep break of slope.
- Springs in a limestone areas, where groundwater flows within large fractures often enlarged by dissolution. These springs can be very large – the outflow of real underground rivers.
- Coastal springs found on beaches where freshwater flows to the surface at the freshwater/saline water interface within the tidal zone.
- Springs which are controlled by faults and fractures. Sometimes the water from this type of spring is from a deep source and can be highly mineralized or geothermal.

There are several pieces of information to assess about a spring before it is developed:

- **The flow rate of the spring** in the rainy season, the end of the dry season and during extended droughts. Community members are the best to judge which springs are most sustainable during the dry season and in times of drought. Detailed community discussions with various groups and key informants are the best way of assessing this information. Sometimes two springs need to be developed: one that is close to the community, but dries in prolonged dry periods, and another that is more sustainable but farther from the community. Key questions are: the time people had to queue to get water; the amount of time it took to fill buckets at different times of the year; how far did people travel to get to this spring etc. Only if the flow is sufficient throughout the year can it be considered as a safe reliable source for a community.
- If more time is available, then **the actual flow of the spring** can be monitored over a season. The flow of a spring can be measured by using a bucket, a pipe to direct the flow and a stop watch, or a V-notch weir if the flow is bigger. Since spring flows varies throughout

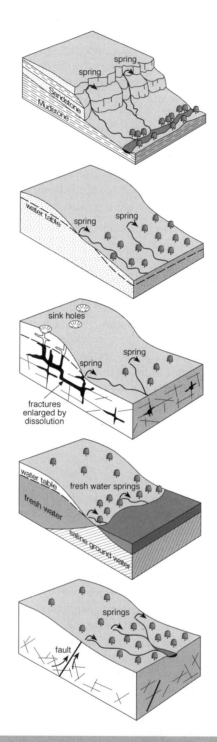

Figure 6.27 Different types of springs: (1) at junction between two different rock types; (2) break of slope; (3) karstic; (4) fresh/saline interface; and (5) fault controlled.

the year, monthly flow measurements over a whole year are needed to assess maximum and minimum discharges. In reality, there is rarely enough time to make these assessments.

- The **quality of the water** at different times of the year. If the yield changes throughout the year, then the quality of the water may change as well. During rainy periods, young rainwater can mix with older groundwater; as the dry season progresses the young rainwater dries out, leaving only the older groundwater to sustain the flow. Springs can be particularly susceptible to microbiological contamination, particularly if the young rainwater makes up a component of flow. Chapter 8 discusses aspects of water quality in more detail. From discussions with the community, it should be possible to find out if there are seasonal changes in water quality. If time allows, quarterly measurements of water quality will be sufficient to map out general changes throughout the year.
- **The catchment area of the spring.** Knowing the catchment area of a spring helps understand threats to it. If boreholes or wells are within the catchment (or just outside it) they can affect the spring flow, and sometimes dry the spring completely. Human or animal activity within the spring catchment can lead to contamination: for example, construction of latrines, application of fertilizers or pesticides, etc. A rough idea of the catchment of a spring can be given, by looking at a topographical map. Starting at the location of the spring, a line is drawn directly up the slope exactly perpendicular to the contour lines.
- **Does the spring move?** Some types of springs can move location, generally up- or downslope. Again, the best method for finding this out is to consult key members of the community. Clues can also be given by examining the spring itself: there may be more than one eye, or a highly diffuse area of vegetation.

6.7.2 Construction

There are two reasons for improving a spring: to harness all the flow of the spring, and to minimize contamination of the spring. A common design for improving a spring is shown in Figure 6 29.

- The **eye** of the spring is excavated to where the spring issues from solid rock. Construction of an intake or catchment may require excavation of a large seepage zone including removal of all overlying soil and weathered regolith.
- An intake pipe is set within large stones around the eye. Care should be taken to have a sufficient size of pipe to cope with high flows during the rainy season. Several pipes are required if the yield is high or the spring diffuse. The pipe is angled downwards.
- The intake pipe is then covered by large stones, gravel and sand and then capped with clay if possible. Turf is then replaced on top.

Figure 6.28 Unimproved spring. Women walk through the water to the back of the spring to try to collect the clean water from the spring source.
Photo: BGS, © NERC 1997.

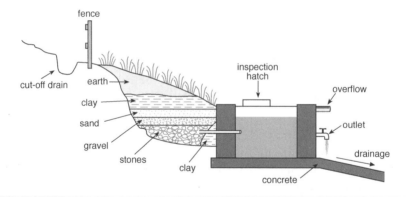

Figure 6.29 Common design of a spring box.
Source: adapted from Davis and Lambert 2002.

- Generally the pipe is led into a spring box. This several important functions: it acts as a collecting tank for low yielding springs; it allows silt to settle out; and it can allow a larger area for people to collecting water. A tank is not always used: sometimes the spring intake pipes are run into a wall which acts as the collecting point.
- A fence should be constructed around the spring area to keep animals away. Usually about 10 m above and 5 m below and to either

side is sufficient. A ditch should be dug above the spring to divert surface runoff and avoid contamination.

Springs are highly vulnerable to pollution. The catchment area should be protected from highly contaminating activities. A good guideline is that at a minimum there should be no pit latrines, graveyards or waste disposal less than 100 m above a spring intake.

6.8 Large-diameter wells

6.8.1 Overview

Well sinking is an ancient craft and, throughout history, wells have provided a perennial source of good-quality drinking water. We now have the technology to drill deep boreholes with relative ease – so can the dug well be considered obsolete? Experience and the results of many research projects would suggest not. The dug well still has a valuable role to play, not only for socio-economic reasons, but also because in many cases it is hydraulically superior.

The main advantage of a large-diameter-well is that it has a large storage capacity. Therefore, for aquifers of low transmissivity, where the rate of flow from the aquifer into the well is slow, water can be abstracted from the

| Figure 6.30 | Collecting water from an improved spring in the Ethiopian Highlands. Photo: BGS, © NERC 2000. |

stored water in the well at a much greater rate than the aquifer alone would allow. The stored water in the well is abstracted once or twice a day and the well allowed to recover to its original level overnight. The large-diameter well therefore acts like a reservoir: storing water gained slowly from the aquifer, and yielding this water at a fast rate when demand is high.

The large volume of the well also allows water to seep in over a much larger surface area, so that more of the aquifer is exploited. In fractured aquifers it increases the likelihood of water-bearing fractures being intercepted, and enables several, previously unconnected, fissure systems to be tapped.

There are also certain socio-economic benefits from utilizing hand-dug wells: no sophisticated machines or tools are needed for their construction, dug wells are invariably cheaper to construct than a modern borehole; communities can easily be involved in the planning and building of the well. Also, since handpumps are not necessary to access the water, the well can be easily maintained for little cost.

However, there are also several disadvantages to the hand-dug well.

- Often it is not appropriate to the hydrogeological environment. If the water-producing fractures are deep (>20 m) it can be difficult, time consuming and expensive to construct a hand-dug well. If the rocks are hard, even with pneumatic hammers the construction of the well can be slow and expensive.
- Hand-dug wells are more susceptible to contamination than boreholes. They are often open, and buckets can introduce contamination. It is also difficult to get a sanitary seal in the top few metres of a hand-dug well. Contamination from shallow soil layers can move down the outside of the well, or even into the well through joins between concrete rings or bricks. Part of the problem is the large area of the well: there is much more opportunity for pathways to develop than in a small-diameter borehole. Another related issue is that in many areas shallow groundwater (which wells exploit) is much more likely to be contaminated than deeper groundwater anyway – regardless of the construction of the well.
- Hand-dug wells can be more susceptible to drought than boreholes. During periods of drought, groundwater levels naturally tend to decline, particularly in shallow aquifers connected to rivers or springs. Also, the increased demand put on individual wells and boreholes as other sources dry up accelerates the decline of water levels.
- Unsuccessful wells can depress communities. Wells can take up to 3 months to construct, and generally use labour from the community. This is a long time to be digging – particularly if no water is found in the end. It can be difficult to motivate a community to try to dig in another location. Some projects have found it useful to drill or auger a trial hole before construction to prove that groundwater is available.

6.8.2 Common designs of large-diameter hand-dug wells

Dug wells often exhibit a high degree of sophistication, sometimes being constructed to depths of over 100 m. In the past, ingenuity and much courage was required to build wells to such depths, but with the advent of reinforced concrete a lot of the risks have been minimized. Wells can be lined with concrete blocks or rings, bricks, laterite blocks, steel sheeting, or even old tractor tyres!

There are several excellent books discussing the engineering aspects of constructing a hand-dug well (see further reading and listed at the end of the chapter). There is no point in repeating that here. Instead we describe the common design and its relevance to the hydrogeology.

A cross-section through a typical modern dug well is shown in Figure 6.31. The well is 1–3 m in diameter and is usually (depending on local

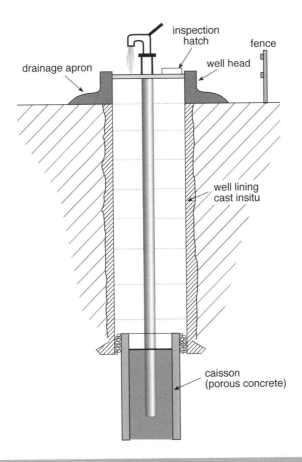

| Figure 6.31 | Schematic diagram of a typical improved hand dug well. |

hydrogeological conditions) between 10 and 20 m deep. The well is lined down to the water table with either bricks or reinforced concrete, to support the surrounding formations. Below the water table caissons, such as concrete rings, are often used to line the well. The rings are pre-cast at the surface near the well and, when set, allowed to sink down into the aquifer under their own weight. Excess material from inside the ring is then excavated and brought to the surface. In more consolidated aquifers (e.g. the fracture zone or basal saprolite), the well can be left open-hole below the water table. This ensures that all water-bearing fractures are being exploited.

If the well is constructed into unconsolidated material, it must be supported as it is being dug. There are two ways of doing this: **shuttering** or **caissoning**. The shuttering method is most useful if only the top few metres is unconsolidated with hard rock below. A large hole is excavated and shutters installed to the top of the stable material. The well is dug as normal below the shutters; once complete, the well is lined up to the ground surface and the shutters removed. For the caissoning method a concrete ring (or tractor tyre or layer of bricks) is laid on the surface. The material inside is dug away and the ring then slowly descends into the hole. Another ring (or tyre or layer of bricks) is joined to the top of the first one and more material removed from inside. In this way the well descends to the appropriate depth. However, with this method it is easy to get a crooked well.

It is easier to get an idea of geology from digging a well than by drilling a borehole. Climbing down an unlined well allows a unique opportunity of observing the hydrogeology undisturbed (see Figure 6.32). A log can be made by slowly being lowered down a well with a tape measure. The geology can be logged, and also seepages and fractures mapped. This can only be done before the well is lined. In addition to this, or if the well is being lined as it is dug, diggers should take and bag representative samples every 0.5 m. These should be analysed in the same way as chip samples (see the section on boreholes).

The wellhead is the upper section of the well, generally extending at least 2 to 3 m below ground level. If the well has been lined with precast rings or bricks, a sanitary seal should be installed here: manufactured bentonite (i.e. pellets) or a cement grout could be poured down to provide an impermeable seal. With concrete lining cast *in situ*, no additional sealing should be required, but care must be taken at the join between different casts to ensure an impermeable seal. A wall is built around the top of the well and often a cover fitted. The wall is vital to keep people safe, and a cover helps to minimize contamination. An apron should be fitted with a runoff channel to take excess water away from the well. This water can be put in a soakaway, or alternatively help to irrigate a small wellside garden. A fence is constructed (or grown) around the well to stop animals congregating.

Figure 6.32	Side of a well before it has been lined, showing weathered sandstone and kaolinite clay layers. Photo: BGS, © NERC 1997.

Wells can be fitted with hand pumps, motorized pump, windlasses or a dedicated rope and bucket. It is never advisable for people to use their own buckets, as this can introduce contamination into the well.

6.8.3 Other designs

A design often found in India is a **dug well-cum-borehole**. As the name suggests this is half borehole, half well. Often the design comes about once a hand-dug well has run dry or more water is required. The borehole penetrates a deeper aquifer to supply the water and (provided the deeper water is under pressure) the dug well acts as a reservoir. If a pump is put down the borehole, the dug well ceases to be of any use, acting only as a pump house, and the storage facilities of the well are lost. Different designs are required depending on the nature of the rocks.

The **collector well** can provide sustainable high yields from low-permeability aquifers. A central shaft is constructed (about 2 m in diameter) as in a normal large-diameter-well. A horizontal drilling rig is then lowered down the well and a series of radials drilled out sideways. This type of well is expensive to construct and requires specialist equipment; however, the benefits can be high. During the prolonged droughts in the 1990s in southern Africa, collector wells proved sustainable where other sources failed.

References, further reading and resources

Ball, P. (2000) Drilled wells. SKAT, St Gallen, Switzerland. Available at: http://www.skat.ch/htn/

Brandon, T.W. (1986) *Groundwater: occurrence development and protection.* Institution of Water Engineers and Scientists, London.

Davis, J. and Lambert, R. (2002) *Engineering in Emergencies.* ITDG Publishing, London.

Driscoll, F.G. (1986) *Groundwater and wells* (2nd edition). Johnson Screens, St Paul, MN.

Fraenkel, P. (1997) *Water-pumping devices* (2nd edition). ITDG Publishing, London.

Rural Water Supply Network: this has detailed resource on different handpumps and also publications on construction and drilling. Available at: http://www.depuran.mhs.ch/

Watt, S.B. and Wood, S.E. (1979) *Hand dug wells and their construction.* ITDG Publishing, Rugby, UK.

US EPA (1976) *National interim primary drinking water regulations.* Environmental Protection Agency. Office of Water Supply. EPA/570/9-76/003, US Government Printing Office, Washington, DC.

7 Assessing the yield of a source

7.1 Why carry out pumping tests?

Pumping tests are one of the most important tools for assessing groundwater resources. They test the response of groundwater in an aquifer to pumping. By carefully measuring and interpreting this response it is possible to deduce various pieces of information: the rough sustainable yield of the borehole or the expected drawdown within the borehole after several months' pumping. From a properly conducted test it is also possible to quantify some of the key aquifer properties of different rocks, such as transmissivity and the storage coefficient. The accumulation of aquifer property data from various tests in an area can then be used to help predict the groundwater potential of different rocks in an area. For example, in several countries, historical databases of pumping tests are regularly consulted by drilling companies before they start work in an area.

The tests involve pumping from a borehole at a controlled rate (hence the name 'pumping tests' – not to be confused with 'pump tests', which test the workings of the pump). The change in water levels in the pumping and surrounding boreholes are then measured and analysed in detail (see Figure 7.1). Tests can last for a few minutes (as in a slug test) or for several weeks in more sophisticated constant-rate tests. The longer a test is carried out, the more information it can give about the aquifer.

Pumping tests can help to answer the following questions:

- **Is the borehole/well 'successful'?** Most water supply projects will have criteria for a successful borehole – usually determined by the borehole sustaining a certain yield, e.g. 10, 20 or 30 litres/minute. A pumping test is the safest way to determine this: it will indicate not only whether the desired yield can be achieved, but also how easily. This can help in judging the sustainability of the borehole.
- **How many people will the borehole or well supply?** Following on from the previous question, if the borehole is not able to deliver the yield defined as successful, a pumping test may indicate whether the borehole can deliver a lower yield – which may supply fewer people. In other cases the pumping test may indicate that the borehole can deliver a much larger yield – which could supply more people or support irrigation.

Figure 7.1 Pumping test being carried out in an exploratory borehole.
Photo: BGS, © NERC 1999.

- **Is it likely to be sustainable in the long term?** Many boreholes constructed during rural water supply programmes fail within a few years. Failure can be caused by many different combinations of factors such as engineering, stress from increased demand, lack of maintenance, poor cost recovery or a decline in groundwater resources. Pumping tests can indicate if hydrogeological conditions are to blame. Although they cannot guarantee that water will be available in several years' time, potential problems can often be identified. Failing that, a test at the time of construction acts as a baseline from which to compare later tests.

- **Have the contractors carried out their job properly?** Since pumping tests can be carried out after the borehole is completed (although before handpumps are fitted), they can be used as a check on work carried out by contractors. Tests can be carried out on selected boreholes to ensure that boreholes described as 'successful' by drilling contractors (under pressure to maximize profits) actually do meet the project success criteria.

There are many different types of pumping test, ranging considerably in the sophistication of equipment, time required, cost and complexity of analysis. Numerous scientific papers and several books describe the different tests and the theory behind them (see the further reading listed at the end of the chapter). In this section we describe some simple borehole tests that we have found most useful in assessing groundwater resources in rural water supply projects. The **bailer test** is a simple short test that gives an indication of 'success'; the **airlift test** gives a very rough indication of borehole yield. **Constant-rate tests** are standard tests used throughout the world. Pumping tests in large-diameter wells are more complex to analyse and not often carried out, but a very simple test to carry out in large-diameter-wells is described towards the end of the chapter.

7.2 Pumping test basics

When a borehole or well is pumped, groundwater stored in the aquifer moves towards the borehole/well. This forms a cone of depression in the water table around the borehole, which gradually moves further out as pumping continues (see Figure 7.2). The size and shape of this cone of depression depends on the pumping rate and also the properties of the aquifer.

7.2.1 Yield and specific capacity

The yield of a borehole is commonly used to describe how successful it is. An accurate definition is the maximum pumping rate a borehole can sustain for a reasonable drawdown (i.e. where the water levels stay above the pump intake). Accurately determining the safe yield of a borehole is not straight-forward and requires a step test to be carried out on the borehole (see resources listed at the end of the chapter). More often than not, the yield quoted for a borehole has been estimated at the time of airlifting (see later in the chapter). Although, this information is better than nothing, it is not a good predictor of the safe yield of the borehole.

Specific capacity is a much more useful parameter than yield. Specific capacity includes a measure of the drawdown in the borehole, and so indicates

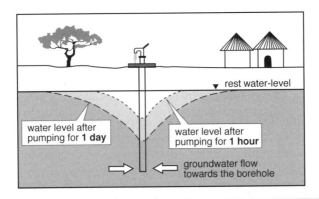

| Figure 7.2 | Development of a cone of depression around a borehole in response to pumping. |

how stressed the borehole is to achieve a certain pumping rate. Specific capacity is defined as is the amount of water that can be pumped out of the borehole per metre of drawdown and is often measured in litres/second per metre. So a specific capacity of 0.1 litres/second per metre means the borehole should be able to sustain a pumping rate of 0.5 litres/second for 5 m drawdown. To measure specific capacity, the borehole should really have been pumping for several days to reach equilibrium. In reality it is often difficult to accurately measure specific capacity in boreholes used for rural water supply. Some projects have got around the problem of not reaching equilibrium by measuring specific capacity after a certain time period (e.g. 2 hours). Different boreholes can then be directly compared. However, it is not much extra work to collect data to give an estimate of transmissivity, a more robust parameter.

7.2.2 Transmissivity and storativity

Most pumping tests are carried out to give an estimate of the transmissivity of the aquifer. Transmissivity is one of the fundamental measures of how good an aquifer is (see descriptions in Chapter 2). Transmissivity indicates how easily groundwater can flow through a rock to a borehole. It is usually measured in m^2/d, and defined as the rate at which groundwater will move through a unit width of aquifer for a unit difference in hydraulic head.

The other fundamental measure of an aquifer is its **storativity** – a measure of how much groundwater can be stored in a rock. Storativity is dimensionless and is defined as the volume of water released from a cubic metre of aquifer after the head in the aquifer reduces by 1 m. In an unconfined aquifer the storativity is often known as the **specific yield**. Storativity can only be analysed from pumping tests with observation boreholes and therefore cannot be determined using data from the pumping borehole alone. However, in most aquifers in sub-Saharan Africa the storage coefficient is usually sufficient to sustain the groundwater for a handpump over the dry season.

One of the most valuable uses of the aquifer parameter transmissivity is to help work out what pumping rate a water point can sustain. Knowing the transmissivity, the maximum allowable pumping rate can be estimated (see Table 7.1). These numbers are based on the following assumptions.

- **The allowable drawdown in the borehole.** This depends on the level of the inflows into the borehole and the depth of the pump. For the example in Table 7.1 two ranges of drawdown are given: 6–8 m and 10–15 m.
- **Rest water levels.** If the water levels decline naturally throughout the dry season – this should be added on to the allowable drawdown. For example, if the water inflow to the borehole is at 20 m below the ground surface and the rest water level naturally declines from 5 m

Table 7.1 How transmissivity is related to borehole yield

Transmissivity (m²/day)	Daily abstraction (litres)	
	Drawdown 6–8 m	Drawdown 10–15 m
0.2	700	1 000
0.5	1 300	2 500
1	2 500	5 000
2.5	5 000	9 000
5	13 000	23 000
10	23 000	40 000

to 8 m throughout the year, then the maximum allowable drawdown would be 12 m.

■ **Storage coefficient.** Water levels in a borehole also depend on the storage coefficient, but are much more sensitive to changes in transmissivity. For most of the semi-confined aquifers used for rural water supply, a storage coefficient of about 0.001 is reasonable. The modelling carried out to give the results in Table 7.1 were based on a storage coefficient of 0.001, and a more conservative value of 0.00001.

■ **Time between recharge events.** Most aquifers are recharged every year during the rainy season. A small amount of recharge (12 mm per year) should be enough to recharge an aquifer sufficiently to compensate for water abstracted for community hand pumps. For modelling purposes, 6 months without rain was used.

■ **Efficiency of the borehole pumping.** For high pumping rates, the drawdown in the borehole is increased because of turbulent flow and friction on the borehole surfaces. For small amount of water abstracted by handpumps, this is rarely a problem.

Using the criteria above, the maximum daily abstraction (taken over a 12-hour period) to give an acceptable drawdown in a borehole at the end of 6 months of pumping is shown in Table 7.1. The results have been calculated for a 6-inch (150-mm) borehole; however, there would be very little difference for a larger or smaller borehole. **Therefore, for the common scenario of a borehole supplying 250 people with 20 litres of water per day, the aquifer must have a transmissivity of at least 1 m²/day.**

7.2.3 Seasonal variations

To give a true idea of sustainability, pumping tests should ideally be undertaken at the peak of the dry season, when water levels are at their deepest. In practice, however, tests are usually done while the contractor is on site, after the borehole has been completed. It is important that the time of year that the test is carried out is taken into consideration when looking at the results. Generally, the deeper the water-producing horizons in a well or borehole, the less they are likely to be affected by change in seasons. If most of the water flowing into a well or borehole is from less than 10 m deep, then a test in the rainy season is unlikely to give an useful information about how the source will behave in the dry season (Figure 7.3).

7.2.4 Pumping test assumptions

Most pumping test analysis has been designed for aquifers that are confined by overlying poorly permeable rocks. This simplifies matters in that groundwater flow within the aquifer is horizontal and also the water is released from compressed storage in the aquifer, and not the dewatering of individual pores. More complex analysis techniques have been designed for unconfined conditions. However, the simpler confined methods can be used in unconfined conditions so long as the drawdown is small compared to the saturated thickness of the aquifer. The bailer test and constant-rate

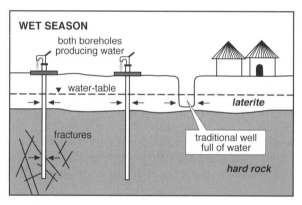

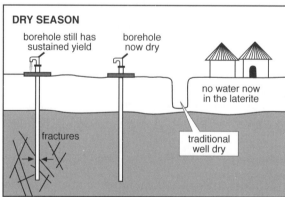

Figure 7.3 How the seasons can affect borehole yield: if a source relies only on shallow water it is much more likely to fail in the dry season, even if it has a high yield during the wet season.

test analysis presented here are for confined situations, but can be used for unconfined aquifers with a high degree of confidence.

Pumping tests generally assume that groundwater flows through pore spaces in the rock. In most hard rocks, however, the water flows through just one or two fractures. Mathematicians have carried out a series of calculations to show that despite the fractured nature of the aquifers, pumping tests and estimations of transmissivity are still valid in most cases – so long as the fractures are not dewatered.

7.2.5 Basic equipment and procedures

Water-level dipper

Fundamental to all pumping tests is the water level recorder (or dipper, as it is usually known). It is the most practical and robust method of measuring rapid changes in water level. The device consists of a two-wire coaxial cable that has an electrode separated by an airgap at the lower end (Figure 7.4). The circuit is completed when both electrodes enter the water, and is indicated by a light or buzzer. The cable is graduated, so depth to water level can be read directly from the cable. Realistically readings can be taken every

| Figure 7.4 | Water level recorder (dipper).
Photo: BGS, © NERC 1997. |

15–30 seconds, although experienced personnel can take readings more often. Sophisticated automatic recorders are available, which rely on pressure transducers and are connected to a computer. They can be temperamental and difficult to fix and are therefore rarely used outside Europe and North America.

Measuring the pumping rate

It is critical to measure the pumping rate during the test. For long, tightly controlled tests, flow meters or gauging weirs are generally used. However for the yields generally encountered for community water supplies, and the accuracy required for the analysis, simple measures using buckets or oil drums are sufficient (see Figure 7.5).

Figure 7.5   Measuring the pumping rate during a short test.
Photo: BGS, © NERC 2000.

Record the time it takes to fill a bucket using the discharge hose from the pumping test. To confirm, repeat at least twice. The pumping rate (in litres per second) is then calculated by dividing the volume of the bucket (in litres) by the time taken to fill it (in seconds). It is important to measure the pumping rate often throughout the test.

As water levels fall during the test, the pumping rate will decline (as the height the pump has to push the water becomes greater). To help analyse the results, this decline must be faithfully recorded, so that an average can be calculated for the test. For small pumps, the change in pumping rate throughout the test can be dramatic. If it declines by more than 30 per cent, stop the test and start measuring the recovery.

7.3 Measuring yield during an airlift

7.3.1 Background

A simple way of roughly estimating the yield of a borehole is to measure the discharge of water during airlifting by the drilling rig. This is a very approximate method and gives no information about the drawdown in the borehole – therefore it is impossible to determine how stressed the borehole is in supplying the yield. It will not give any indication about the sustainability of the borehole. Sadly, this is often the only method used to assess whether a borehole will be able to sustain the required yield.

One of the main reasons for measuring the yield during an airlift is to see whether the borehole is likely to be productive and therefore whether it is worthwhile installing screen and casing. It can also be useful for assessing what size of pump to use for a proper pumping test. The information is 'free' since all boreholes must be airlifted after drilling anyway to get rid of rock chippings ands reduce the scum on the sides of the borehole (see Chapter 6). Table 7.2 summarizes the advantages and disadvantages of assessing yield during airlift.

Table 7.2 Advantages and disadvantages of measuring yield during airlift

Advantages	Disadvantages
'Free' information since doesn't require extra time or testing	Highly inaccurate
Can be carried out by drillers	Doesn't measure water levels in the borehole
Gives an indication of yield before putting in screen	
No lengthy interpretation required	

7.3.2 Procedure

Airlifting involves forcing air from a compressor down the borehole. The air discharges through a perforated pipe set well below the water level. The air forces the water upwards and out of the borehole. Compressed air is dangerous, and all fittings and pipes must be of the correct size and rating for pressures used.

To measure yield during airlifting, the water blown from the hole must be channelled away from the top of the borehole to stop re-circulation. This can be achieved by making a small bund around the top of the borehole with the rock chippings. The water is channelled in one direction and through a pipe (an old piece of casing). A hole is dug in the ground to allow a bucket to stand upright beneath the pipe. The time for the bucket to fill is measured with a stopwatch and the flow rate calculated (see Figure 7.6). As the flow rate often varies during airlifting, it should be repeated several times.

7.4 The bailer test

7.4.1 Background

Simple bailer tests have been carried out on boreholes for many years. Water is removed from a borehole with a bail and the water level is then allowed to

Figure 7.6 Measuring yield during development of a borehole by airlifting.
Photo: BGS, © NERC 1998.

recover. The time of recovery is then interpreted in some way to give an indication of whether the borehole has been 'successful'. Until recently they were generally analysed qualitatively or with simple, empirical rules of thumb. Analysed in this way, these tests are of little use and generally inaccurate. However, several years of research in Nigeria by BGS and WaterAid led to a much improved bailer test that is based on sound scientific and practical principals. It has undergone trials in various parts of Africa and found to be almost as efficient as longer constant-rate tests at predicting borehole success and aquifer properties.

The bailer test has been designed to meet the following criteria:

- **Simple and rapid to carry out.** The test does not require sophisticated equipment or engineering skill to conduct. Community members can participate in the test, which can be completed within one hour.
- **Cheap and robust equipment.** Much of the equipment can be constructed locally (apart from the dipper) and can easily be transported in the back of a Land Rover or pickup truck.
- **Appropriate level of information.** The test can be interpreted simply, without computers or complex analysis, to indicate whether a borehole is likely to easily sustain a handpump. Additional information on aquifer properties can be interpreted from the data produced by the test if desired.
- **Effective for rural water supply.** The test has been designed specifically for poor aquifers (where transmissivity typically ranges over $0.1–10\,\mathrm{m^2/d}$). This translates to the aquifer properties required to sustain the yield from a handpump.

However, the test has certain limiting factors to (see Table 7.3 for a summary of the advantages and disadvantages). It relies on being able to pull out several bails of water per minute from the borehole, which becomes difficult if the water levels are deeper than about 10 m. The test is designed only for boreholes. In large-diameter wells, the bailers would not affect the water

Table 7.3 Advantages and disadvantages of the bailer test

Advantages	Disadvantages
Rapid to carry out (<1 hour)	Water-levels must be shallow
Equipment can mostly be manufactured locally and is robust	Does not give as reliable information as a longer constant rate test
Interpretation and analysis of the test results are straightforward	Interpretation relies on having to look up tables
Can be carried out before screen and casing have been installed	
Data can be analysed at a later date to give estimates of transmissivity	

levels sufficiently to be able to measure changes. Traditional large-diameter well methods should be used instead (see later in the chapter).

7.4.2 Procedure

Equipment

The equipment required to carry out a test is shown in Figure 7.7. All should be available locally apart from the water level dipper.

- The bailer is a long cylindrical bucket that can easily fit down a borehole; it should contain 4–5 litres of water. It can easily be made from 3-inch (75-mm) steel pipe, which would allow about 4.4 litres from a 1-m length. The volume of the bucket can be easily calculated using the formula $\pi r^2 l$, where r is the inner radius of the bailer; l is the inner length of the bailer; and π is 3.14. Two bailers should be made, to allow pumping to be carried out at a reasonable rate. A 20-m rope is attached to the top of the bucket.
- A watch (preferably a stopwatch) is required to measure the time of pumping and recovery.
- A prepared notebook or standard form (see Appendix 2) is used to record data during the test.
- The most sophisticated equipment required is a dipper (see earlier in the chapter).

Carrying out the test

The field procedure for carrying out a bailer test is straightforward and can readily be undertaken with community help. The procedure is outlined below.

- The rest water table is measured in the borehole and the datum, from where all readings are to be taken, is chosen and recorded

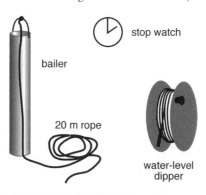

stop watch

bailer

20 m rope

water-level dipper

Figure 7.7 Equipment required to carry out a bailer test.

(e.g. the top of the casing). The water levels must be at rest before the test, so the test should not be conducted the same day as drilling or development of the borehole.

■ Bailer A is lowered down the borehole; as the full bail is removed, the stopwatch is started. A second bail is removed using Bailer B as the water in Bailer A is emptied. This procedure continues for 10 minutes, during which time 20–50 bails should have been abstracted, depending on the depth to the water level. A good guide-line figure to aim for is 40 bails in 10 minutes. (Although an even pumping rate is not essential, the test will be more accurate if the rate of removal of the bails is fairly constant throughout the test.) Since removing the bails becomes more onerous as the drawdown increases, bail removal should be paced during the first half of the test.

■ Bailing must stop at exactly 10 minutes. The stopwatch is immedi-ately reset and water levels measured every 30 seconds for a further 30 minutes. A data form for recording and analysing data is given in Appendix 2.

7.4.3 Interpretation and analysis

The data can be analysed at various levels of complexity, varying from a quick estimate of 'success' to a more reliable estimate of the transmissivity of the aquifer using a computer program. In this manual we describe only the simplest analysis. However, as long as copies of the datasheets are kept, more sophisticated analysis could be performed at a later stage. (Further analyses to give estimates of transmissivity can be carried out using the computer program BGSPT – see resources listed at the end of the chapter.)

The interpretation given here is a 'yes, no or maybe' answer to the question 'can the borehole supply a village water supply?' This yes/no/maybe analysis is based on a borehole having a transmissivity of $1 \text{ m}^2/\text{day}$ and storage coefficient of greater than 0.00005. The borehole should therefore be able to 250 people with 20 litres/day over a 6-month dry season (see Table 7.1). To interpret the test, the following procedure must be followed. A worksheet is given in Appendix 2 and a worked example in Figure 7.9.

■ Calculate the pumping rate (p-rate) for the test in litres per minute by dividing the volume of water abstracted (in litres) by the length of the test in minutes (usually 10 minutes).
■ Calculate drawdowns for the test, by subtracting the rest water level from all the water levels measured in the test.
■ Record the maximum drawdown (d_{max}). This should be the first drawdown after bailing stopped.
■ Calculate d_{50} by halving the maximum drawdown (i.e. $d_{50} = d_{max}/2$) and d_{75} which is the time for the drawdown to recover to a quarter of the maximum value (i.e. $d_{75} = d_{max}/4$).

Figure 7.8 Bailer test being carried out by community members at Edumoga, Nigeria. Photo: BGS, © NERC 1998.

- Read from the data the time (t_{50}) for d_{50} and the time (t_{75}) for d_{75}.
- Estimate the borehole diameter. If the borehole is open hole or is cased but with no gravel pack, then the diameter is the drilled diameter. If the borehole already has a gravel pack then the diameter of the borehole is somewhere between the casing diameter and the drilled diameter. Since the porosity of gravel is usually about 30 per cent, the diameter can be approximated by the equation

  0.3 × (drilled diameter − casing diameter) + casing diameter.

- Use the pumping rate (in litres per minute) and the estimated borehole diameter to find the correct column in the Table 7.4.

time since bailing stopped (mins)	water-levels (m below top casing)	drawdown (m)	
30 secs	9.43	2.065	← dmax
45 secs	9.29	1.925	
1 minute	9.175	1.81	borehole diameter = 6 ins
1 m 15 s	9.06	1.695	rest water level
1 m 30 s	8.965	1.6	before test = 7.365 m
1 m 45 s	8.88	1.515	10 minutes bailing with
2 mins	8.798	1.433	standard bail
2 m 15 s	8.725	1.36	39 bails removed = 17 litres
2 m 30 s	8.663	1.298	per minute
2 m 45 s	8.595	1.23	
3 mins	8.539	1.174	dmax = 2.065 m
3 m 15 s	8.485	1.12	t_{50} = 3 m 45 secs
3 m 30 s	8.435	1.07	t_{75} = 9 min 30 secs
3 m 45 s	8.39	1.025	← d50
4 mins	8.348	0.983	
4 m 15 s	8.307	0.942	From table 7.4: dmax < 5.7 m
4 m 30 s	8.269	0.904	t_{50} < 12 mins
4 m 45 s	8.237	0.872	t_{75} < 28 mins
5 mins	8.203	0.838	
5 m 30 s	8.143	0.778	
6 mins	8.097	0.732	
6 m 30 s	8.048	0.683	**Therefore, borehole should**
7 mins	8.012	0.647	**easily sustain a handpump**
7 m 30 s	7.981	0.616	
8 min	7.95	0.585	
8 m 30 s	7.919	0.554	
9 mins	7.888	0.523	
9 m 30 s	7.86	0.495	← d75
10 mins	7.836	0.471	
10 m 30 s	7.811	0.446	
11 mins	7.791	0.426	
12 mins	7.766	0.401	
12 m 30 s	7.752	0.387	
13 mins	7.742	0.377	
1 m 30 s	7.725	0.36	
14 mins	7.716	0.351	
14 m 30 s	7.703	0.338	
15 mins	7.69	0.325	

Figure 7.9 Worked example of data interpretation from the bailer test.

If the measured values of d_{max}, t_{50} and t_{75} for the test are all less than the values in Table 7.4, then the borehole is likely to be successful. If the measured values are greater than the guideline values then the borehole is unlikely to be sufficient for 250 people. If some of the values are greater and

Table 7.4 Table for assessing the success of a borehole from a bailer test. If the maximum drawdown and time for half and three quarters recovery are all less than quoted here (for the correct borehole diameter and pumping rate) then the borehole is likely to sustain a handpump for 250 people with 20 litres a day each

Diameter of the borehole ↓	Pumping rate in → litres per minute	7	10.5	14	17.5	21
	(Number of standard bails)*	(16)	(24)	(32)	(40)	(48)
4 inch	Max drawdown (m)	3.5	5.3	7.1	8.8	10.6
	time for half recovery (mins)	6	6	6	6	6
	time for three-quarters recovery (mins)	14	14	14	14	14
5 inch	Max drawdown (m)	2.9	4.3	5.7	7.1	8.5
	time for half recovery (mins)	9	9	9	9	9
	time for three-quarters recovery (mins)	21	21	21	21	21
6 inch	Max drawdown (m)	2.3	3.4	4.6	5.7	6.9
	time for half recovery (mins)	12	12	12	12	12
	time for three-quarters recovery (mins)	28	28	28	28	28
8 inch	Max drawdown (m)	1.5	2.3	3.1	3.8	4.6
	time for half recovery (mins)	19	19	19	19	19
	time for three-quarters recovery (mins)	46	47	47	47	47

*Standard bailer is 4.4 litres (1 m long 3 inch pipe)

Table 7.5 Table for assessing the success of an irrigation borehole from a bailer test, where success is defined as 40 m^3/day for a drawdown of 10–15 m. If the maximum drawdown and time for half and three quarters recovery are all less than quoted here (for the correct borehole diameter and pumping rate) then the borehole is likely to be successful

Diameter of borehole		Pumping rate in litres/min (number of standard bails)*				
		7 (16)	10.5 (24)	14 (32)	17.5 (40)	21 (48)
4 inch (100 mm)	d_{max} (m)	0.87	1.3	1.73	2.17	2.6
	t_{50} (min)	1	1	1	1	1
	t_{75} (min)	3	3	3	3	3
5 inch (125 mm)	d_{max} (m)	0.82	1.23	1.64	2.05	2.46
	t_{50} (min)	1	1	1	1	1
	t_{75} (min)	3	3	3	3	3
6 inch (150 mm)	d_{max} (m)	0.77	1.16	1.56	1.94	2.32
	t_{50} (min)	2	2	2	2	2
	t_{75} (min)	4	4	4	4	4
8 inch (200 mm)	d_{max} (m)	0.68	1.02	1.36	1.71	2.04
	t_{50} (min)	3	3	3	3	3
	t_{75} (min)	7	7	7	7	7

* Standard bailer is 4.4 litres (1 m length of 3 inch pipe).

drawdown and recovery curve for two different aquifers. In the poor aquifer, where a borehole can barely support a handpump, the initial part of the recovery is dominated by the diameter of the borehole – not the aquifer properties.

To get an approximate estimate of transmissivity (within about 25 per cent) only data after recovery time t_0 should be used: t_0 in minutes is calculated using the formula $t_0 = 25000 \times r_c^2/T$, where r_c is the effective radius of the borehole in metres (see bailer test section for information on how to calculate this radius) and T is the transmittivity. For example, for a 6-inch (150-mm) borehole in a low-transmissivity aquifer (roughly $1\,\text{m}^2/\text{day}$), over 2 hours of recovery would be needed before the data become sufficiently useful to estimate the transmissivity. If however, the aquifer is better (transmissivity of $10\,\text{m}^2/\text{day}$) the recovery data would be useful after 20 minutes.

There is, of course, a circular argument here: you need to know the transmissivity before knowing how long to measure the recovery for! This is a good reason for roughly analysing the drawdown data from a test to get an idea how long the recovery data should be measured for. Techniques for analysing drawdown data are given later in the chapter.

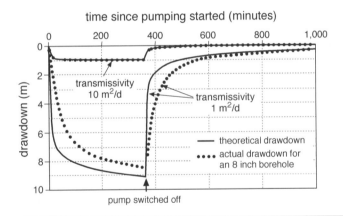

| Figure 7.10 | Effect of well storage on the shape of drawdown and recovery curves in two aquifers with different transmissivity. For low transmissivity aquifers only the later data will give a reasonable estimate of transmissivity. |

For a more accurate measurement of transmissivity (within 10 per cent) the formula $t_0 = 36\,000 \times r_c^2/T$ should be used to calculate the time that recovery data becomes useful for estimating transmissivity. For example, for a 6-inch (150-mm) borehole in a low transmissivity aquifer (roughly $1\,\text{m}^2/\text{day}$) over 3 hours of recovery would be needed before the data become sufficiently useful to estimate the transmissivity to within 10 per cent.

7.5.4 Carrying out a pumping test

Before the test begins

- The water levels in the borehole should be steady – therefore wait at least 12 hours from previous drilling, pumping or airlifting, or if rest water levels were recorded before airlifting, until the water levels have recovered to their original level.
- Record the location of the test (e.g. latitude and longitude from a GPS, village name, borehole name) and also the date and time of the test.
- Install the appropriate pump. Generally the pumping rate should be about 25–50 per cent greater than the maximum rate of the pump to be installed. For example if a handpump with yield of 0.2 litres/second is to be installed, the borehole should be tested at greater than 0.3 litres/second. The pump should be positioned several metres below the deepest water levels expected during the test. Ensure that there is a non-return valve on the pump, so that when the pump is switched off the water in the rising main or hose does not immediately fall down the borehole.
- Make sure the discharge hose is a few tens of metres from the borehole (can be closer for a Whale® pump where discharge is small) and properly controlled. In water-scarce areas people will generally collect the water that is pumped, so ensure that this is done in an orderly fashion.
- Measure the rest-water level using a dipper and clearly mark the measuring point on the borehole casing.

During the test

- Start pump and stopwatch simultaneously. If something goes wrong with the pump in the first few minutes stop the test, wait for the water levels to recover back to the rest water level and start again.
- Measure water level every 30 seconds for the first 10 minutes, every 1 minute until 30 minutes; every 5 minutes to 2 hours and every 10 minutes after that. Always write down the exact time a reading was taken; if you are late in taking a reading, write down the real time, not the time you were planning to take at.
- Periodically measure the pump rate using the simple methods discussed earlier. Also measure the pumping rate if there is a noticeable change in the rate of drawdown, the pump sounds different, or the discharge appears different. If the pumping rate has changed by more than about 30 per cent from the beginning of the test, stop the pump and start to measure the recovery.
- For a borehole to be equipped with a handpump, the test should last at least 5 hours.

- Switch off the pump (note total time of pumping) and immediately restart the stopwatch. Measure recovery in same fashion as drawdown (i.e. 30 seconds for the first 10 minutes, etc.).
- Continue to measure recovery for between 2 and 3 hours (Figure 7.11). Do not remove the pump. In poor aquifers (transmissivity around $1 \text{ m}^2/\text{day}$) only the later recovery data will give a good estimate of transmissivity (see earlier). The time in-between measurements can be a useful time for plotting up the data for the test. In this way it may be possible to identify when sufficient data has been collected.

As with all fieldwork, keeping a neat and detailed notebook is essential. At the beginning of the test, or start of recovery, readings are taken every few seconds, so it is important to be prepared. It can help to have the times for the first few readings already marked in the notebook (although it is import-

Figure 7.11   Once pumping has stopped, recovery should be measured for up to 4 hours.
Photo: BGS, © NERC 1998.

ant to amend these if a reading is not actually taken at that time), or get someone else to help write down the readings. Figure 7.12 shows an example of a notebook for a drawdown and recovery test.

7.6 Analysing constant-rate tests

7.6.1 General

Analysis of constant-rate pumping test data can be carried out using graph paper and a calculator. Special semi-log graph paper is required (and is available to be photocopied in Appendix 2). If a computer is available, a simple spreadsheet (such as Microsoft Excel) can be used. Much of the analysis can be carried out during the test itself. Later in the pumping or recovery phases of the test, water level measurements are made every 10 minutes, allowing plenty time between readings to plot the data and carry out the analysis. More complicated methods of analysis involving specialist computer programs or matching curves are described in other books and scientific papers. However,

---

Date   : 16 April 2001
Village   : Omollo 44° 322'N 9° 212'E
Borehole number : NK43 Test started at 8.15 am
                         Water levels measured
                         from top casing
                         Stephen Obilla

Two Whale pumps
Rest water level = 4.3 m
Height of casing = 0.32 m

Time	Water level	
30 secs	4.43	
1 min		
1 min 30 secs	4.52	
2 mins	4.62	1 min 38 secs to fill 15 litre bucket
2 mins 30s	4.71	
3 mins	4.80	
3 mins 30s	4.895	
4 mins	4.98	1 min 37 secs to fill 15 litre bucket
4 mins 30 s	5.07	
5 mins	5.155	
6 mins	5.31	
7 mins	5.445	

Figure 7.12 Example of a notebook for the beginning of a constant-rate pumping test.

for the level of information required for tests on handpump village water supplies these more complicated analyses can be rarely justified.

The best quality data to analyse from a pumping test with no observation boreholes is the recovery data (the water levels recorded after the pump has been switched off). This is because the recovery smoothes out any small changes in pumping rate and after the first few seconds there are no errors due to well losses. One of the most common analysis methods, and the one described here, is the **Theis recovery method**. The method will give an estimate of transmissivity, and an experienced eye can also detect other borehole behaviour from the shape of the graph.

Useful information can also be gathered from analysis of the drawdown data measured during pumping. Although not as reliable as recovery analysis for estimating transmissivity, the presence of fractures or hydraulic barriers are easier to detect from drawdown data. The most common graphical methods for analysis the data is known as **Jacob's method**. The theory behind both Jacob's and the Theis recovery method is given in the resources referred to at the end of the chapter.

The two analysis methods depend on plotting data on a semi-log graph. This type of graph has two very different axes. On one axis (usually the y-axis) the numbers increase arithmetically – 1, 2, 3, 4, 5, etc. On the x-axis the numbers increase logarithmically – 1, 10, 100, 1000, etc. Semi-log paper is available for photocopying in Appendix 2. This type of graph is required because groundwater tends to respond logarithmically to pumping. Water-levels decline rapidly at the beginning of a test and decline less and less as the pumping proceeds and the cone of depression moves out into the aquifer.

7.6.2 Recovery analysis: Theis recovery

In Appendix 2 there is a worksheet to help record data from the test, and also some graph paper to help plot the data. A summary of the analysis method is given here.

- For the recovery part of the test, calculate the residual drawdown (s') by subtracting the rest water level (measured before pumping started) from the measured water levels.
- The time elapsed since the start of the recovery is known as t'. For each recovery water level calculate the time elapsed since the very start of the test (t). For example, if the pump was pumping for 360 minutes before it was switched off, and recovery water levels were measured at 0.5, 1 and 1.5 minutes, t would be 360.5, 361 and 361.5 minutes respectively, and t' could be 0.5, 1 and 1.5 (see Figure 7.13).
- Divide t by t' (i.e. t/t').
- Plot the residual drawdown s' against t/t' on semi-log paper – t/t' on the log scale, with s' on the arithmetic scale. Photocopy the semi log

paper in Appendix 2 or use tracing paper. Residual drawdown should be in metres. The data should plot roughly as a straight line (see Figure 7.14).

■ Draw a best-fit line through the data, using mostly data from low t/t' values. High t/t' values are affected by well storage and changes in pumping rate at the end of the test. It is usual to look for a line that is trending towards $t/t' = 1$.

■ Measure $\Delta s'$ from the best-fit line. $\Delta s'$ is the difference in drawdown over one log cycle of time (a log cycle is either 1–10, 10–100 or 100–1000). See the worked example in Figure 7.15.

■ Calculate the average pumping rate (Q) for the pumping test in m³/day. If the pumping rate has steadily declined over the test, then the average pumping rate will be the rate in the middle of the test. If the pumping rate was variable throughout the test, then the average pumping rate will need to be calculated more carefully by estimating the amount of time it was pumping at each rate. To change from litres/second to m³/day, multiple by the number of seconds in a day (60 × 60 × 24) and divide by the number of litres in a cubic metre (1000).

■ Substitute Q (in m³/day), and $\Delta s'$ (in m) into the formula below to find the transmissivity, T (measured in m²/day):

$$T = 0.183Q/\Delta s'$$

t¹-time since start of recovery (mins)	t-time since start of pumping (mins)	t/t¹	wls (m)	s¹
0.25	360.25	1441	9.17	1.85
0.5	360.5	721	9.085	1.765
0.75	360.75	481	9.005	1.685
1	361	361	8.933	1.613
1.25	361.25	289	8.873	1.553
1.5	361.5	241	8.815	1.495
1.75	361.75	207	8.76	1.44
2	362	181	8.715	1.395
etc.....				

Rest water level = 7.32 m
time of pumping = 360 minutes

Figure 7.13 Calculating t/t' and s' for the Theis recovery method. The numbers in bold are directly measured from the test; the numbers not in bold are calculations.

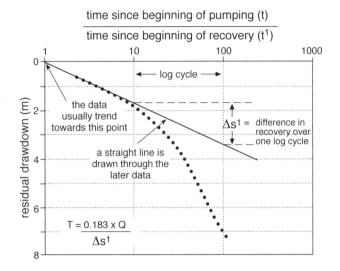

Figure 7.14 Analysing recovery data using the Theis recovery method.

Other information can be obtained by looking at the shape of the recovery curves. Figure 7.16 shows several examples of recovery curves from different tests carried out in rural water supply projects. Leakage, fractures and well storage can all be distinguished. However, it is generally easier to identify these characteristics from the drawdown data, discussed in the next section.

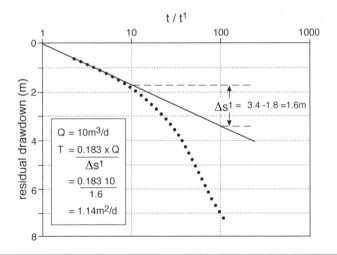

Figure 7.15 Worked example for the Theis recovery method. This borehole will just sustain a hand pump yield of about 5000 litres per day.

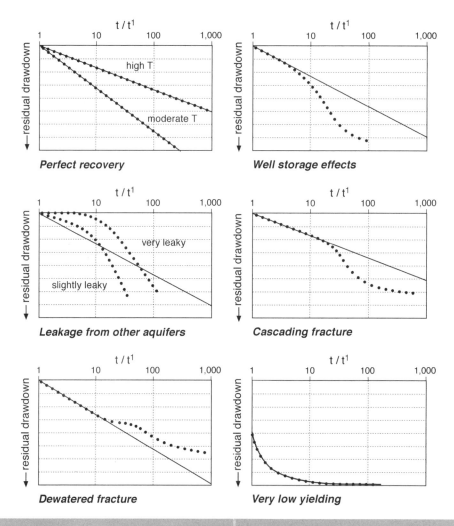

Figure 7.16 Common causes of deviations from the theoretically perfect Theis recovery curve.

7.6.3 Drawdown analysis

In Appendix 2 there is a worksheet to help record data from the test, and also some graph paper to help plot the data. A summary of the analysis method is given here.

- Plot the water levels from the start of the test to when the pump is switched off against time on semi-log paper – time on the log scale, with water levels on the arithmetic scale (see Figure 7.17). Photo-copy the semi-log paper in Appendix 2, or use tracing paper. The time is the number of minutes since pumping started; drawdown should be plotted in metres. The data should plot roughly as a straight line.

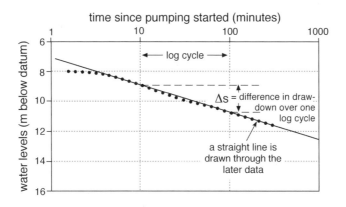

Figure 7.17 Analysing drawdown data using the Jacob method.

- Draw a best-fit line through the data – using mostly the middle or later data (see the worked example in Figure 7.18).
- Measure Δs from the best-fit line. Δs is the difference in water levels (in metres) over one log cycle of time (a log cycle is either 1–10, 10–100 or 100–1000).
- Calculate the average pumping rate (Q) for the pumping test in m^3/day. To change from litres/second, multiple by the number of seconds in a day ($60 \times 60 \times 24$) and divide by 1000 (the number of litres in a cubic metre).

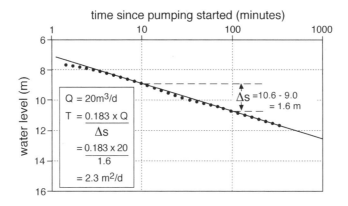

Figure 7.18 Worked example for the Jacob drawdown method.

- Substitute Q (in m^3/day), and Δs (in metres) into the formula below to find the transmissivity T (measured in m^2/day):

$$T = 0.183Q/\Delta s$$

235

As discussed above, estimating the transmissivity using drawdown data from the pumping borehole can be fairly unreliable because of changes in pumping rate and well losses – recovery data is generally taken in preference to it. However, useful information on the borehole behaviour can be interpreted from the shape of the drawdown curve.

In an ideal situation the drawdown on a semi-log graph should plot as a straight line, with some deviation at the beginning due to well storage. Any changes in pumping rate will cause a change in gradient in the line – these should be noted. If the gradient of the line increases (and is not due to a change in pumping rate) a fracture may have been emptied, or the cone of depression may have intersected an impermeable boundary.

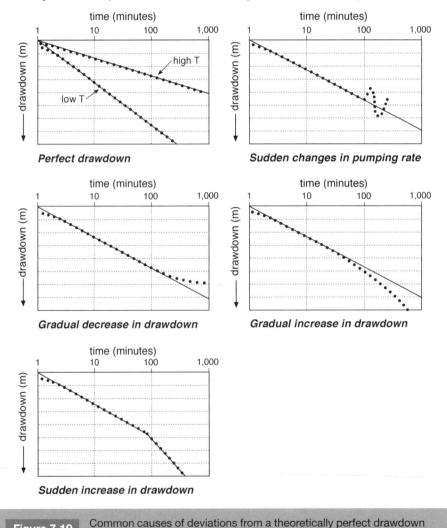

| Figure 7.19 | Common causes of deviations from a theoretically perfect drawdown curve. |

The following deviations from the standard Jacob straight line are commonly observed. Figure 7.19 illustrates the common deviations.

- Before attributing the changes to either the borehole or aquifer, the effects of changes in pumping rate or rainfall during the test must first be discounted. Gradual decreases in pumping will decrease the rate of drawdown. More severe problems with the pump (such as the pump switching off for several minutes) will show up as more dramatic fluctuations in water levels. If the borehole is shallow, and the test long, rainfall can occasionally cause fluctuations in drawdown curves − these can be seen as a rise in water levels.

- **Gradual decrease in drawdown.** Aquifers showing this sort of effect are often said to be **leaky**. Drawdown decreases because some extra water is being added to this aquifer. This may be leaking from overlying deposits, from the unsaturated zone, from aquifers below the borehole, or even from within the aquifer itself from small pores to the flowing fractures. Leakage is generally an encouraging sign, and indicates more water within the system. Transmissivity should be calculated from before the leakage is observed. If a test is only 5 hours long, it is unlikely that much leakage will be observed.

- **Gradual increase in drawdown.** A gradual increase in drawdown usually indicates that the aquifer properties away from the borehole are poorer than those immediately surrounding the borehole. This is occasionally observed with boreholes sited in valleys − as the cone of depression moves outwards and away from the valley the aquifer properties reduce and the drawdown increases. A second reason for this response is the dewatering of shallow parts of the aquifer as the test proceeds; this can be particularly the case if the drawdown is high relative to the depth of the borehole (e.g. 10 m drawdown in a 25-m deep borehole). This is not an encouraging sign, and indicates there is probably less water in the system. The test should be continued until the drawdown stabilizes into a straight line on the semi-log plot and transmissivity calculated for this part of the test.

- **Sudden increase in drawdown.** A sudden increase in drawdown (often known as a **dog leg**) can result from the dewatering of an important fracture, or (less commonly) the intersection of a hydraulic barrier. This is of serious concern and indicates that the borehole may dry up after heavy usage or during the dry season. However, the borehole may still be sustainable: (1) if the transmissivity calculated after the fracture has dewatered is still sufficient to sustain a handpump (>1 m^2/day); or (2) if the dewatered fracture is deep and the pumping rate for the test is much higher than the intended operational pumping rate.

7.7 Large-diameter wells

It is difficult to carry out rigorous pumping tests in large diameter wells. The large amount of water stored within the well masks much of the behaviour of the aquifer. When the well is emptied, water is taken mainly from storage in the well, and then the rate of recovery (particularly in low-permeability rocks) is based not only on the recovering water levels in the aquifer, but on the volume of the well. Various techniques have been developed to get around this problem; however, the analysis is generally too complicated to be done without a computer. This level of analysis is outwith the scope of this manual, but readers can take it further by using the program BGSPT, and reading the associated manuals (see resources listed at the end of the chapter).

However, the performance and behaviour of wells can be directly measured by monitoring the recovery of water levels in a well after it has been pumped. A simple test, taking only a few hours, can help understand how the source is performing.

- Before starting this test it is important that the well has not been pumped for about a day, so that the water levels have fully recovered. If the well is the main source of water for a community, it is difficult for it to remain untouched for more than about 12 hours. The well should be left to recover overnight and the test carried out first thing in the morning.
- Mark a point to take readings from and measure the rest water level in the well.
- The well is then pumped as rapidly as possible until nearly empty. A suction pump (with foot valve) is often suitable for this sort of test and could dewater a well in a few minutes. In water-scarce areas the water should not be pumped to waste, but collected by the community.
- The volume of water pumped from the well, and also the time taken to empty the well, should be recorded.
- Once the pump has been switched off, a stopwatch should be started and recovery of the water levels recorded: every 30 seconds for first 10 minutes, every 1 minute until 30 minutes, every 5 minutes to 2 hours and every 10 minutes after that.
- The test can stop once the well has recovered to about 75 per cent of its original water level.

Without a computer, it is only possible to interpret the test qualitatively. The data can be plotted on graph paper and the shape of the recovery noted. At its simplest, the quicker the well recovers to its original level, the better the well. If recovery is roughly linear over the first half of the test, it is possible to calculate the inflow into the well. The volume of well filled within the linear period is estimated using the formula $\pi r^2 h$, where r is the radius of the well and h is the recovery during the period, and divided by the time over which the recovery occurred.

Wells must be tested at different times of the year. A test carried out during the rainy season will not predict how the well will fare in the peak of the dry season. Figure 7.20 shows a series of tests carried out on a 10-m deep well into laterite and mudstone. In the wet season, the permeable laterite is saturated and the well recovers very quickly. By the middle of the dry season, the laterite is dry and recovery is much slower. By the end of the dry season, the only inflow to the well is from small fractures in the mudstone, consequently the well has not recovered even after one day. This source, although excellent in the rainy season and early dry season, is not able to meet the community needs at the most critical time of year. The well should either be deepened, or another source (such as a borehole) developed.

If it is not possible to directly monitor the well (for example if you want a quick assessment of how the well performs at the peak of the dry season, and it is now raining heavily) then the community will be able to provide this information. The following questions can be helpful:

- How many buckets (of what size) can be taken at different times of year?
- When do people collect water (in water-scarce areas people will collect water at night)?
- How long are the queues?
- Does the water change in taste or colour throughout the year?

Figure 7.20 Drawdown and recovery for a pumping test carried out in the same well at different times of the year.

Further reading and resources

Barker, J.A. and Macdonald, D.M.J. (2000) A manual for BGSPT: programs to simulate and analyse pumping tests in large-diameter wells. British Geological Survey Technical Report WC/00/17. Available at: http://www.bgs.ac.uk

Butler, J.J. (1997) *The design, performance and analysis of slug tests.* Lewis Publishers, New York.

Fetter, C.W. (2001) *Applied Hydrogeology* (4th edition). Prentice Hall, Englewood Cliffs, NJ.

Kruseman, G.P. and deRidder, N.A. (1990) Analysis and evaluation of pumping test data. International Publication 47, Institute for Land Reclamation and Improvement, The Netherlands.

USGS Aquifer test software: http://water.usgs.gov/pubs/of/of-02197/

8 Water quality aspects of rural water supply

8.1 Quality of water for drinking – 'safe' water supplies

Since water is essential for life, the first priority is that it should be made available – even if the quality is not entirely satisfactory. This is, however, not the whole story, and more recent statements (such as in the United Nations Millennium Development Goals) refer to the right of communities to have access to an adequate supply of safe water. In this context, 'safe' is taken to mean water that:

- does not represent a significant health risk
- is of sufficient quantity to meet all domestic needs
- is available continuously to all of the population
- is affordable.

This can be summarized as **quantity, quality, continuity, coverage** and **cost**.

This chapter discusses the quality aspects of rural water supply. Both microbiological and chemical constituents can cause health risks, so we cannot really describe a supply as safe unless we know about both. Groundwater may contain natural constituents of health concern, the most important of which are arsenic and fluoride. Although groundwater within aquifers is generally of good microbial quality, it can become contaminated if protective measures at wells, boreholes or springs are not well constructed or maintained. Further problems occur where infiltrating recharge carries mobile and persistent chemical pollutants from agriculture, waste disposal or industry. All these potential constraints are serious, but the control of microbiological quality remains the highest priority for the World Health Organization (WHO) because of the potentially devastating consequences of waterborne infectious diseases. For rural water supplies, treatment of water is rarely possible, so the emphasis is on adequate protection measures so that the quality of water provided at the pump remains good.

In this chapter, the main threats to safe water supply caused by both microbiological and chemical quality are described. Information is provided to help predict quality problems and to assess likely pollution hazards. No detailed information is given on sampling methods as these vary according to the equipment used (which should come with detailed instructions for taking samples). Some guidance is provided on general monitoring strategies.

8.2 Drinking-water guidelines and standards

The World Health Organization (WHO) has, since the 1950s, been the component part of the UN system with responsibility for providing guidelines on the quality of drinking-water. International standards for drinking-water were first prepared by WHO in 1958 and revised in 1963 and 1971. In the 1980s, the philosophy and content was changed significantly to become the first edition of the WHO *Guidelines for Drinking-water Quality*, published in 1984. Work to revise the guidelines started in 1989 and a second edition was published in 1993–97. The third edition, which is largely web-based and regularly updated to take account of new information on health impacts, is in the final stages of preparation in 2004 (see resources listed at the end of the chapter).

Drinking-water guidelines and standards (see Box 8.1) are derived from the careful collection and interpretation of published evidence of health impacts. This is not a straightforward process, as much of the evidence comes from the observation of acute toxic effects of high intakes of chemicals in animals. It can be difficult to extrapolate these animal results to

---

BOX 8.1 Guidelines and standards

- **Guidelines** are advisory – based solely on the potential impacts on human health of the substances and organisms considered. The WHO guidelines are intended as a basis for national authorities to help develop drinking-water standards and regulations that are appropriate to the country's own socio-economic conditions and water quality situation. The guidelines recognize the desirability of adopting a risk-based approach whereby the development of standards by individual governments is a careful process in which the health risks are considered alongside the technical and economic feasibility.
- **Standards** imply fixed and often legally binding obligations for compliance, and take into account social, economic, environmental, political and financial considerations. Fixed standards achieve little or nothing unless they can be implemented and enforced. When national standards are being established, consideration must be given to practical measures, such as finding new sources of water supply to replace those whose quality is unacceptable, installing treatment and developing adequate water quality monitoring programmes.

humans, and to make the jump from acute high doses used in the tests to the effects of long-term low doses generally found in water supplies. Because of these uncertainties, large safety factors are usually incorporated into the guidelines. The values established are subject to regular evaluation and may be revised in the light of new health evidence, as has happened in recent years for lead and arsenic. Examples of guideline and standard values for some of the most important chemicals relevant to rural water supplies are given in Table 8.1.

Table 8.1a contains parameters with direct health significance and Table 8.1b lists parameters which may have aesthetic effects that cause complaints from consumers. They may then reject a new supply, perhaps in favour of a polluted traditional surface water source. We can see from Table 8.1 that there is general consistency between the WHO guidelines and the European and US standards, reflecting broad consensus about the health hazards. The websites and publications of the three agencies quoted can provide the most up-to-date values, and the WHO guidelines in particular have helpful supporting technical documentation. The web addresses are listed at the end of this chapter.

The situation for organic parameters is more complicated. There are many hundreds of synthetic organic compounds (and new ones are always being developed) for use in a wide range of industrial processes and as pesticides. Rather than providing a very long list here of the different kinds, the situation can be summarized as follows:

- **Industrial compounds:** chlorinated solvents, aromatic hydrocarbons and other compounds with guidelines or standards ranging from less than one to several hundred µg/litre, based on specific toxicity.
- **Pesticides:** many groups of compounds, with WHO guidelines and US EPA standards ranging from less than 0.05 µg/litre for the most toxic, 2–10 µg/litre for the majority, and 20–40 µg/litre for less toxic compounds. In contrast, the EC has taken a non-toxicity-based approach to pesticide standards in drinking-water, instead setting a value of 0.1 µg/litre for all compounds and 0.5 µg/litre for total pesticides detected. This was effectively a surrogate zero concentration, based on analytical capabilities in the late 1970s when the Drinking-water Directive was being prepared by the EC.
- **Disinfection by-products:** trihalomethanes and compounds such as bromate, chlorate and chlorophenols, with guidelines and standards mostly in the range 10–100 µg/litre.

Dependable analysis of synthetic organic compounds is expensive and requires considerable investment in equipment and training. Therefore, it is best to consider them only where they are known or suspected of being problematic: perhaps in peri-urban areas, where there is dispersed small-scale industry, intensive cultivation or disposal of solid or liquid waste. In these areas, further information should be sought from the resources and

Table 8.1 (a) Drinking water guidelines and standards for selected inorganic parameters that are of direct health significance

Parameters	WHO[a]	EU[b]	US EPA[c]	Notes
Arsenic (µg/l)	10	10	10	reduced from 50 µg/l
Boron (mg/l)	0.3	1.0	–	
Cadmium (µg/l)	3.0	5.0	5.0	
Chromium (µg/l)	50	50	100	
Copper (mg/l)	2.0	2.0	1.3	
Cyanide (µg/l)	70	50	200	
Fluoride (mg/l)	1.5	1.5	4.0	Varies with climate
Lead (µg/l)	10	10	15	
Nitrate (mg/l as NO$_3$)	50	50	45	
Nitrite (mg/l as NO$_2$)	3.0	0.5	3.3	

(b) Drinking water guidelines and standards for selected inorganic parameters that may cause consumers to reject a supply

Parameters	WHO[a]	EU[b]	US EPA[c]	Why parameter is included
Colour (TCU[d])	15	Acceptable	15	Appearance
Turbidity (NTU[e])	5	Acceptable	5	Appearance, disinfection
Aluminium (mg/l)	0.2	0.2	0.05–0.2	Deposition, discolouration
Ammonia (mg/l)	1.5	0.5	–	Odour, taste
Iron (mg/l)	0.3	0.2	0.3	Staining
Manganese (µg/l)	100	50	50	Staining
Sulphate (mg/l)	250	250	250	Taste, corrosion
Chloride (mg/l)	250	250	250	Taste, corrosion
Hydrogen sulphide (mg/l)	0.05	–	–	Odour, taste
Hardness	–	–	–	Scum and scale formation
pH	–	6.5–9.5	6.5–8.5	Low pH: corrosion; high pH: taste and soapy feel
Zinc (mg/l)	3.0	–	5.0	Appearance, taste
Total dissolved solids (mg/l)	1000	–	500	Taste

[a] WHO (1993).
[b] EU (1998).
[c] US EPA (2003).
[d] Time colour unit.
[e] Nephelometric turbidity unit.

further reading listed at the end of the chapter. The three major sets of guidelines and standards (WHO, EU, US EPA) include many specific organic compounds.

Unless there is strong evidence to the contrary, most effort in rural water supply programmes should be directed towards inorganic chemical and microbiological constraints on the safety of the supplied water. With respect to microbiological quality, the guidelines and standards specify a complete absence of indicator organisms such as *E. coli*, enterococci or other thermotolerant coliform bacteria, and this remains the dominant concern in provision of safe drinking-water.

8.3 Microbiological quality of groundwater supplies

8.3.1 Pathogens and pathways

Water can transport many different pathogenic micro-organisms. Those of most concern occur in the faeces of humans and some animals; infection is caused when someone who is susceptible consumes contaminated water. These waterborne pathogens can be classified into four broad groups according to their physical, chemical and physiological characteristics. In order of increasing biological complexity, these groups are viruses, bacteria, protozoa and helminths. The transmission of the last of these in groundwater is unlikely because of their large size in relation to the pore sizes and microfractures in aquifer materials (ARGOSS 2001), and they do not need to be considered further here. The three other groups contain important organisms that can be found in groundwater (Table 8.2), and have major health implications.

The types and numbers of the various pathogens in a groundwater supply are highly variable and depend on the following factors:

- incidence and seasonality of disease in the community
- sanitation methods in the community
- characteristics of the groundwater system
- the type and construction of the water point.

The severity of health impacts varies greatly, as do the infective doses (which can be as little as a single pathogenic organism), and different people may be more susceptible to disease, according to their immune

Table 8.2 Pathogens of concern in groundwater

Viruses	Bacteria	Protozoa
Coxsackievirus	*Escherichia coli*	*Cryptosporidium parvum*
Echovirus	*Salmonella* spp.	*Giardia lamblia*
Norovirus *(formerly Norwalk)*	*Shigella* spp.	
Hepatitis	*Campylobacter jejuni*	
Rotavirus	*Yersinia* spp.	
Enteric adenovirus	*Legionella* spp.	
Calicivirus	*Vibrio cholerae*	

status, prior exposure and nutritional status. This is why the basis for most guidelines and standards for drinking-water quality is a total absence of pathogens.

Most of the faecal pathogens affecting human health are transmitted by the faecal–oral route. Transmission may occur by a variety of pathways, as shown in Figure 8.1, and so to reduce the risks to health, interventions are needed:

- in **sanitation and excreta disposal**, to remove faeces from the environment
- in **water supply**, to prevent consumption of water containing pathogens
- in **hygiene education**, to prevent transmission from contaminated hands to food or water.

These interventions help to form barriers to transmission by the routes shown in Figure 8.1. The left-hand side of this figure is the transmission route of concern for groundwater, and it is put into the context of the source→pathway→receptor concept in Figure 8.2. If there is to be the potential for pollution of a receptor (in this case a well or borehole with a handpump), there needs to be both a source and a pathway. In this example, the sources are the pit latrine and the activities of people or animals around the pump. The pathways are either naturally occurring through the inter-granular pores and fractures in the soil and rock (the **aquifer pathway**), or manmade pathways arising because of failures in the design or construction of the receptor (the **local pathway**).

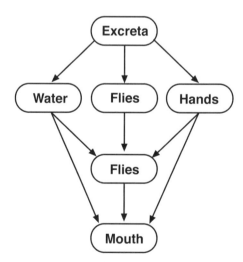

| **Figure 8.1** | Principal elements of faecal–oral disease transmission. |

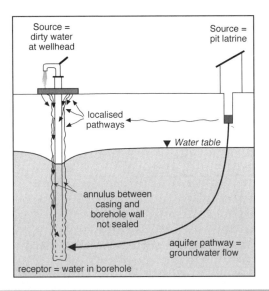

Source=
dirty water
at wellhead

Source=
pit latrine

localised
pathways

▼ Water table

annulus between
casing and
borehole wall
not sealed

aquifer pathway =
groundwater flow

receptor = water in borehole

Figure 8.2	Source→pathway→receptor concept for groundwater pollution.
	Source: modified from ARGOSS 2001.

The approach outlined in the following section for assessing the potential for microbial pollution by these two routes is based heavily on that developed by ARGOSS (2001).

8.3.2 Assessing the potential for microbial pollution through the aquifer

In projects where onsite sanitation exists, or is being installed, and there is control over the siting, design and construction of the supply sources, then an assessment of the potential for pollution through the aquifer pathway can be very useful. As this manual is primarily concerned with rural water supplies rather than sanitation, this section focuses on siting and design of the water supplies rather than the sanitation facilities. More detailed discussions of sanitation facilities can be found in Franceys et al. (1992) and Mara (1996).

The steps required to assess the potential for microbial pollution of groundwater supplies via the aquifer pathway are shown in Figure 8.3 and details of the information required are given below. Figure 8.3 provides an indication of the suitable groundwater supply options in each case.

STEP 1 Collect background information. This requires general characterization of the local hydrogeological environment, the depths at which aquifers are likely to occur, and typical minimum depths to the water table (by measuring water levels in wells or boreholes, from local knowledge or from records held in government agencies or

Step 1: Collect background information

Step 2: Assess attenuation within unsaturated zone

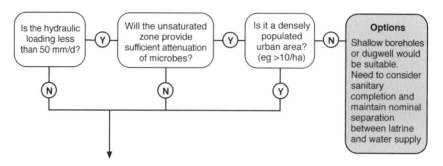

Step 3: Assess attenuation with depth below water table

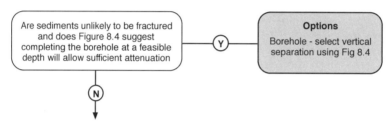

Step 4: Assess attenuation with lateral separation in aquifer

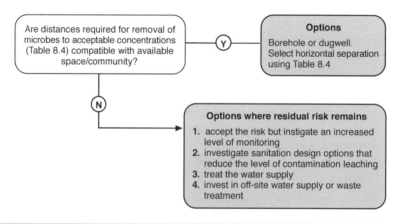

Figure 8.3 Steps for assessing the potential for microbial pollution through the aquifer. *Source:* ARGOSS 2001.

projects). It also requires information on the types of sanitation used or planned.

STEP 2 Assess attenuation potential in the unsaturated zone. A conservative approach is to assume that if the hydraulic loading is greater than 50 mm/day, then there is significant potential for pathogens to reach the water table. At a loading of >50 mm/day sufficient wetting occurs that hydraulic conductivity increases, travel times are shortened and attenuation capacity reduced. Loadings of <50 mm/day are usually associated with latrines (simple, ventilated, composting, urine separation and pour-flush), and loadings of >50 mm/day with septic tanks and aqua privies. Even if the hydraulic loading is <50 mm/day, there may still be potential for pathogens to reach the water table depending on the nature of the soil and material in the unsaturated zone.

The matrix in Table 8.3 provides an indication of the potential for pathogens to reach the water table. A safety factor is incorporated to allow for uncertainty in classifying rock type and estimating the depth to water table, which should be from the base of the pit. For highly permeable sediments and where fractures are suspected to occur, attenuation in the unsaturated zone cannot be relied on, and it is necessary to proceed to step 3.

STEP 3 Assess attenuation with depth below the water table. Placing the screen at greater depth in a borehole will increase the travel time of water and pollutants from the onsite sanitation, and this may be sufficient to reduce the potential for pollution to occur. While even small increases in the depth to the screened section can extend the travel time by tens or hundreds of days in unconsolidated granular materials, vertical fractures in consolidated aquifers can provide

Table 8.3 Assessment of pollution potential after attenuation in the unsaturated zone (ARGOSS 2001)

Rock types forming the unsaturated zone	Depth to water table (minimum depth, metres below base of pit)		
	<5	5 - 10	>10
fine silt, sand and clay			
weathered basement[1]			
medium sand			
Coarse sand and gravel			
sandstones, limestones, fractured rocks			

[1] where weathered material is soft and easily dug. If the weathered material remains competant and potentially fractured, it should be considered as fractured rock.

significant potential for microbial organisms to reach the water table at unacceptable levels

low to very low potential for microbial organisms to reach the water table at unacceptable levels ie. travel time through the unsaturated zone greater than 25 days rapid pathways from the water table. The vertical separation needed to provide adequate travel times can be calculated from Figure 8.4, in which a pumping rate of 0.25 litres/second can be used for a typical handpump supply.

The option of increasing the depth to the screened section is attractive because increasing the vertical separation allows the horizontal separation to be reduced to a nominal value and the borehole can then be located conveniently close to the users. However, this is only effective if there are no local pathways of contamination (see below). Where vertical separation is not sufficient to protect the source, then it is necessary to proceed to step 4.

STEP 4 Assess attenuation due to lateral groundwater movement. The horizontal separation needed is the distance that groundwater would travel in 25–50 days. Each aquifer type has a broad range of hydraulic conductivities, and although a narrower band of more likely values can be used to estimate the required separation, higher velocities are possible and horizontal separation estimates are subject to considerable uncertainty.

Values for the parameters required can be obtained from Table 8.4. The maximum hydraulic conductivity and minimum porosity values should be used to provide a conservative estimate of lateral separation. The estimated lateral separation may not provide adequate attenuation if there are thin strata of high conductivity, e.g. sands within a layered alluvial sequence, or if the aquifer is fractured. Where this is the case, or where, in more densely populated areas, there is just not enough space for adequate separation, the potential for pollution will remain, and the options available are listed at the bottom of Figure 8.3.

8.3.3 Assessing the potential for microbial pollution through local pathways

Often the most likely contamination of a groundwater supply is via local pathways that bypass the aquifer. These can be through the headworks or along shallow permeable soil layers and down the side of the borehole casing or well lining (Figure 8.2). Following the source→pathway→ receptor approach outlined above, the threat of pollution can be reduced in two ways:

- minimize activities which might cause pollution and keep potential pollution sources away from the immediate vicinity of the supply
- ensure that the sanitary completion of the source described in Chapter 6 is properly designed, constructed and maintained.

Assessing the sanitary conditions of the headworks and surroundings

Sanitary inspection procedures have been developed for assessing the condition of the headworks (see Box 8.2 and the resources listed at the end

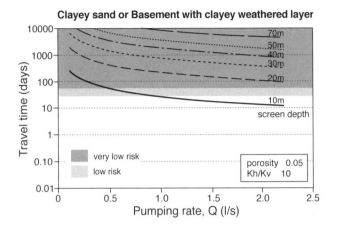

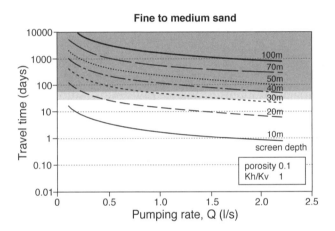

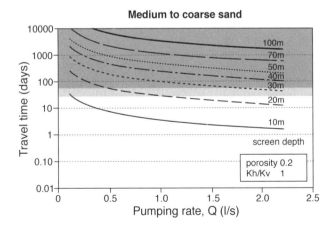

Figure 8.4 Depth to screen and travel times for different aquifers. K_h/K_v is the ratio between aquifer permeability in the horizontal and vertical directions.
Source: ARGOSS (2001).

Table 8.4 Typical aquifer properties and feasibility of using horizontal separation

Rock types	Typical porosity	Typical K_h/K_v ratio[a]	Range of likely hydraulic conductivity (m/day)	Feasibility of using horizontal separation	Lateral separation for low potential for pathogen arrival at water supply
Silt	0.1–0.2	10	0.01–0.1	Yes	Up to several metres[b]
Fine silty sand	0.1–0.2	10	0.1–10	Yes, should generally be acceptable[1]	Up to several metres[b]
Weathered basement (not fractured)	0.05–0.2	1–10	0.01–10	Yes	Up to several metres[b]
Medium sand	0.2–0.3	1	10–100	Uncertain, needs site-specific testing and monitoring	Tens to hundreds of metres
Gravel	0.2–0.3	1	100–1000	Not feasible	Up to hundreds of metres
Fractured rocks	0.01	1	Difficult to generalize, velocities of tens or hundreds of m/day possible	Not feasible	Up to hundreds of metres

[a] Ratio of horizontal to permeability to vertical permeability.
[b] Select a minimum separation to avoid localized contamination.
Source: ARGOSS (2001).

of the chapter). An example of a sanitary inspection form for a borehole with a handpump is shown in Figure 8.5. Equivalent forms for other types of water supplies, together with useful notes for completing the forms are provided by Howard (2002). In the example shown here, questions 1–3 refer to potential sources of faeces in the environment, questions 4–6 refer to indirect factors and questions 7–10 refer to direct pathway factors.

Although easy and rapid, sanitary inspections need to be undertaken reasonably frequently because the pollution threats change with time. For example, development may occur around the water supply or the condition of the wellhead deteriorate through lack of maintenance. Most importantly, some of the risk factors are far more critical in the rainy season than the dry season, and inspections are certainly required in both. Examples of good and poor surface condition are shown in Figure 8.6.

BOX 8.2   Sanitary inspections

Sanitary inspections provide an easy but effective, risk-based approach to monitoring wellhead protection. The use of standardized and quantifiable approaches makes it possible to compare the results obtained by different inspectors, allows an overall risk score to be developed, identifies priority sites for remedial actions and permits comparisons between different supply types – wells, boreholes and springs – once the data have been converted into a percentage risk.

Sanitary inspections are designed as a series of simple questions with yes/no answers tailored to the type of supply source (Lloyd and Helmer 1991; Howard 2002). The questions are worded so that a positive answer indicates the presence of a pollution threat or risk factor and is allocated a score, with no score being given for a negative answer. Adding the positive answers yields an overall sanitary risk score. The three main types of risk factors are (Howard 2002):

- **Hazard factors** from which pollution can be derived, and are a measure of the sources of faeces in the environment. Examples include latrines, sewers, solid waste dumps and animal wastes.
- **Pathway factors** that allow microbial pollution to enter the groundwater supply source, but do not provide the faecal matter. Pathway factors are often critical in determining whether pollution will occur, as the presence of a hazard may not correlate with observed pollution if no pathway exists. Examples of pathway factors include leaking pipes, eroded catchment areas and damaged plinths or headworks.
- **Indirect factors** enhance the development of pathway factors, but do not either directly allow water into the supply, nor form a source of faeces. Examples include lack of fencing or poor surface water diversion and drainage.

Assessing sanitary protection below the ground surface

The questions in the sanitary inspection deal comprehensively with the condition of the headworks and surroundings, but this is not the complete pathway. Below ground, the likelihood of a pollution pathway depends on the construction of the well or borehole and the nature of the surrounding aquifer material (Figure 8.2). Particularly critical is the presence or absence of a properly installed sanitary seal of the type described in Chapter 6, which should fill the annular space between casing or well lining and aquifer to below the permeable soil layers (usually to at least 3 m below the ground surface).

The sanitary inspection of an operating supply is unable to determine the presence or condition of this seal, and it is necessary to check the

---

I.   **Type of Facility**   **BOREHOLE WITH HANDPUMP**

1.   Village

2.   GPS

3.   Code Number

4.   Date of visit

5.   Water sample taken?..............Sample No. ....TC/100ml..........

II. **Specific Diagnostic Information for Assessment**

1.   Is there a latrine within 10 m of the borehole?   Y/N

2.   Is there a latrine uphill of the borehole within 100 m?   Y/N

3.   Are there any other sources of pollution within 10 m of the borehole?   Y/N
     (e.g. animal breeding, cultivation, roads, industry etc.)

4.   Is the drainage faulty, allowing ponding within 2 m of the borehole?   Y/N

5.   Is the drainage channel cracked, broken or need cleaning?   Y/N

6.   Is the fence missing or faulty?   Y/N

7.   Is the apron less than 1 m in radius?   Y/N

8.   Does spilt water collect in the apron area?   Y/N

9.   Is the apron cracked or damaged?   Y/N

10. Is the handpump loose at the point of attachment to the apron?   Y/N

                                              Total score of risks   ../10

Risk score : 9-10 =Very high;   6-8 = High;   3-5 = Medium;   0-3 = Low

III. **Results and Recommendations:**

The following important points were noted: (list Nos. 1-10)

Signature of Health Inspector/Assistant:

Comments

| Figure 8.5 | Example sanitary inspection form for a borehole equipped with handpump. *Source:* Howard 2002. |

construction or completion report form of the borehole or well. However, even if a suitable sanitary seal was specified and the completion form confirms its installation, experience suggests that this is one construction step where shortcuts and cost savings are sometimes made, especially by commercial contractors who are under pressures of time or cost. The certainty

Figure 8.6 Top is an example of cracked headworks, lack of drainage and standing water seeping back under the plinth. Bottom shows a properly completed borehole with a drainage apron.
Photo: BGS, © NERC 1986.

with which its reported presence can be accepted depends on the closeness of supervision of the final steps of the construction process.

If absence of a seal is known or suspected, then the presence of fine-grained unconsolidated materials which readily collapse against the casing to seal the annulus reduces the likelihood of a pathway, especially if the water table and screen are at appreciable depths. For consolidated, fractured formations, however, installation of a sanitary seal to below the soil layers is critical and wells or boreholes without seals should be considered as high risk.

8.3.4 Managing microbiological contamination using sanitary inspections

Communities, projects and water supply and health surveillance agencies can use sanitary inspections (Box 8.2) as a management tool. They provide a broad perspective on the hazards of pollution and the effectiveness of operation and maintenance of the water supplies. If certain hazard factors dominate, then this can help direct efforts in remedial actions and improvement so that the invariably limited maintenance resources can be best used. This knowledge can also help to improve the training of communities, project staff or pump operators. Further, the results of sanitary inspections can provide additional criteria for assessing the advantages and disadvantages of different types of supply sources for national, local or project planning (Bartram 1999; Howard et al. 2003).

If sanitary inspections and sampling for microbiological analysis are both carried out at the same supply sources, then the results can be evaluated together to provide a more effective way of prioritizing which supplies should be improved. To do this, the faecal coliform counts are first classified and then plotted against the sanitary inspection scores. Table 8.5 gives a faecal coliform classification for a study in Indonesia from which Figure 8.6 is reproduced – but any subdivisions suitable for the specific circumstances can be selected.

There should be a general linear relationship between overall sanitary risk score and observed level of pollution, with the points plotting in a broad band from supplies requiring no action in the bottom left to those requiring urgent action in the top right. Fewer points should fall in the top left or

Table 8.5 Faecal coliform classes for an Indonesian case study

Grading	Count/100 ml	Risk
A	0	No risk
B	1–10	Low risk
C	11–100	Intermediate to high risk
D	101–1000	Gross pollution; high risk
E	>1000	Gross pollution; very high risk

Source: Lloyd and Helmer (1991).

bottom right. For those in the bottom right (none in this example), where high risk from the sanitary survey is not borne out by observed faecal contamination, remedial action is still required although the risks have not led to pollution. For those in the top left of Figure 8.7, having high coliform counts without the presence of many risk factors, re-sampling should be undertaken; if the high counts are confirmed then remedial action is indicated. However, without high risk scores from the sanitary inspection it may be hard to identify where and how to improve the source, and a more thorough inspection should be undertaken at the time of the re-sampling.

If the sanitary inspection scores and the coliform counts do not give a general linear relationship then there is likely to be an important factor that is not being picked up by the sanitary inspections, or the sampling for coliforms is flawed. The sanitary inspection method and sampling procedures should be reviewed.

Field experience of the use of sanitary inspections shows that more often moderate to high risk scores are not borne out by observed faecal contamination. Observed deterioration of the plinth, apron, drainage or pump fixing may not yet have become a pollution pathway or, if it has, the sanitary seal below may be doing its job. Alternatively, inspectors may be unnecessarily scoring risk factors and, thereby overestimating the risk of pollution.

The results of sanitary inspections and microbial analyses have also been used to assess whether pollution is derived more from poorly sited or constructed sanitation facilities than from ingress of polluted water around the supply itself; i.e. comparing the aquifer pathway and the local pathway. Statistical approaches for relating individual risk factors to water quality measurements range from reporting frequency of risks in relation to water

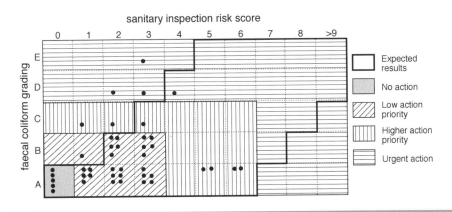

Figure 8.7 Combined sanitary inspection and faecal coliform grading, handpumps >10 m deep, Indonesia.
Source: Lloyd and Helmer 1991.

quality targets, to the use of contingency tables and logistic regression (see resources listed at the end of the chapter). Using this approach, leaching from onsite sanitation was found to be the more important in rural areas of Moldova (Melian et al. 1999) and Karachi (Rahman 1996) whereas poor sanitary completion was the dominant factor in parts of Guinea (Gelinas et al. 1996), Kenya, Mozambique and Uganda (Barrett et al. 2000; Howard et al. 2003). Where the relationship between sanitary inspection risk factors and microbiological analyses is less clear, then other factors such as rainfall and population density (as an indicator of faecal loading) may be important.

Although sanitary inspections are clearly useful, nevertheless, the results need to be interpreted with the following factors in mind:

- Risk factors are treated as having equal weighting, although in practice this is unlikely to be the case.
- Some risk factors are less important in some supply types than others.
- Some supply types are more difficult to protect than others.
- Account has to be taken of the fact that boreholes and wells are likely to be installed in different pollution risk environments – i.e. dug wells where water tables are shallower.
- Account has to be taken of the pollution vulnerability of the aquifer when comparing different supply types, locations or projects.

8.3.5 Testing microbiological quality

In the ideal situation, a laboratory infrastructure and sampling capacity is established which allows samples for microbiological analysis to be returned to central, provincial or district laboratories within a few hours of being taken. In practice, in countries poorly served by roads and transport links (especially those with rural populations dispersed over large areas) it is just not feasible to meet the high personnel and transport costs required. The resulting problems of sample storage and preservation often, therefore, rule out this approach, and simple but robust and reliable field kits have been developed for routine microbiological testing of faecal coliform indicators, and these are now widely used. Almost all comprise a form of portable incubator powered by a rechargeable battery to test for faecal coliforms using the membrane filtration method (Bartram and Balance 1996).

The use of field kits may allow local project staff and communities to be involved in the monitoring. Also, since the results are available quickly it is easier to carry out necessary remedial action than if samples had to be sent to a remote laboratory. The use of field kits is likely to mean that, in general, a smaller number of analyses are undertaken at a larger number of sites, and this may be especially useful for dispersed, rural groundwater supplies.

However, it also may mean that, within a monitoring programme, a larger number of people are carrying out the sampling and analysis, so the training requirements may actually be greater than for a laboratory-based approach. This is an important consideration to remember, as the perception might be that 'simple' and portable field test kits mean a lesser need for training.

Detailed descriptions of field kits and sampling procedures can be found in the relevant literature (see resources at the end of the chapter) and in the manufacturers' manuals for specific kits. There are, however, some key points of guidance that are generally applicable (Howard 2002):

- Adequate preparation is essential for successful fieldwork. The kit should be checked, the relevant parts sterilized and sufficient consumables and reporting sheets packed.
- A realistic sampling itinerary should be planned. Many kits can incubate to 16 samples at once, but as the filters should be left only for between 1 and 4 hours, this leaves a 3-hour sampling period, including travel between sites. Sampling should not be rushed, however, and it is better to take fewer samples whose results are reliable rather than many that are unreliable.
- Great care must be taken in sterilizing the equipment before setting out for the field and in maintaining sterile conditions during sampling.
- Most field kits enable other water quality surveillance parameters to be measured at the same time, such as pH, turbidity and chlorine residuals (see Table 8.6).

Table 8.6 Some of the additional measurements made by field microbiological kits

Turbidity	A measure of the suspended solids present in the water. Important because bacteria are often attached to suspended particles, and high turbidity may reduce the effectiveness of chlorination (Table 8.1). Characteristic of rapid infiltration through karstic aquifers in the rainy season
Disinfection residual	Only applies to supplies that have been disinfected by chlorination. A small amount, the 'chlorine residual', is left in the water to safeguard against contamination during distribution, and should be detectable. Absence when expected may reflect inadequate chlorination and should be followed up
pH	If the pH is too high, chlorination will be less effective as some of the chlorine reacts to try to restore the pH to neutral. Low pH may promote mobility of metals and other parameters. Optimum pH range 6.5–8.5 (Table 8.1) but some hydrogeological environments, e.g. weathered crystalline basement, are characterised by groundwater with natural pH as low as 4.5–5.0

8.4 Chemical quality constraints on water supply

8.4.1 Natural, background or baseline groundwater quality

Groundwater has traditionally been regarded as having good natural quality. For most of the geological environments described in the manual this is true, but this does not mean that natural groundwater quality is always good. The natural quality can vary from one rock type to another and also within aquifers along groundwater flow paths. Because groundwater movement can be slow, and residence times long, there is scope for chemical interaction between the water and the rock material through which it passes.

Natural groundwater quality changes start in the soil, where infiltrating rainfall dissolves carbon dioxide to produce weak carbonic acid which can remove soluble minerals from the underlying rocks. At the same time, soil organisms consume some of the oxygen dissolved in the rainfall.

In temperate and humid climates, groundwater in the outcrop areas of aquifers is often low in overall chemical content, with igneous rocks usually having less dissolved constituents than sedimentary rocks. In arid and semi-arid regions, evapotranspiration rates are much higher, recharge is less, flow paths longer, and residence times much greater – this results in much higher levels of natural mineralization (often dominated by sodium and chloride). In some desert regions, even if groundwater can be found, it may be so salty as to be undrinkable, and the difficulty of meeting even the most basic domestic requirements can have serious impacts on health and livelihoods. The outcome of all of these processes is that the background or baseline quality of groundwater, unaffected by the impact of human activities, varies considerably.

Nine major chemical constituents – sodium (Na), calcium (Ca), magnesium (Mg), potassium (K), bicarbonate (HCO_3), chloride (Cl), sulphate (SO_4), nitrate (NO_3) and silicon (Si) – make up about 99 per cent of the solute content of natural groundwaters. The concentrations of these constituents give groundwaters their hydrochemical characterization, and the proportions reflect the geological origin and groundwater flow regime. However, it is the presence (or absence) of the remaining 1 per cent – the minor and trace elements – that can occasionally give rise to health problems or make the water unacceptable for human use. Figure 8.8 indicates which chemicals are essential for humans and which are harmful.

Geology controls much of the natural distribution of chemicals in the environment: particular chemicals are associated with particular rock types and it may be possible to estimate the likelihood of occurrence of certain chemicals on the basis of the underlying geology. In addition, natural variations in pH and oxygen status are important and conditions of concern are not restricted to deep environments. Extremes of (low or high) pH or the absence of oxygen (called **reducing conditions**) can promote the

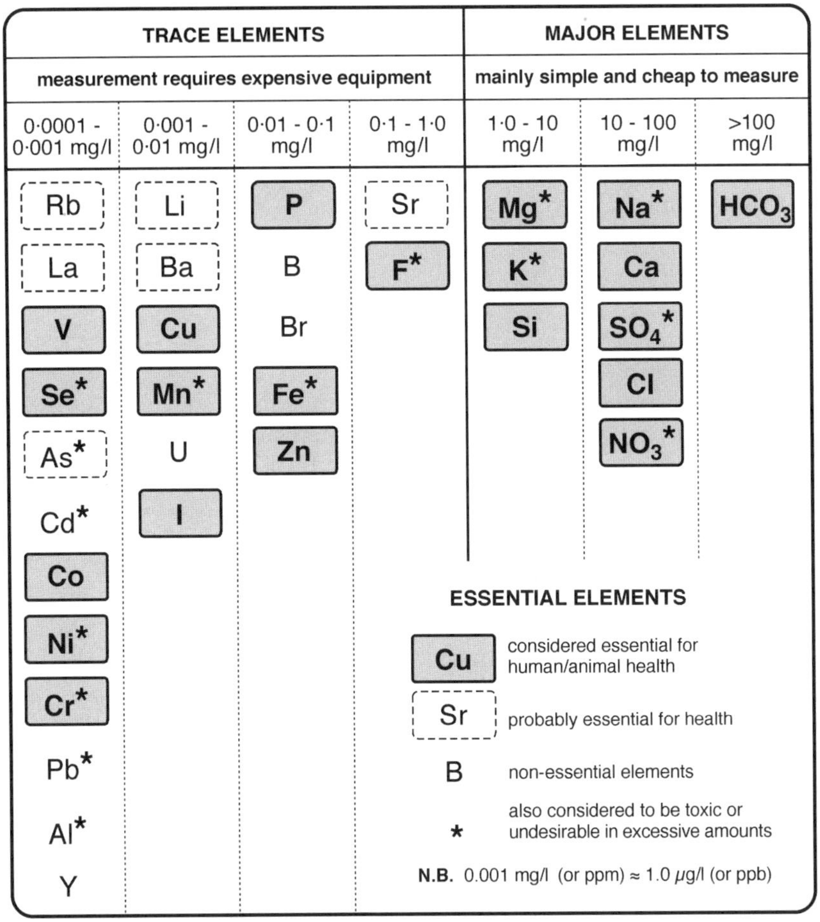

TRACE ELEMENTS				MAJOR ELEMENTS		
measurement requires expensive equipment				mainly simple and cheap to measure		
0·0001 - 0·001 mg/l	0·001 - 0·01 mg/l	0·01 - 0·1 mg/l	0·1 - 1·0 mg/l	1·0 - 10 mg/l	10 - 100 mg/l	>100 mg/l
Rb	Li	P	Sr	Mg*	Na*	HCO_3
La	Ba	B	F*	K*	Ca	
V	Cu	Br		Si	SO_4*	
Se*	Mn*	Fe*			Cl	
As*	U	Zn			NO_3*	
Cd*	I					
Co						
Ni*						
Cr*						
Pb*						
Al*						
Y						

ESSENTIAL ELEMENTS

Cu — considered essential for human/animal health

Sr — probably essential for health

B — non-essential elements

* — also considered to be toxic or undesirable in excessive amounts

N.B. 0.001 mg/l (or ppm) ≈ 1.0 μg/l (or ppb)

Figure 8.8 Health effects of different constituents found in groundwater.
Source: Foster et al. (2000); Edmunds and Smedley (1996)

mobilization of metals and other parameters of health significance such as arsenic.

In this section we discuss the main chemicals in groundwater that can cause health problems: arsenic and fluoride (the greatest problems of all inorganic constituents); nitrate (mainly from sanitation or agriculture) and metals which can be mobilized when the pH is extreme.

First, however, it is worth mentioning an important community health problem related to drinking-water quality – iodine deficiency. Iodine is essential for a healthy diet (Figure 8.8) but the rocks of the earth's crust are relatively depleted in iodine, compared to the higher concentrations in the oceans. Rainfall originating from the oceans has adequate amounts of iodine compared to continental rain; therefore the problem is largely one of the continental interiors. The scale of the problem is large, and it has been estimated that up to 1 000 million people are at risk from iodine deficiency, of whom some 200–300 million suffer from goitre and some 6 million may be affected by cretinism. Adding iodine to table salt is the most common way of alleviating the problem.

8.4.2 Fluoride

Health effects

Fluoride is essential for healthy living (Figure 8.8) and hence fluoride causes health concerns when concentrations in drinking-water are too low as well as when they are too high. Fluoride has been found to have a significant mitigating effect against dental caries and it is widely accepted that some fluoride presence in drinking-water is beneficial. Optimal concentrations are around 1 mg/litre. However, chronic ingestion of concentrations much greater than the WHO guideline value of 1.5 mg/litre (Table 8.1) is linked with development of dental fluorosis and, in extreme cases, skeletal fluorosis. High doses have also been linked to cancer, although the evidence for this is much less clear.

Based on experience in Sri Lanka, one of the affected countries, Dissanayake (1991) summarized the likely impacts from long-term consumption of fluoride-bearing water as:

<0.5 mg/litre: dental caries
0.5–1.5 mg/litre promotes dental health
1.5–4 mg/litre dental fluorosis
>4 mg/litre dental and skeletal fluorosis
>10 mg/litre crippling skeletal fluorosis

Dental fluorosis is by far the most common health effect and, as it has greatest impact on growing teeth, children under the age of 7 are particularly vulnerable. So, if children in a project area seem to have very yellow or brown mottled teeth, then this could indicate that fluorosis is a problem and the water should be tested for fluoride. In practice, other factors such as general health and nutritional status also have an impact.

Occurrence in groundwater

The dominant controls on fluoride concentrations in groundwater are:

- geology
- contact times with fluoride minerals
- groundwater chemical composition
- climate.

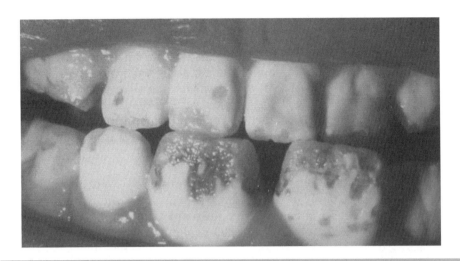

Figure 8.9 Example of dental fluorosis.
Photo: © Vladislav Poverosnuk.

Fluoride in water derives mainly from dissolution of natural minerals in the rocks and soils through which it passes. The most common fluorine-bearing minerals are fluorite, apatite and micas, and fluoride problems tend to occur where these elements are most abundant in the host rocks. Groundwaters from crystalline rocks, especially granites, are particularly susceptible to fluoride build-up because they often contain abundant fluoride-bearing minerals. Alkaline granites rich in potassium and sodium present a special problem in East Africa. In active volcanic terrains, fluoride in groundwater may also derive from mixing with fluids from hot springs and volcanic gases, which can contain concentrations of several tens to hundreds of milligrams of fluoride per litre. In contrast, some sandstones have very low concentrations of fluorine and hence resident groundwaters may be low in fluoride.

Reaction times with aquifer minerals are also important. High fluoride concentrations can build up in groundwaters that have long residence times in the host aquifers. Surface waters usually have low concentrations, as do most shallow groundwaters from hand-dug wells as they represent young, recently infiltrated, rainwater. Deeper (older) groundwaters from boreholes are more likely to contain high concentrations of fluoride. Exceptions can occur locally in active volcanic areas where both surface water and shallow groundwaters can have high concentrations derived from hydrothermal activity. High fluoride concentrations are also a feature of arid climatic conditions where groundwater flow is slow and reaction times between water and rocks are enhanced. Fluoride build-up is less pronounced in the humid tropics because of high rainfall inputs and their diluting effect on groundwater chemical composition.

A low calcium concentration in groundwater is one of the major controls on the concentrations of fluoride. Calcium [Ca^{2+}] limits the fluoride [F^-] concentrations in the water by forming the mineral calcium fluoride (CaF_2). Therefore, high-fluoride groundwaters typically (though not always) have sodium and bicarbonate as the dominant dissolved constituents, with relatively low calcium and magnesium concentrations. Such water types also generally have high pH values (>7) and these can be useful proxy indicators of potential problems but, where fluoride problems are anticipated, the parameter itself will need to be measured.

Most groundwaters have low or acceptable concentrations of fluoride (<1.5 mg/litre), but high-fluoride groundwaters are found in many parts of the developing world, and many millions of people rely on groundwater with concentrations above the WHO guideline value. The worst affected areas are arid parts of northern China (Inner Mongolia), India, Sri Lanka, West Africa (Ghana, Ivory Coast, Senegal), North Africa (Algeria), South Africa, East African Rift (Kenya, Uganda, Tanzania, Ethiopia), northern Mexico and central Argentina. In the early 1980s, it was estimated that around 260 million people worldwide (in 30 countries) were drinking water with more than 1 mg/litre of fluoride (Smet 1990). In India alone, endemic fluorosis is thought to affect around 60 million people and is a major problem in 17 out of the country's 22 states, especially Rajastan, Andra Pradesh, Tamil Nadu, Gujarat and Uttar Pradesh. In Sri Lanka, fluoride problems have a strong geographical control linked to climatic conditions, with high-fluoride waters being restricted to the dry zone on the eastern side of the island (Dissanayake 1991).

Testing for fluoride

Simple fluoride analysis can be carried out by colorimetry or ion-selective electrode. Low-cost pocket colorimeters are available for field testing of fluoride and can be supplied as kits with reagent solutions. Alternatively, the ion-selective electrode is a rapid and accurate test of free fluoride concentrations and also requires relatively little equipment (fluoride and reference electrodes, ion meter, standard solutions). It is not strictly a field test technique as the electrode requires pre-calibration using known standard solutions, and samples are therefore best analysed in batches in a local laboratory.

Fluoride removal

Most low-technology methods of fluoride removal rely on precipitation or adsorption/ion-exchange processes. Probably the best-known and established method is the Nalgonda technique, commonly used in India, in which a combination of alum and lime, together with bleaching powder, is added to high-fluoride water. The mixture is stirred and left to settle, and fluoride is subsequently removed by flocculation, sedimentation and filtration. The method can be used at domestic scale (in buckets) or community scale (fill-and-draw type defluoridation plants), has moderate costs and uses materials that are usually easily available. Other precipitation methods include the use of gypsum, dolomite or calcium chloride. Most of the methods (except gypsum) are capable of reducing fluoride in treated water to below the WHO guideline value.

The most common ion-exchange removal methods are activated carbon, activated alumina, ion-exchange resins (e.g. Defluoron-2), plant carbon, clay minerals, crushed bone or bone char. Activated alumina and bone materials are among the most effective appropriate-technology removal methods, but have drawbacks: activated alumina may not always be available or affordable, and bone products are not readily acceptable in many cultures. Other highly efficient methods of removal include electrodialysis and reverse osmosis. These are technically difficult and expensive, and are less suitable for application in developing countries. Most methods designed for village-scale fluoride removal have some drawbacks in terms of removal efficiency, cost, local availability of materials, chemistry of resultant treated water and disposal of treatment chemicals. Local circumstances will dictate which methods, if any, are the most appropriate. In practice, remediation techniques meet with varying degrees of success, depending on efficacy, user acceptance, ease of maintenance, degree of community participation, availability and cost of raw materials.

Alternatively, water quality can potentially be improved by careful siting boreholes or wells, or by groundwater management. Factors to be considered in choosing sites are local geology and local information about variations in groundwater fluoride concentration with depth (however, it should be appreciated that deeper boreholes may eventually draw shallow fluoride-bearing water down to greater depths, and vice versa). Fluoride-affected areas are often quite extensive, so that finding suitable alternative sites close enough to the users may not be feasible. Management options include optimizing pumping rates (especially where there exists the possibility of mixing of groundwater with deep hydrothermal solutions, enhanced at high pumping rates), and possibilities for artificial recharge of low-fluoride surface water to produce dilution within the aquifer.

8.4.3 Arsenic

Health effects

Arsenic has long been recognized as a toxin and carcinogen. Long-term ingestion of high concentrations from drinking-water can give rise to a number of health problems, particularly skin disorders such as pigmentation changes (dark/light skin spots) and keratosis (warty nodules, usually on the hands and feet). Additional symptoms include more serious dermatological problems (e.g. skin cancer and Bowen's disease); cardiovascular problems (hypertension and heart disease) and Raynaud's syndrome; blackfoot disease and gangrene; neurological, respiratory, renal and hepatic diseases as well as diabetes mellitus. Internal cancers, particularly of the lung, bladder, liver, prostate and kidney have also been linked with arsenic in drinking-water (Smith et al. 1998). It can take years for arsenic-related health problems to become apparent, which helps to explain why many of the problems in developing countries have only recently emerged despite prolonged ground-water use. Many of the advanced and most serious clinical symptoms are incurable. Others can be treated if a supply of low-arsenic drinking-water is provided at a relatively early stage. Early detection of arsenic in drinking-water and provision of low-arsenic alternatives is therefore critical to health, and the element warrants special monitoring in susceptible groundwaters.

Following the accumulation of evidence for the chronic toxicological effects of arsenic in drinking-water, the recommended and regulatory limits of many authorities have been reduced. The WHO guideline value for arsenic in drinking-water was reduced in 1993 from 50 µg/litre to 10 µg/litre, and the US and EC standards have been similarly reduced (Table 8.1). The figure is based largely on analytical capability, although from risk alone it would probably be lower still. At present, most developing countries continue to use 50 µg/litre as a national standard often because of limited analytical capability.

Occurrence in groundwater

Arsenic is mobilized in the environment by a combination of natural processes such as weathering reactions, biological activity and volcanic emissions, as well as through a range of human activities, including mining, industry and agricultural use of arsenical pesticides. It occurs naturally in a number of geological environments, and is common in active volcanic regions where it is present in some geothermal fluids. It occurs in sulphide minerals precipitated from hydrothermal fluids, in pyrite accumulated in sedimentary environments, and in association with iron oxides which are also common in sedimentary environments. The occurrence of arsenic in groundwater is complex – only an introduction can be given here – and more detailed information can be found in the resources given at the end of the chapter.

Of the various sources of arsenic in the environment, drinking-water probably poses the greatest threat to human health. Groundwaters are generally more vulnerable to accumulation of high arsenic concentrations than surface waters because of the increased contact between water and rocks, and most (as yet) unidentified high-arsenic occurrences are likely to be in groundwater. Groundwaters usually have arsenic concentrations below 10 µg/litre but they may exceed 1 mg/litre in some conditions (Smedley and Kinniburgh 2001). Most high-arsenic groundwaters are naturally derived, either due to the oxidation/reduction and pH conditions in aquifers or due to inputs from local geothermal sources.

Figure 8.10 Woman in Bangladesh with Keratosis as a result of drinking water with a high arsenic concentration.
Photo: BGS, © NERC 2002.

Arsenic problems may also occur in areas affected by mining of coal and metals associated with sulphide minerals. Both mining effluent and geo-thermal waters often have arsenic concentrations in the milligram/litre range and can cause major increases in concentrations in surface waters and groundwaters. Unlike affected major aquifers, these tend to be relatively localized and easily identified. Contamination from industrial sources may also be severe locally, but such cases are comparatively rare.

Arsenic forms anionic (negatively charged) species in water which are stable in soluble form at the neutral to alkaline pH (6.5–8.5) characteristic of most groundwaters. However, under normal pH conditions, arsenic is strongly adsorbed onto sediments and soils, particularly iron oxides, as well as aluminium and manganese oxides and clays. These are common con-stituents of aquifers and are the reason why most groundwaters have low arsenic concentrations. At elevated pH (for example in the loess aquifers of Argentina) arsenic species are less strongly adsorbed to mineral surfaces and concentrations in groundwater can be a problem.

Arsenic occurs in two oxidation states in water. In reduced (no oxygen, anaerobic) conditions, it is dominated by the reduced form, arsenite, As(III) and in oxidizing conditions by the oxidized form, arsenate, As(V). Arsenate is strongly adsorbed and is therefore less mobile than arsenite.

High arsenic concentrations in groundwater are therefore mainly found where adsorption is naturally inhibited under either two aquifer conditions:

- Strongly reducing (no oxygen, anaerobic) groundwaters where arsenite dominates and hence adsorption to iron oxides is less favourable. Iron oxides themselves may also dissolve in such conditions, which may release further arsenic.
- Oxidizing (aerobic) aquifers with high pH (>8), typically restricted to arid or semi-arid environments. Such groundwaters commonly also have high concentrations of other potentially toxic elements such as fluoride, boron, uranium, vanadium, nitrate and selenium.

The precise mechanisms of arsenic release in groundwater are not yet fully understood but two further criteria appear to be necessary for the development of regionally significant high arsenic concentrations in groundwaters from these environments. Affected sedimentary aquifers recognized so far tend to be geologically young (i.e. sediments deposited in the last few thousand years), and contain groundwaters characterized by slow flow conditions, either because of low hydraulic gradients (low-lying areas such as flat alluvial basins and the lower parts of deltas) or lack of active rainfall and recharge (arid areas, closed basins).

Examples of anaerobic aquifers affected by arsenic include the alluvial and deltaic aquifers of Bangladesh, West Bengal and Nepal (formed by erosion of the Himalaya in the last few thousand years), and alluvial and lake sediment aquifers of northern China, deltaic sediments of Vietnam, alluvial sediments of Cambodia, parts of Taiwan and the Danube basin in Hungary. Examples of oxidizing aquifers, where elevated pH is associated with arsenic problems, are the loess aquifers of central Argentina and parts of Chile (formed over the last few thousand years largely by wind erosion of Andean rocks) and alluvial aquifers of northern Mexico and parts of the south-western USA (Smedley and Kinniburgh 2002).

Arsenic problems in mining and mineralized areas occur because of the oxidation of sulphide minerals (especially pyrite and arsenopyrite) which can contain very high concentrations of arsenic and which oxidize by aeration, particularly by the disturbances created by the mining activities themselves. Arsenic problems have been recorded in sulphide-mining areas in many parts of the world, but are particularly well documented in parts of Thailand, Ghana, the USA and Canada.

Areas where potential future arsenic problems may be identified include:

- large low-lying present-day alluvial and deltaic basins composed of young sediment where groundwater flow is slow or stagnant and where anaerobic conditions prevail (possibilities include the lower reaches of the Indus valley, Pakistan, the Mekong, and possibly the lower reaches of the Nile and Niger deltas)

- inland basins with young sediments in arid and semi-arid areas (such as unsurveyed areas of northern China)
- sulphide-mineral rich areas, particularly metal-and coal-mining areas (occurring in basement aquifers in for example parts of Africa, including Ghana, South Africa, Zimbabwe and India)
- geothermal areas (possibilities include the East African Rift, although no arsenic data are known for the region).

Features of the different types of high-arsenic groundwater environment are shown in Figure 8.11.

Field testing for arsenic

Arsenic has traditionally not been included on lists of elements routinely analysed by water quality laboratories in developing countries and so some high-arsenic groundwaters undoubtedly remain to be identified. Discovery of arsenic contamination on a large scale in Bangladesh has highlighted the need for a rapid assessment of the situation in similar aquifers worldwide, and the revision of drinking-water standards and guidelines for arsenic has also prompted the need for its inclusion in water quality monitoring programmes.

Aquifers with identified arsenic problems typically have a high degree of variability in concentrations, both laterally within relatively short distances (metres to kilometres), and with depth. This means that ideally, in susceptible aquifers, each source used for drinking-water needs to be tested to ensure its fitness for use. In affected aquifers such as those of Bangladesh, this means several million boreholes. Laboratory analysis is preferable, but difficult on such a large scale. Field test kits are an alternative, but need to be simple, rapid, inexpensive and reliable to use. Most field test kits employ the reduction of arsenite and arsenate by zinc to give arsine gas, which is then used to produce a stain on mercuric bromide paper. Such tests have had poor sensitivity, being barely able to analyse concentrations reliably at less than 100 µg/litre. Test kits have improved significantly in recent years in response to the growing appreciation of the extent of the problem and the lowering of guideline values and the best can now measure down to less than 10 µg/litre. Even so, stringent quality control of analyses using field test kits needs to be carried out by a structured programme of laboratory cross-checking.

Arsenic concentrations may change (often increase) with pumping as groundwater from further away moves towards the borehole intake. Therefore, samples should ideally be taken from pumping boreholes and monitored regularly.

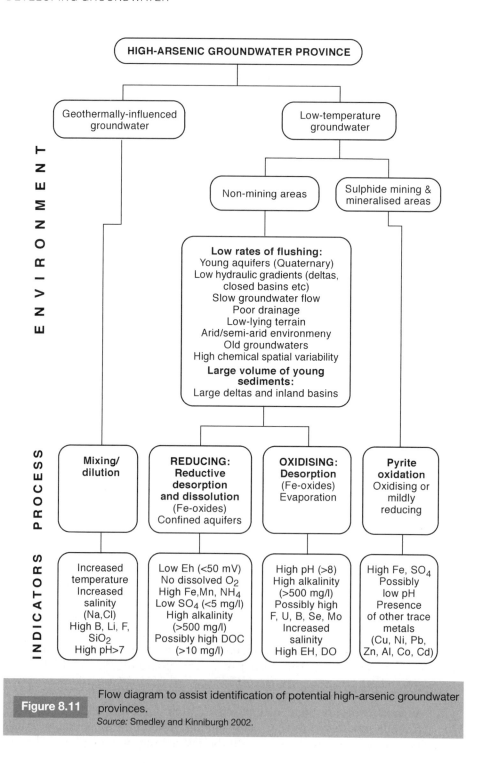

Figure 8.11 Flow diagram to assist identification of potential high-arsenic groundwater provinces.
Source: Smedley and Kinniburgh 2002.

Remediation techniques and supply of low-arsenic drinking-water

A number of solutions have been suggested for arsenic-affected areas, but no single solution is appropriate to all: social and community preferences, as well as technical feasibility, need to be taken into account. In areas where arsenic problems may be suspected but data are lacking, a broad-scale randomized survey of selected boreholes is required to identify the scale of the potential problem. In areas of known arsenic problems such as Bangladesh and West Bengal, effort is being concentrated on the identification of safe boreholes by sampling – since even in severely affected areas not all wells within a given aquifer are contaminated at greater than the national standard concentration.

Groundwater should not be abandoned completely without further evaluation, because surface water sources without high arsenic may suffer from gross bacteriological pollution. In Bangladesh, a comprehensive study has shown that of some 3500 groundwater samples collected nationally, 25 per cent were above 50 µg/litre and 35 per cent above 10 µg/litre (BGS and DPHE 2001). There is also the possibility of selective use of uncontaminated sources for drinking and cooking and contaminated sources for washing and other domestic uses, but in some areas such a high percentage of boreholes may be contaminated that other alternatives need to be found.

The most commonly used methods for treating high-arsenic waters at community and municipal level are the addition of coagulants such as alum or potassium permanganate. Alum is readily available in most countries but has the drawback of leaving residual aluminium and sulphate in treated waters and is not very efficient for waters above pH 7.5. Alum is being promoted for domestic use in Bangladesh using a two-bucket (alum, potassium permanganate and sand) system. Potassium permanganate is added to the reducing waters to oxidize ferrous iron to ferric iron and arsenite to arsenate, and thereby facilitate arsenic removal (since arsenate is easily adsorbed to iron oxides). Ferric chloride can also be used but is more expensive. The efficacy of the various treatments depends on a number of factors, including the original arsenic concentrations and the overall water chemistry. Activated alumina is also used in some areas to remove arsenic by adsorption, though this is also expensive and not so suitable for developing countries. Treatment of affected groundwater in Bangladesh and West Bengal is also being tried at household level using pots with various adsorption media (e.g. sand coated with iron oxide, gravel, clay, brick chips) with varying success.

For iron-rich, anaerobic (oxygen-poor) groundwaters, arsenic may be removed by simply leaving water for a period (overnight) to allow aeration and settling of iron oxide (passive sedimentation). However, the efficiency of arsenic removal by this method is highly variable and it is less effective than the adsorption methods referred to above. In Bangladesh, removal efficiency of about 30 per cent has been shown using this simple method, but efficiency varies as a function of iron concentrations, arsenic concentrations and arsenic/iron ratios. Removal will be less effective where arsenic concentrations and arsenic/iron ratios are high. The method is not effective for aerobic (oxygen rich) groundwaters because iron concentrations are invariably low. All village-scale treatment methods require considerable care to avoid bacterial contamination.

In thick alluvial sequences such as those in Bangladesh and West Bengal, older aquifers at greater depth (>150 m) contain groundwater with mainly low arsenic concentrations and have in places been developed for drinking-water supply. The great spatial variability in arsenic concentrations also offers some possibilities for alternative siting at a local, village scale. However, lateral and depth variations in arsenic concentrations are not universally predictable in different aquifers. For example, the widespread occurrence of low-arsenic groundwaters at depth in Bangladesh and West Bengal is not yet confirmed, and requires a detailed investigation of subsurface hydrogeological and geochemical conditions. Provision of deeper boreholes involves significant extra cost, and current understanding of the spatial variation at a local scale does not allow accurate prediction of the locations of low-arsenic groundwater sources. In reducing (anaerobic) aquifers, shallow, open hand-dug wells often have low arsenic concentrations whilst boreholes only a few metres deeper have much higher concentrations. The difference is probably due to maintenance of aerobic conditions in the open well and also to regular flushing of the shallowest parts of the aquifer close to the water table by recharge of recent rainwater. Arsenic concentrations below 50 µg/litre are typical of hand-dug wells in Bangladesh and West Bengal as well as in Ghana, but careful attention needs to be given to bacteriological quality of water from open dug wells, as they are more vulnerable to pollution from the surface.

In areas with alternative sources of water, it is possible to develop them, provided that they do not suffer from gross bacteriological contamination. In areas with sufficient rainfall, rainwater harvesting may be possible, at least seasonally. Even if this is only possible for drinking and cooking water for 6 months of the year, it can significantly reduce the long-term exposure to arsenic. Surface water usually has low arsenic concentrations (generally much less than 10 µg/litre) but may suffer from serious bacterial contamination. On a larger scale, piped-water supplies distributing treated river water are being installed in some arsenic-affected areas (e.g. West Bengal). In time, this may be the most secure and reliable approach of all, but it is expensive and not suitable immediately for most large, dispersed rural communities.

8.4.4 Iron and manganese

High concentrations of iron and manganese in groundwater are a widespread and sometimes underrated constraint on rural water supply. Both iron and manganese may cause rejection of water by consumers because of the colour that develops when iron changes from the ferrous to the ferric state on contact with air (and therefore oxygen). When this happens the water can stain clothes, utensils and food, and may also taste bitter. Although this is not of direct health significance, health problems may arise if communities decide not to use these improved supplies because of the staining and taste, and return instead to old polluted sources. WHO has therefore suggested that concentrations in drinking-water above 0.3 mg/litre for iron and 0.1 mg/litre for manganese may give rise to complaints from consumers, and has set a provisional health guideline for manganese of 0.5 mg/litre (Table 8.1).

Iron and manganese can be found in most hydrogeological environments, but are only dissolved in groundwater under reducing (anaerobic) conditions. Solubility also increases in low-pH groundwaters. Given the correct conditions, concentrations of dissolved iron may reach more than 10 mg/litre. Weathered crystalline basement regions are particularly prone to low pH and high iron concentrations.

High iron content is easily detected. As the water is drawn to the surface it may be completely clear, but on exposure to the atmosphere the dissolved iron is oxidized to produce an objectionable reddish-brown colour and with time a precipitate forms.

There is evidence that the use of galvanized iron pump components and mild steel borehole casing can make the situation worse, adding iron and zinc to the water by corrosion. Therefore, iron concentrations in water drawn from boreholes with a high ferrous metal component may increase with time even if an analysis at the time of construction indicated an acceptable concentration. Research in the weathered basement aquifers in Malawi, showed that boreholes with PVC casing and plastic pump components produced water with significantly lower iron concentrations than their equivalents with mild steel and galvanized iron in the same hydrochemical environment (Lewis and Chilton 1984). Corrosion of steel casing and cast iron pump components is a major problem in areas of aggressive groundwater with low pH, reducing conditions or high salinity, and has a major impact on borehole life, handpump performance and maintenance costs.

8.4.5 Nitrate

Health effects

The primary health concern regarding nitrate and nitrite is the occurrence of methaemoglobinaemia, the so-called **blue baby syndrome**. Nitrate is converted to nitrite in the stomach of infants, and nitrite can oxidize haemoglobin (Hb) to methaemoglobin (metHb), which is unable to transport oxygen around the body. This reduced oxygen transport becomes clinically manifest when metHb concentrations reach 10 per cent or more of normal Hb concentrations, compared to the normal 1–3 per cent. The condition, called methaemoglobinaemia, produces symptoms of lethargy, shortness of breath and the bluish skin colour and causes cyanosis and, at higher concentrations, asphyxia and death. Reduction of nitrate to nitrite by gastric bacteria is greater in infants because of low gastric acidity, and can reach 100 per cent compared to 10 per cent in adults and children more than 1 year old. The concentration of nitrate in breast milk is relatively low, but bottle-fed infants of less than 3 months are at risk because of the potential for exposure to nitrate/nitrite in drinking-water and the relatively high intake of water in relation to body weight. The greater reduction of nitrate to nitrite in young infants is not well quantified, but it appears that gastro-intestinal infections can increase the conversion from nitrate to nitrite, and health problems are therefore more likely where bacteriological quality of drinking-water is also poor.

Although many studies have been carried out, the weight of evidence is strongly against there being an association between nitrite and nitrate exposure in humans and the risk of cancer (WHO 1998). Based on the risk of methaemoglobinaemia in infants, the WHO has set a drinking-water guideline value of 50 mg/litre for nitrate and a provisional value of 3 mg/litre for nitrite (Table 8.1). Further, because of the possibility that nitrate and nitrite could occur together in drinking-water, the sum of the ratios of the concentrations of each to its guideline value should not exceed 1.

Occurrence in groundwater

Nitrate is one of the most commonly identified groundwater pollutants. It rarely originates from rocks, but indicates pollution from human activities. Nitrate (NO_3^-) is the main form in which nitrogen occurs in groundwater, although dissolved nitrogen may also be present as nitrite (NO_2^-), ammonium (NH_4^+), nitrous oxide (N_2O) and organic nitrogen. The chemical and biological processes of the nitrogen cycle govern the concentration, form and behaviour of nitrogen in water. In this cycle, atmospheric nitrogen gas is converted to organic nitrogen compounds by nitrogen fixers such as blue-green algae and some bacteria, such as those in the root nodules of leguminous plants. Nitrogen in organic form and ammonium can be converted by bacteria under aerobic conditions into nitrite and nitrate, a process termed **nitrification**. Nitrate in anaerobic systems can be reduced by other strains of bacteria to nitrous oxide or nitrogen gas; this is **denitrification**.

The chemical form of nitrogen in groundwater is therefore controlled by the presence or absence of oxygen in the water (known as the **redox condition**). In aerobic water, nitrogen occurs as nitrate or nitrite ions. Nitrate is stable over a considerable range of conditions and is very mobile in water. Concentrations of nitrate in groundwater typically range from 0 to 15 mg/litre NO_3, compared to the guideline value of 50 mg/litre (Table 8.1). Concentrations above 15 mg/litre usually indicate pollution from human activities, but natural concentrations of up to 100 mg/litre have been observed in some arid parts of the world such as the Sahel region of North Africa (Edmunds and Gaye 1997) and the interior of Australia (Barnes et al. 1992). In anaerobic water, nitrogen occurs as ammonium rather than nitrate. Ammonium and organic forms of nitrogen are unstable and ammonium is strongly adsorbed to clay particles, which limits its subsurface mobility. Natural concentrations of ammonium in groundwaters are usually below 0.2 mg/litre. In confined aquifers, if conditions are anaerobic, nitrate is converted to nitrogen gas by denitrification but nitrite or ammonium may persist.

Sources of nitrate pollution in groundwater

Growth in food production in the most rapidly developing countries has been accompanied by rapid increases in nitrogen fertilizer use during recent years, and application rates have tripled since 1975. With this more widespread and more intensive use of fertilizers, however, comes the possibility that the land will receive more nitrogen than the crops can use, and the excess can pollute surface water runoff or drainage, or leach from the store of nitrogen in the soil to underlying aquifers and pollute groundwater. There is a wide variation in nitrate leaching losses from agriculture, resulting from differences in soil and crop types, fertilizer application rates and irrigation practices. High rates of nitrogen leaching from the soil can be anticipated in areas where soils are permeable and aerobic, and nitrogen applications are made to relatively short duration crops, e.g. vegetables or wheat (Figure 8.12).

The nitrogen loading will be greatest where cultivation is intensive and double or triple cropping is practised. Especially high nitrogen leaching can occur from soils where irrigation is excessive and not carefully controlled. Nitrate concentrations well in excess of the 50 mg/litre drinking-water guideline have been observed in groundwater beneath intensively cultivated land in both temperate and tropical regions and for a wide range of hydrogeological environments and crop types. Areas of livestock concentration can also be a source of groundwater pollution by discharge of effluents, leaching from manure heaps, leaking slurry storage pits and slurry or manure spreading. Consideration should always be given to the possibility of nitrate pollution in areas of intensive cultivation or livestock farming.

Sewage and wastewater disposal is also a major source of nitrate in groundwater. Nitrogen is present in sewage in a range of reduced and organic forms, such as ammonia and urea. In rural, peri-urban and many urban areas without water-borne sewerage systems, the major pollution concern is associated with unsewered sanitation units such as septic tanks, cesspits and latrines. Estimates of the likely nitrate concentrations in infiltration from these installations can be made, as shown in Box 8.3.

Figure 8.12 Intensive agriculture on sandy soils can lead to high amounts of nitrate leaching to groundwater.
Photo: © BGS, NERC 1996.

Leachate arising from solid waste disposal is a highly mineralized mixture of inorganic and organic compounds. In humid tropical conditions leachate can be generated in relatively large volumes potentially leading to extensive groundwater plumes. Leachate is generally anaerobic and may contain a high concentration of ammoniacal nitrogen. Such nitrogen is readily absorbed to clay mineral in the aquifer and may not migrate for large distances, but it can also be oxidized in the aquifer, giving rise to high concentrations of nitrate. As an example, groundwater in drinking-water wells in two suburbs of Ibadan and Lagos were found to have very poor water quality, including unacceptable concentrations of nitrate and ammonia, ascribed to local waste disposal sites (Ikem et al 2002). A study at Chiang Mai, Thailand found that even 10 years after an open waste dump had been closed and covered with soil, there was still evidence for pulses of contaminants, included nitrate, moving away from the site in the rainy season. During the dry season the aquifer became anaerobic and nitrate was only detected at a few points (Morris et al. 2003).

Distinguishing sources of nitrate

Because there are several potential sources of nitrate in groundwater, and they may occur together in the same area, it may be desirable to distinguish between them so that pollution control measures are directed at the right source. The simplest indication can come from looking at the ratio of nitrate concentrations and other waste components, such as chloride. The ratio of

BOX 8.3 Estimating nitrogen leaching from unsewered sanitation

Estimates of the possible concentrations of nitrate in local groundwater recharge in areas of unsewered sanitation can be made for aerobic ground-water systems using the following equation derived by Foster and Hirata (1988):

$$C = (4400 \, a \, A \, f)/[0.365 \, A \, U + (10 \, I)]$$

where C is the concentration in mg/litre of nitrate in the recharge (expressed as NO_3), a is the amount in kilograms of nitrogen excreted per person each year (usually about 5 kg), A is the population density in persons/ha, f is the proportion of the excreted nitrogen leached to groundwater (reflects and integrates both the condition of latrines and the vulnerability of under-ground to nitrogen leaching), U is the non-consumptive portion of total water usage in litres per person/day, i.e. the amount returned to the sanitation system, and I is the natural rate of infiltration for the area in mm/year.

Most of the parameters can be easily estimated: the only two that may be difficult are f and I. In shallow aerobic aquifers f is usually in the range of 0.2–0.6 (the higher values for highly fractured aquifers with latrines in poor conditions and lower values for good latrines in fine unconsolidated material). I is the effective rainfall in an area. Some sort of estimate can be given by knowing the rainfall and evaporation.

Example of a rural community:

$a = 5$ kg

$A = 10$ people/ha

$f = 0.4$

$U = 20$ litres per person/day

$I = 200$ mm/a

The concentration of nitrate in the recharge = 42 mg/litre

nitrate to chloride in groundwater affected by unsewered sanitation is often about 2:1. In groundwater affected by nitrate leached from agriculture the ratio is often much higher – sometimes as high as 8:1.

A strong positive correlation between high nitrate and microbial pollution can be taken as an indicator of pollution from sanitation or waste disposal. Boron or optical brighteners from laundry detergents (in domestic waste-water) and zinc (where sewage contains industrial effluent) can also act as indicators that high nitrate concentrations originate from sewage.

More complex methods using nitrogen isotopes can be used to distinguish the potential sources of nitrate contamination (Girard and Hillaire-Marcel

1997). This can be used to distinguish between nitrogen derived from inorganic fertilizers and animal or sewage wastes. Determination of nitrogen stable isotope ratios is very expensive and outside the scope of routine water quality sampling in rural water supply programmes.

Testing for nitrate

Nitrate should be tested for quickly, since it can degrade in the sample bottle. When samples are taken for nitrate it is important that no air is present in the sample bottle, the water has been filtered (using a 0.45-μm filter) and the sample is kept cool.

Test strips are available for use in the field which give semi-quantitative results. These cover the sensitivity range 0–50 mg/litre for NO_3 and 0–3 mg/litre for NO_2. Nitrate can also be determined in the field using an ion-selective electrode. This has a limit of detection of about 0.2 mg/litre, but chloride and bicarbonate interfere when present in concentrations of more than 10 times the nitrate.

8.4.6 Heavy metals

Health effects

The heavy metals for which there are health-based guidelines include cadmium, lead, nickel, chromium and copper. Cadmium is notorious for its high renal toxicity due to its irreversible accumulation in the kidneys. Lead is a strong neurotoxin in unborn, newborn and young children, leading to irreversible impairment of intelligence. Lead easily crosses the placenta. The threshold of neurotoxic concern has decreased over the last 20 years and drinking-water standards and guidelines for lead have been revised accordingly to their present 10 μg/litre (Table 8.1). Nickel has high allergenic potential. Chromium is found in the environment in two states, Cr^{3+} and Cr^{6+}. The latter is toxic and originates only from human activities. Copper is an essential trace element (Figure 8.8) with an optimum daily oral intake of 1–2 mg per person. Concentrations above 2 mg/litre could lead to liver cirrhosis in babies if water of this concentration is used to prepare bottle-feeding formulas.

Sources and occurrence in groundwater

Heavy metals are natural constituents of groundwaters originating from the weathering and solution of numerous minerals. Natural concentrations are typically low – copper 10–20 μg/litre, nickel <10 μg/litre, lead <5 μg/litre, cadmium and chromium <1 μg/litre – but concentrations can increase above guideline values locally in groundwater from rocks containing metal-bearing ores. Metal concentrations in groundwater can be increased by mining, mineral processing, metal smelting and finishing, waste disposal in spoil heaps and tailings ponds and by other industrial processes and waste disposal. The leather-processing industry in particular is a well-documented source of chromium pollution of groundwater. Acidification of soils and rainfall by air pollution lowers pH and may encourage the mobilization of heavy metals.

Heavy metals can only be realistically analysed in a laboratory. To be sure that dissolved rather than suspended particulate or colloidal concentrations are measured, samples should be filtered (using a 0.45-μm filter) and acidified using nitric acid.

8.4.7 Total dissolved solids (TDS)

Groundwater with high TDS is an often unrecognized problem in rural water supply. Table 8.1 has the guideline value of 1000 mg/litre on account of taste. Higher concentrations can taste salty and can turn people away from a supply. However, high TDS can have several other problems: it can cause problem to certain crops, particularly high-value market garden crops; it make it difficult to get soap to lather; and most importantly it can cause serious corrosion of any metal within the borehole. Mild steel casing or rising main can be quickly corroded, rendering the borehole useless. Figure 8.12 show the rising main from a borehole with TDS of 2000 mg/litre after only 1 year.

It is very easy to identify high TDS in a borehole by measuring the SEC (specific electrical conductivity). The SEC measurement in mS/m at 25 °C is multiplied by 0.7 to give a rough estimate of TDS. In high TDS areas, steel fittings should not be used. Plastic casing, rising main and pump fittings should all be considered.

8.4.8 Taking samples for inorganic analysis

Although this chapter is not designed to give a step-by-step guide for sampling groundwater, this section describes some of the general procedures that should be followed for taking samples to characterize the inorganic chemistry. The resources listed at the end of the chapter give more information on taking samples and interpreting the data.

Detailed chemical analysis can only be undertaken in a laboratory, with samples that have been collected in a controlled manner. However, some field measurements are essential to help interpret the data. If a laboratory of sufficient standard is not available in country, then samples may have to be sent abroad for analysis. Once the chemistry of an area is known, then field measurements of key parameters may be sufficient to identify any problems.

Ideally, the source to be sampled should be regularly pumping, so that the water in the borehole is not stale. If the source has not been pumping

Figure 8.13 Corroded rising-main from a high TDS borehole.
Photo: BGS, NERC 1997.

recently, the borehole volume should be emptied three times before taking a sample and all the field measurements should be stable.

Field measurements

- The pH, temperature, SEC and bicarbonate content should always be measured in the field. This is because the pH and bicarbonate concentration will change once the sample has been placed in a bottle.
- Electrical conductivity and pH are measured using meters – it may take several minutes for the meter to stabilize. Bicarbonate is measured using a digital titrator.
- If an airtight connection can be made to the borehole (either by connecting to the discharge hose from a test pump, or the end of a handpump) then the dissolved oxygen content and the *Eh* can be measured (see Figure 8.14). These will give you information about the redox conditions in the aquifer – i.e. if the water is reducing (anaerobic) or oxidizing (aerobic).
- All field equipment should be calibrated daily, and regularly checked through the day. Buffer and standard solutions are required for calibration.

| **Figure 8.14** | Measuring pH and dissolved oxygen with a flow through cell and an airtight connection to the handpump. |

Photo: BGS, NERC 2002.

- After each measurement, the equipment should be washed. If no distilled water is available, then the probes can be washed in the water that is just about to be sampled.
- If a laboratory is not available then certain parameters can be measured in the field using specific equipment: fluoride, nitrate and arsenic can all be adequately measured in the field under optimal conditions.
- As in all fieldwork it is essential to keep a good notebook. The name of the borehole, GPS, date and time, pumping history etc. should all be recorded as well as the method used for taking the sample and any other relevant information.

Taking samples

- All equipment should be thoroughly washed in the sample water (syringe, filter holders, etc.).
- The samples must first be filtered using a 0.45-µm filter. The sample bottle should be thoroughly washed and rinsed three times (including the inside of the lid) in the filtered sample water.
- Two samples should be taken: one that has been filtered and then acidified to keep all the cations in solution, and another that has been filtered but not acidified (for analysis of anions at some laboratories). Aristar grade nitric acid (1 per cent of the volume of the sample)

should be used for acidification; it may be difficult to locate in some countries, but university laboratories often have a supply.

- The sample bottles should be filled right to the top, so that no air is in the bottle, and the lid firmly closed.
- The samples must now be kept cool and out of sunlight. Keeping them in a domestic fridge is normally adequate.
- It is important to label the sample bottle using a permanent (water-proof!) marker. The number, date, whether it has been filtered or acidified, and some of the field data should be included on the label.
- Samples should be transported to the laboratory as soon as possible for analysis.

8.5 Assessing the potential for chemical pollution of groundwater

8.5.1 A framework for defining pollution potential

A logical approach to defining the potential for groundwater to become polluted by human activities is to think of it as the interaction between the **pollutant load** applied to the land surface as a result of human activity and the **aquifer vulnerability**, which is determined by the characteristics of the strata separating the aquifer from the land surface.

This general approach is used the world over to develop groundwater protection strategies. Adopting this approach, it is possible to envisage situations in which the aquifer is highly vulnerable, but there is little or no danger of pollution because there is no pollution load, or vice versa. Both are consistent in practice. The former might occur on an uninhabited coral limestone island, and the latter where an urban area with many small pollution sources is separated from an underlying deep aquifer by a thick sequence of impermeable clays or silts. The interaction is shown simply as a relative assessment of pollution potential in Figure 8.15, which has been modified from that developed by Foster and Hirata (1988). Thus a combination of a high pollutant load and high aquifer vulnerability provides the most extreme pollution potential in the top right corner of the figure.

Whether the pollution potential derived in this way will be translated into serious degradation of water quality at a groundwater supply will depend on several factors. These include the mobility and persistence of the pollutants within the groundwater flow regime and the scope for further dilution in the saturated zone. The economic and financial scale of the impact will depend on the value of the groundwater resources affected, which includes the investment and operating costs in abstracting the water and delivering it to consumers, and the cost of finding alternative supplies, as well as the broader societal and environmental value of the groundwater where, for example, there are many small-scale community or private wells and boreholes in rural areas.

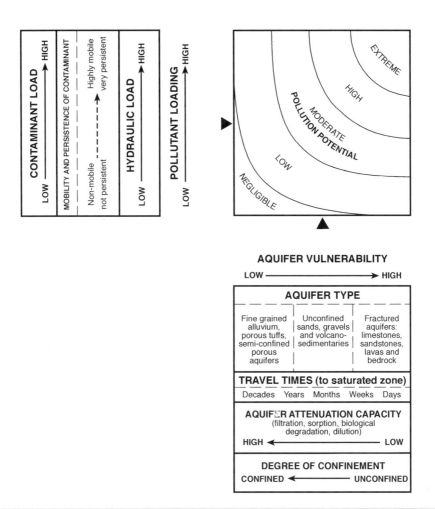

Figure 8.15 Overview of how the factors affecting aquifer vulnerability and contaminant loading combine to indicate pollution potential.

8.5.2 Vulnerability to pollution

The concept of vulnerability to pollution has been in common usage by hydrogeologists for more than 30 years. The general intention was to show that the subsurface environment can protect groundwater from pollution, but that this capacity varies from place to place (Vrba and Zaporozec 1994). Thus the fundamental principle of vulnerability is that some parts of the land surface are intrinsically more vulnerable to pollution than others, and this can be depicted in map form as a function of hydrogeological conditions, usually in relative rather than absolute terms. While this concept has been accorded broad acceptance over the years, there is not really a universally agreed definition. One of the most commonly used is:

Vulnerability comprises the properties of the strata separating a saturated aquifer from the land surface which determine the sensitivity of that aquifer to being adversely affected by pollution originating at the land surface.

This 'intrinsic' vulnerability is determined by the hydrogeological characteristics of the soil and rocks above the water table, and is largely independent of the transport properties of specific contaminants. Many hydrogeologists have commented on the limitations of this approach because every contaminant behaves differently, and some have advocated the use of 'specific' vulnerability maps for individual contaminants or groups of contaminants, such as nitrate, pesticides or atmospheric deposition. However, although it would be more scientifically robust to evaluate specific vulnerability for each individual contaminant, this is impractical as there are neither sufficient data nor adequate human resources to do so (Vrba and Zaporozec 1994; Foster et al. 2002). Specific vulnerability maps are, therefore, rarely prepared, whereas mapping of intrinsic vulnerability is widely established.

Development of a generally accepted definition of vulnerability does not mean that there should always be a standardized approach to its depiction. Hydrogeological environments and user requirements in terms of scales are too diverse to be dealt with in a standardized way. Vulnerability is not an absolute term – it cannot be directly measured. Rather it is a simplification in relative terms of the complex and varied conditions that determine travel times from the ground surface to the water table. Aquifer vulnerability can be subdivided simply into five broad classes (Box 8.4). Extreme vulnerability is associated with aquifers having a high density of open fractures and with shallow water tables, which offer little chance for pollutant attenuation.

BOX 8.4   Broad classification of aquifer vulnerability

- **Extreme:** Vulnerable to most water pollutants with relatively rapid impact in many pollution scenarios.
- **High:** Vulnerable to many pollutants, except those highly absorbed and/or readily transformed, in many pollution scenarios.
- **Moderate:** Vulnerable to some pollutants, but only when continuously discharged or leached.
- **Low:** Only vulnerable to the most persistent pollutants in the long-term, when continuously and widely discharged or leached.
- **Negligible:** Confining beds are present and prevent any significant vertical groundwater flow.

After Foster et al. (2002)

For preliminary assessment purposes, specific areas can be assigned to these broad classes based on information about the hydrogeological environments described in Chapter 2, since they differ greatly in the time taken for recharge entering at the land surface to reach groundwater (Table 8.7).

The main factors affecting intrinsic vulnerability are:

- the physical, chemical and biological composition of the soil
- the physical, chemical and biological characteristics of the geological materials in the unsaturated zone, especially their hydraulic conductivity and ability to transmit water and their capacity to retard or remove pollutants
- the depth to groundwater
- the rainfall and recharge.

Table 8.7 Groundwater pollution vulnerability of the main hydrogeological environments

	Hydrogeological environment	Typical travel times to water-table	Attenuation potential of aquifer	Pollution vulnerability
Weathered crystalline basement	Unconfined	Days–weeks	Low	High–extreme
	Semi-confined	Weeks–years	Moderate	Moderate
Consolidated sedimentary aquifers	Porous sandstones	Weeks–years	High	Moderate–high
	Karstic limestones	Days–weeks	Low	Extreme
	Mudstones	Months–years	High	Moderate
Coastal limestones	Unconfined	Days–weeks	Low–moderate	High–extreme
Major alluvial and coastal basins	Unconfined	Weeks–months	High–moderate	Moderate
	Semi-confined	Years–decades	High	Low
Loess	Unconfined	Days–months	Low–moderate	Moderate–High
Small, dispersed, unconsolidated sediments	Unconfined	Weeks–years	Moderate–low	High–Moderate
Intermontane deposits	Unconfined	Months–years	Moderate	Moderate
	Semi-confined	Years–decades	Moderate	Moderate–low
Extensive volcanic terrains	Lavas	Days–months	Low–moderate	High–extreme
	Ash/lava sequences	Months–years	High	Low

Source: Morris et al. (2003).

The soil zone is usually regarded as one of the principal factors in the assessment of groundwater vulnerability and the first line of defence against pollution. Because of its potential to attenuate a range of pollutants; it plays a critical role when considering vulnerability to diffuse sources of pollution such as agricultural fertilizers, pesticides and acid deposition. The soil has a particularly important position amongst vulnerability factors because the soil itself is vulnerable. The soil's function as a natural protective filter can be damaged rather easily by such routine activities as cultivation and tillage, irrigation, compaction and drainage. Human activities at the land surface can greatly modify the existing natural mechanisms of groundwater recharge and introduce new ones, changing the rate, frequency and quality of groundwater recharge. This is especially the case in arid and semi-arid regions where there may be relatively little and infrequent natural recharge, but also applies to more humid regions.

Most importantly, there are many human activities that might cause pollution in which the soil is removed or otherwise bypassed, and for these the component of protection provided by the soil does not apply. Many of these concerns are dominantly urban, but in the rural water supply context, the hazard from unsewered sanitation has been highlighted already, and disposal of household waste into old brickpits from which the protecting clay layer has been excavated is another example to look out for.

Below the soil, the unsaturated zone is very important in protecting the underlying groundwater, especially where soils are thin and/or poorly developed. The main unsaturated zone properties that are important in vulnerability assessment are the thickness, lithology and vertical hydraulic conductivity of the materials. The thickness depends on the depth to the water table, which can vary significantly due to local topography and also fluctuates seasonally, and both these have to be taken into account when determining thickness. The distribution of hydraulic conductivity and its role in determining groundwater flow rates is particularly important. Porosity, storage properties, and groundwater flow direction may also be important, and another supplementary parameter in some types of aquifers and circumstances may be the depth and degree of weathering of the upper part of the unsaturated zone.

Degree of confinement is also an important factor in determining vulnerability. Concern about groundwater pollution relates primarily to unconfined aquifers, especially where the unsaturated zone is thin because the water table is at shallow depth. Significant risk of pollution may also occur in semi-confined aquifers, if the confining aquitards are relatively thin and permeable. Groundwater supplies drawn from deeper and more fully confined aquifers will normally be affected only by the most persistent pollutants and in the long-term.

The above is intended to provide general awareness in a rural groundwater supply context of the idea that some aquifers are more vulnerable than others, rather than detailed guidance on assessing vulnerability, for which numerous methods have been developed. These fall into three broad categories:

■ those that use indices to weight critical factors (e.g. DRASTIC and GOD)
■ overlay methods, which display interpreted information but do produce combined indices (e.g. the UK and Irish methods)
■ complex models of the physical, chemical and biological processes in the unsaturated zone.

The approach in the third category is used mainly for site specific pollution, since there are rarely sufficient data available to develop models over wider areas. Details of methods in the first two categories are given in the further reading listed at the end of the chapter (Vrba and Zaporozec 1994; Foster et al. 2002).

8.5.3 Assessment of pollution loading

Returning to the assessment of pollution loading (Figure 8.15), a series of questions that need to be asked in such assessments is shown in Table 8.8. The information needed to provide the answer has to come from a survey or inventory to identify, locate and characterize all likely pollutant sources, including where possible their historical evolution. Much of the work in developing approaches to these surveys and assessments has come from investigations in urban and industrial localities. In rural areas, the most obvious pollution source of concern is likely to be unsewered sanitation, which is comprehensively dealt with in this chapter. Intensive agriculture with irrigation and use of fertilizers and pesticides, solid waste disposal and salinization problems arising from irrigation are other activities that can cause groundwater pollution. Further discussion of data collection procedures and design and implementation of pollution inventories is provided in Zaporozec (2001) and Foster et al. (2002).

8.6 Monitoring groundwater quality in rural supplies

Since groundwater quality can affect people's health, monitoring of groundwater quality should be an essential component, albeit usually a small one, in all rural water supply programmes. Unfortunately this is not always the case, and monitoring is often omitted, often because the financial and institutional arrangements are not in place to allow it to happen, or because 'monitoring' is not seen to have any direct benefits or because it is so big a topic that it is difficult to know where to start.

Although regular monitoring is not usually within their scope or budget, rural water supply projects have an obligation to provide an essential starting point by collecting groundwater samples at the time of test pumping a completed well or borehole, or commissioning a protected spring. These

Table 8.8 Assessment of pollution loading

Question to be answered	Component of assessment
Which pollutant?	Assess the human activities present and their possible associated pollutants Type of human activity: agriculture, sanitation, industry, mining, waste disposal, landfills The distribution of potential pollution sources associated with these activities: point, multi-point, line or diffuse Types of pollutant: nitrogen, pesticides, pathogens, metals that might be generated by these activities
How much of the pollutant?	Estimate the amount of pollutant released from these human activities
How does the pollution enter the ground?	Assess the mode of pollutant disposition in the subsurface environment Estimate the hydraulic loading – the volume of fluid comprising or containing the pollutants (e.g. irrigation water) which helps to drive the pollutant into the ground Estimate the depth below ground at which pollutant is discharged (leaking sewers or tanks, latrines) or leached (agriculture, landfills, mine waste, wastewater reuse)
What concentrations?	Assess the intensity of pollution in local recharge Estimate the likely pollutant concentrations relative to WHO Guideline values Estimate the proportion of recharge affected at this concentration which can vary from high for agriculture to low for landfills, waste disposal, industrial effluents and spills
How mobile and persistent?	Assess the ease of pollutant transport and the likely degree of attenuation from the properties of the pollutant and the soil and aquifer material; Consider the likely scope for it to be eliminated or degraded Consider the likely scope for it to be retarded by adsorption
How long does the pollution last?	Assess the probable duration of the pollutant loading Consider the probability that the pollutant will be discharged to the subsurface Consider the period over which the pollutant loading will last, from very short for many accidental spillages or leaks to years for sanitation, agriculture, landfills

should be analysed for major and minor ions to characterize the general hydrochemistry and for trace elements of health significance such as fluoride and arsenic. The results should be archived with the rest of the completion information for each water supply source. Testing new rural water supply points for microbiological quality must wait until the permanent pump has been installed and is operating; the possibility of contamination during construction means that earlier testing has no relevance. Testing should be combined with a first sanitary inspection to confirm that the pump has been properly installed and the associated plinth, apron and drainage measures have been adequately constructed.

While this is not the place to embark on a lengthy discussion of what is indeed a large and complex topic, nevertheless we can at least identify some of the key questions to be posed in setting up a regularly, ongoing, monitoring programme:

- **Why?** Objectives, who will use the data and for what – regulatory standards, water uses, health related
- **Who?** Project? Government? Health ministry? Water authority? Communities? Central or local?
- **Where?** Which boreholes, wells or springs? Network density, shallow or deep groundwater? Public water supplies or other?
- **When?** How frequently? Seasonal influences – wet and dry season?
- **What?** Which parameters should be monitored? Health related, specific indicators etc.
- **How?** Sampling procedures and analytical procedures, data handling and presentation.

Some of these questions have multiple answers, because a monitoring programme can have several objectives, or there may be several different type of monitoring programme. Here we are mainly concerned with the surveillance of rural water supplies in relation to drinking-water quality. Some of the broader answers to the questions may need to be provided well beyond project or even programme level, and it is unrealistic for those involved in project implementation to take this on.

In areas where troublesome concentrations of health-related parameters are possible or expected, then water samples should certainly be collected during test pumping or even, if they can be analysed in the field, when sufficient water is encountered during drilling. If high concentrations are measured, consideration can be given to abandoning the partially-completed well or borehole before the extra expense of installing the hand-pump is incurred and, more importantly, before the community begins to consume poor quality water. If the community has provided significant contributions to construction, either in cash or in kind, and in choosing the site, then this decision is not an easy one and needs careful handling within the project. If testing can be done during drilling, then the cost of lining the well or borehole may also be saved; in any case a strategy to deal with water quality needs to be incorporated into project or programme planning.

References, further reading and resources

ARGOSS (2001) Guidelines for assessing the risk to groundwater from on-site sanitation. British Geological Survey Commissioned Report CR/01/142. Available at: http://www.bgs.ac.uk

Barnes, C.J., Jacobson, G. and Smith, D.G. (1992) The origin of high-nitrate groundwaters in the Australian arid zone. *Journal of Hydrology*, **137**, 181–97.

Barrett, M., Howard, G., Pedley, S., Taylor, R. and Nalubega, M. (2000) A comparison of the extent and impacts of sewage contamination on urban groundwater in developing and developed countries. In: Chorus, I., Ringelband, U., Schlag, G. and Schmoll, O. (eds.) *Water, sanitation and health*. IWA Publishing, London, pp. 179–86.

Bartram, J. (1999) Effective monitoring of small drinking-water supplies. In: Cotruvo, J.A., Craun, G.F. and Hearne, N. (eds.) *Providing safe drinking-water in small systems*. Lewis, Washington, pp. 353–65.

Bartram, J. and Balance, R. (1996) *Water quality monitoring: a practical guide to the design and implementation of freshwater quality studies and monitoring programmes*. E & FN Spon, London.

BGS and DPHE (2001) Kinniburgh, D.G. and Smedley, P. L. (eds.) *Arsenic contamination of groundwater in Bangladesh*. British Geological Survey Technical Report, WC/00/19. Available at: http://www.bgs.ac.uk

Brassington, R. (1998) *Field hydrogeology*. John Wiley & Sons, Chichester, UK.

Dissanayake, C.B. (1991) The fluoride problem in the groundwater of Sri Lanka – environmental management and health. *International Journal of Environment Studies*, **19**, 195–203.

Edmunds, W.M. and Gaye, C.B. (1997). Naturally high nitrate concentrations in groundwaters from the Sahel. *Journal of Environmental Quality*, **26**, 1231–9.

Edmunds, W.M. and Smedley, P.L. (1996) Groundwater geochemistry and health: an overview. In: Appleton, J.D., Fuge, R. and McCall, G.J.H. (eds). *Environmental geochemistry and health*. Special Publication 113, Geological Society, London, pp. 81–105.

EU (1998) European Union drinking-water standards. Council Directive 98/83/EC on the quality of water intended for human consumption. Available at: http://www.europa.eu.int/comm/environment/water/water-drink/index

Foster, S.S.D. and Hirata, R. (1988) *Groundwater pollution risk assessment: a methodology using available data*. WHO-PAHO Technical Manual, CEPIS, Lima, Peru.

Foster, S.S.D., Chilton, P.J., Moench, M., Cardy, F. and Schiffler, M. (2000) Groundwater in rural development. World Bank Technical Paper No 463. World Bank, Washington DC. Available at: http://www-wds.worldbank.org/

Foster, S.S.D., Hirata, R., Gomes, D., D'Elia, M. and Paris, M. (2002) *Groundwater quality protection: a guide for water utilities, municipal authorities and environment agencies*. World Bank, Washington. Available at: http://www-wds.worldbank.org/

Franceys, R., Pickford, J. and Reed, R. (1992) *A guide to the development of on-site sanitation*. WHO, Geneva.

Gelinas, Y., Randall, H., Robidoux, L. and Schmit, J.-P. (1996) Well water survey in two districts of Conakry (Republic of Guinea) and comparison with the piped city water. *Water Resources*, **30**(9), 2017–26.

Girard, P. and Hillaire-Marcel, C. (1997) Determining the source of nitrate pollution in the Niger discontinuous aquifers using the natural $^{15}N/^{14}N$ ratios. *Journal of Hydrology*, **199**, 239–51.

Howard, G. (2002) *Water quality surveillance*. WEDC, Loughborough University. Available at: http://wedc.lboro.ac.uk/

Howard, G., Pedley, S., Barrett, M., Nalunbenga, M. and Johal, K. (2003) Risk factors contributing to microbiological contamination of shallow groundwater in Kampala, Uganda. *Water Research*, **37**, 3421–9.

Ikem, A., Osibanjo, O., Sridhar, M.K.C. and Sobande, A. (2002) Evaluation of groundwater quality characteristics near two waste sites in Ibadan and Lagos, Nigeria. *Water, Air and Soil Pollution*, **140**(1–4), 307–33.

Lewis, W.J. and Chilton, P. J. (1984) Performance of sanitary completion measures of wells and boreholes used for rural water supplies in Malawi. In: *Challenges in African hydrology and water resources*. IAHS Publication 144, 235–48.

Lloyd, B. and Helmer, R. (1991) *Surveillance of drinking-water quality in rural areas*. Longman, Harlow, UK.

Mara, D. (1996) *Low-cost urban sanitation*. John Wiley & Sons, Chichester, UK.

Melian, R., Melian, N., Gouriev, A., Moraru, C. and Radstake, F. (1999) Groundwater quality and rural drinking-water supplies in the Republic of Moldova. *Hydrogeology Journal*, 7, 188–96.

Morris, B.L., Lawrence, A.R., Chilton, P.J., Adams, B., Calow, R. and Klinck, B.A. (2003) *Groundwater and its susceptibility to degradation: A global assessment of the problems and options for management*. Early Warning and Assessment Report Series RS 03–3. United Nations Environment Programme, Nairobi, Kenya. Available at: http://www.unep.org/DEWA/water/

Rahman, A. (1996) Groundwater as a source of contamination for water supply in rapidly growing megacities in Asia: case of Karachi, Pakistan. *Water Science and Technology*, **34**(7–8), 285–92.

Smedley, P.L. and Kinniburgh, D.G. (2001) Source and behaviour of arsenic in natural waters. Chapter 1 in: Yamamura, S. (ed.) *UN Synthesis Report on Arsenic*, WHO, Geneva. Available at: http://www.who.int/water_sanitation_health/en/

Smedley, P.L. and Kinniburgh, D.G. (2002) A review of the source, behaviour and distribution of arsenic in natural waters. *Applied Geochemistry*, **17**, 517–68.

Smet, J. (1990) Fluoride in drinking-water. Chapter 6 in: Frencken, J.E. (ed:) *Proceedings of the symposium on endemic fluorosis in developing countries: causes, effects and possible solutions*. NIPG-TNO, Leiden, pp. 51–85.

Smith, A., Goycolea, M., Haque, R. and Biggs, M.L. (1998) Marked increase in bladder and lung cancer mortality in a region of Northern Chile due to arsenic in drinking-water. *American Journal of Epidemiology*, **147**, 660–9.

Smith, G.D., Wetslaar, R., Fox, J.J., van de Graaff, R.H.M., Moeljohardjo, D., Sarwono, J., Wiranto, Asj'ari, Sri R., Tjojudo, S. and Basuki (1999) The origin and distribution of nitrate in groundwater from village wells in Kotagede, Yogyakarta, Indonesia. *Hydrogeology Journal*, 7, 576–89.

US EPA (2003) Drinking-water standards. Available at: http://www.epa.gov/safewater/standards

Vrba, J. and Zaporozec, A. (eds.) (1994) *Guidebook on mapping groundwater vulnerability*. International Association of Hydrogeologists, Heise, Hannover, Germany.

WHO drinking-water guidelines. Available at: http://www.who.int/water_lsanitation_l-health/en/

WHO (1993) *Guidelines for drinking-water quality* (2nd edition). WHO, Geneva.

WHO (1998) *Guidelines for drinking-water quality* (2nd edition): *Addendum to Volume 2, Health criteria and other supporting information*. WHO, Geneva.

Zaporozec, A. (ed.) (2001) *Groundwater contamination inventory: a methodological guideline*. UNESCO, Paris.

9 Learning lessons

9.1 Why lesson-learning is important

Many communities are subjected to repeated mistakes made by a succession of rural water supply projects. The following scenario is not uncommon: one project team comes to a village, drills several boreholes, finds no water and disappears. Several years later, another project team, with different funding comes to the village, tries again and fails. This pattern can continue until a sustainable water point is found, either through science or good luck, or the area is avoided as it is known to be difficult. One of the main reasons for continued low success rates of water projects is the lack of time set aside to learn lessons from our own, and others', experience. Central to this process is the mundane process of keeping, and making available, records from all aspects of our projects.

Therefore, once the water point is completed, and the water quality assured, a little time should be set aside to look after the data generated. The information gathered from constructing a water point, even if that water point is unsuccessful, is of great value. There is no other way of finding out how groundwater occurs in an area than by drilling and testing boreholes, examining the geology, carrying out geophysical surveys and undertaking a water quality assessment. The routine procedures described in this manual, used in the first instance to provide information about the success and potential sustainability of an individual water point, can be used to construct the bigger picture of how groundwater occurs across the whole project area, supporting other projects and programmes.

Much of what is said here should be obvious from preceding chapters. Here we recap and expand on Chapter 4 (reconnaissance) with a focus on how raw data (unanalysed facts and figures) can be converted into information (analysed data in a form useful for decisions) and ultimately, knowledge (assimilated and understood information).

9.2 The uses and users of project data

Before looking at issues of data management, it is important to remind ourselves of the end uses and users of the data. An understanding of user requirements – within and beyond the project – should always inform what we do. The harvesting and storage of data is not the end goal!

First and foremost, the collection of data has value within the project itself. As more data are generated, groundwater development maps (described in Chapter 4) can be revised and produced in more detail. This can enable more informed choices to be offered to communities with greater confidence. Other options can be offered in areas where groundwater resources are known to be problematic, or investigations commissioned to help overcome problems which have been identified from reviewing the data.

However, data generated on a project also has value to others beyond any current or future application on that particular project. Adding to the stock of publicly available good data is vital. There are many potential 'data stakeholders' with various interests and needs. These stakeholders may range from international donors and UN agencies to individual communities.

- **National government** can use data to help develop national planning tools and maps, such as water resources maps, drought maps, coverage maps, etc. Data are also required to help make water supply audits and to provide information to UN agencies and donors.
- **Regional/district hydrogeologists** can make significant use of hydrogeological data to develop an understanding of how groundwater occurs in an area; this understanding can then be used to guide decisions on individual projects in their region. Priority areas can also be identified using the data, and areas for which little information is available.
- **The private sector**, including drilling companies, need information on how easy/difficult it is to find and develop groundwater resources in an area, and what methods are most cost-effective. Data are most useful where compiled into hydrogeological maps and regional reports.
- **NGOs and other partner organizations** also need information on how easy or difficult it is to find groundwater in an area, what methods need to be used to develop water resources and what technologies are likely to be viable.
- **Communities** need information on any boreholes/wells constructed in the community to help with the maintenance of any working source, or to make sense of any failures.

The most efficient way of ensuring that all stakeholders have access to the data they require is through national or regional databases. The more data that is put into a system, the more useful it can become to all users. Therefore any individual project needs to find out about the procedures and systems already in place for submitting and retrieving data and make sure they are followed. In many countries, however, data storage and retrieval systems have fallen into disuse (in part) because data remain with individual projects and the cycle of data pooling and data retrieval starts to break down.

This has been made worse by the decentralization of government which has led to the fragmentation of records that were previously held nationally. Where this is the case, projects will need to find other ways of sharing and accessing data. These may include workshops for rural water supply stakeholders, where a day can be set aside to share experience and learn lessons, and other formal or informal networks.

9.3 Storing useful information – a project perspective

To be useful, information should be recorded in a usable format and then stored in a number of safe, but accessible locations. This should not be a difficult task, or cost much in terms of time or resources to a project – it is just being conscious of how precious this information is to the project, and other potential users. If contractors are carrying out the work it is necessary that all field data and related information are lodged with the project. Sometimes arguments can arise about data ownership. Contractors who undertake geophysical surveys, geological logging and pumping tests may be reluctant to part with data. This is partly due to time constraints; more serious, however, is the belief that knowledge and information is power. The concern may be that another contractor will use the geophysical data to site additional boreholes. As a basic rule, whoever pays for the work to be carried out should have access to the data, although they may also be retained by the contractor. For clarity, this should be written into every contract.

BOX 9.1   What data should be kept?

- Geological field notes for the area and any other reconnaissance data.
- Data from any geophysical surveys (and their location).
- The drilling report (including all data relating to the drilling, construction and geological/geophysical logging of the borehole as described in Chapter 6) including all dry holes.
- Data and results from the pumping tests.
- Information from sanitary inspections, etc. and from the water quality assessment.

To build up as full a regional picture as possible, it is vital to hold on to detailed information from unsuccessful boreholes. This information is as useful as that from a successful borehole: it should help build up a picture of areas with poor groundwater resources and, therefore, help to offer better informed choices to communities based on an understanding of what options are feasible in different areas. This will save the project time and money, and help build the confidence of communities in the project.

It is also useful to write a summary (less than one page) of the data, just highlighting the important facts for the source and as a quick reference. An example is given in Box 9.2.

BOX 9.2   Summary data

- Georeference data: longitude and latitude or local grid reference
- Name: Okumbgo, borehole OB37a
- Geology: weathered crystalline basement (granite)
- Siting methods: borehole sited using ground conductivity: EM34 with 20-m separations – where conductivity (horizontal coils) was greater than 10 mS/m
- Drilling: borehole drilled to 36 m; 100 mm open hole
- Construction: surface casing pressure grouted to 10 m through soil and highly weathered zone
- Test pumping: 6 hour pumping test gives transmissivity of 4 m²/day from recovery;
- Water quality: TDS 150 mg/litre, pH 6.8 – no other constituents measured
- Sanitary inspection: no obvious signs of contamination within 50 m
- Installed pump: India Mark 3 hand pump set at 25 m.

Project data do not need to be stored on computer. A well-ordered paper filing system should be the foundation for any database of the information. Each borehole should be given a unique number, to avoid confusion between different sources. It is also useful to check when filing that all appropriate information is present; e.g. coordinates, drilling report, geophysics reports, pumping tests, etc. This is the best opportunity to gather the data together – if it is not done at this stage it is unlikely to actually happen and the data will be lost. Chapter 4 describes a geographical information system (GIS), which is an excellent computerized method of storing and analysing data.

As a safeguard against loss, copies of data should be held by various people. This could include the contractor, partners, donors, appropriate ministry and communities.

9.4   Making use of information

Once some data has been collected it can start to be used to help give a better understanding of the hydrogeology of an area and how to improve the success of this and other projects. In this section we suggest various ways in which data collected on the project can be interpreted to provide information and improve knowledge: Here are several ideas:

- Review the effectiveness of siting techniques by comparing geophysical surveys with actual geological logs and borehole success.
- Refine the initial groundwater development maps made for the area during the reconnaissance phase to create a more definitive groundwater development plan.
- Make predictions about areas with similar conditions.
- Develop a better understanding of why wells and boreholes fail.
- At a national level develop planning tools, such as drought maps, or national water resources maps and inform rural water supply policy.

9.4.1 Review siting methods

After several tens of boreholes have been drilled, or wells dug, it can be useful to examine the effectiveness of the siting techniques. For example, geophysical surveys can be compared with the actual drilling logs to see if any consistent patterns emerge. It is particularly important to examine the geophysical surveys of unsuccessful boreholes: are there any features of the geophysical log or geological log that explain why the boreholes were unsuccessful?

In Malawi, the Mangochi project has used this review process to good effect (Robins et al. 2003). By collecting and interpreting data from all drilling, the methods used to site future boreholes were refined and the success rate gradually improved from 40 per cent to more than 75 per cent.

9.4.2 Making groundwater development maps

With good data, it is possible to make excellent groundwater development or hydrogeological maps. To do this, essentially the same process as described in Chapter 4 (Reconnaissance) is followed – except this time you have much more data, and information that you know you can trust. Local groundwater development maps were made for Oju and Obi local government areas (Nigeria) after 50 boreholes had been drilled throughout the area (Davies and MacDonald 1999). Given a small amount of training, the maps were then used by the local government water and sanitation unit to offer realistic options to communities for improved water supplies, ranging from rainwater harvesting to borehole drilling and well construction. After the maps had been in use for several years and more than 100 water points had been constructed, the success rate rose from less than 20 per cent to more than 80 per cent. Figure 9.1 shows local community members using the groundwater development map.

Groundwater development maps can also be useful training aids. They can facilitate discussions with local partners and also communities. In Oju and Obi (see above) they were used in conjunction with simple models to show why boreholes were more successful in some areas and inappropriate in others.

Figure 9.1 Local government officials in Nigeria using a groundwater development map.
Photo: BGS, © NERC 2000.

9.4.3 Making predictions for other areas

Often a detailed study in one area can have direct benefits to other areas with similar geology. If a project has generated sufficient data to develop a thorough understanding of how groundwater occurs across an area, it is a small step to develop general rules for this type of rock which can be translated to other areas. Such a study is often carried out in combination with research establishments or universities, who can help interpret the project data. This knowledge can then be shared through workshops, scientific papers or direct training.

An excellent example of this knowledge transfer has occurred with the development of groundwater resources in crystalline basement. This type of rock (which covers 40 per cent of the land area of sub-Saharan Africa) was once thought not to contain any usable groundwater. However, after sharing the lessons from various research and rural water supply projects in the 1970s and 1980s the methods of developing groundwater in these rocks have become well known (Wright and Burgess 1992).

9.4.4 Develop an understanding of why wells and boreholes fail

Depressingly many boreholes are not functioning 5 years after they were first constructed; in some places the failure rate is two out of three boreholes drilled. Why do so many wells and boreholes fail? There are three main reasons.

- **Poor construction or source location.** This is a common problem: often boreholes are claimed to be successful without carrying out a yield test, or have not been constructed well enough to exclude sand. This should not be an issue for boreholes or wells constructed using the guidelines in this manual. However, an examination of the borehole records will reveal the construction of the borehole and whether it was suitable for the job.

- **Drought or declining water levels.** Successful boreholes can fail because of changes in the availability of groundwater in the surrounding rocks. There are two ways in which this can occur: natural decline in a borehole in response to droughts, or pumping out more groundwater than is naturally replenished every year. These two factors are often linked: during droughts, abstraction from boreholes often increases which exacerbates the natural decline in water levels (Calow et al. 1997). Many people believe that problems of drought and declining water levels will become more extreme as a result of the impact of climate change.

- **Lack of maintenance.** Boreholes and wells need to be regularly maintained. The rubbers and seals on handpumps must be changed, connecting rods looked after and holes in the rising main detected and fixed. This cannot happen on its own, but needs interested and qualified personnel and also small amounts of money. Much research and many, many projects have shown that the single most important factor for reliable maintenance is a sense of ownership by the community. The community must have the responsibility for the borehole and handpump and be able to raise small amounts of money to buy spare parts.

9.4.5 Developing planning tools

Hydrogeological data can be interpreted to provide planning tools which may be used by policy makers and planners. Raw data, or hydrogeological interpretations, can be combined into more user-friendly maps which give a broad indication of conditions across a region or a country. One of the most common planning criteria used by central governments and donors is **coverage**, i.e. the percentage of the population in various districts with access to improved water supplies.

More sophisticated examples of using groundwater data to make user-friendly planning tools are the development of national groundwater availability or groundwater potential maps, water security and drought maps (see Figure 9.2). Although these tools are much too general to plan individual projects, they can be very useful to help policy makers or politicians make decisions about broad areas of investment, and to communicate complex

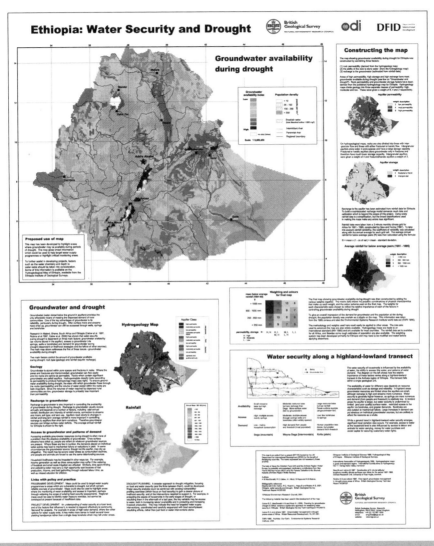

Figure 9.2 Black and white scan of a water security and drought map produced for Ethiopia.
Source: Calow et al. 2002.

ideas to non-specialists. If these tools can be underpinned with good-quality data from actual projects, they can ensure that those with the power to make decisions are actually doing so with the help of the lessons learned from projects throughout the country.

References, further reading and resources

Calow, R.C, Robins, N.S., MacDonald, A.M., Macdonald, D.M.J., Gibbs, B.R., Orpen, W.R.G., Mtembezeka, P., Andrews, A.J. and Appiah, S.O. (1997) Groundwater management in drought prone areas of Africa. *International Journal of Water Resources Development*, **13**(2), 241–61.

Calow, R.C., MacDonald, A.M., Nicol, A., Robins, N.S. and Kebede, S. (2002) *The struggle for water: drought, water security and rural livelihoods*. British Geological Survey Commissioned Report, CR/02/226N.

Davies, J. and MacDonald, A.M. (1999) *Final Report: the groundwater potential of the Oju/Obi area, eastern Nigeria*. British Geological Survey Technical Report WC/99/32.

Robins, N.S., Davies, J., Hankin, P. and Sauer, D. (2003) Groundwater and data – an African experience. *Waterlines*, **21**(4) 19–21.

Appendix 1

Identifying different rocks

Recognizing different rocks in the field is fundamental to understanding the hydrogeology of an area. In this appendix we give a short introduction to the field identification of different types of rocks – this is a large and complex subject, so only a brief overview can be given here. References to some of the many detailed resources available about the identification and classification of rocks are given at the end of the section. We have included several pages of colour photographs to help recognize some of the most common rocks.

A1.1 Getting samples

Bedrock is often concealed beneath soil or other unconsolidated materials such as sands or gravels. Chapter 5 gives some suggestions of where to look for good fresh rock samples – for example in river valleys or road cuttings. Rock formations are often better exposed in arid areas or in areas that have been subjected to glaciation. In a groundwater project, rock samples tend to come from three sources:

- **Samples from rock outcrops** (see Chapter 4): here it is important to get fresh samples, so use a geological hammer to get a good sample or to split a rock to get a fresh surface to examine.
- **Rock chip samples** (see Chapter 6): these are small rock chippings produced from drilling.
- **Cores** (see Chapter 6): cores of rock from boreholes are an excellent way of examining the geology but are rarely used on groundwater development projects.

The character of rock units can be highly variable over short distances. If the intention is to collect a sample that is representative of a rock unit, it is important to establish how much the rock varies in character in the local area.

A1.2 The tools of the trade

The basic equipment required to identify and describe rocks in the field is simple, low cost, and will last for many years. The following items are essential:

- hand lens with a magnification of ×8 or ×10
- geological hammer (this needs to be appropriate to the task in hand; if you're working in crystalline rocks you'll need a large hammer in order to collect good samples, whereas in sedimentary rocks a smaller hammer may suffice)
- penknife for splitting small samples and testing hardness
- reference charts and field books for assessing grain size and diagrams to aid correct determination of lithology
- safety glasses and gloves
- notebook in which to record observations ands sample locations.

If possible, it is very helpful to have the following:

- GPS to accurately locate the position of samples
- colour charts to accurately record colour
- dilute hydrochloric acid (0.1 molar, or 10 per cent HCl) if possible to identify carbonate rocks
- camera
- bags and markers for storing samples.

Chapter 6 describes some of the additional equipment required when logging rock chip samples while drilling.

A1.3 Describing and recognizing rocks

When presented with a rock or chip sample it is important to have a structured methodology for describing the sample to help recognize what it might be. For each sample the following should all be noted: the texture of the rock, colour, the type of minerals present, how weathered the sample is and any structures or features.

A1.3.1 The texture of the sample

Consolidation

The first observation to make is whether the rock is consolidated or not. This will be obvious from the area and the drilling process. For example, in unconsolidated sediments, wells and boreholes tend to collapse, and small pits for extracting sand may be present.

Porosity

It is straightforward to assess whether the rock sample is crystalline, with limited porosity, or granular with pore spaces between grains. A hand lens is used to examine the grains and look for porosity. Crystalline rocks are usually igneous or metamorphic; thoroughly cemented limestones may also be crystalline. Sandstones and siltstones are granular and their porosity will depend on the grain size and the amount of cement between grains.

Grain size

Grain size is an important measure, particularly in sedimentary rocks: coarser grained sands or sandstones tend to be better aquifers. A hand lens and ruler (or grain size chart) is essential for accurate estimation of grain size. Figure A1.1 shows a grain size chart that can be photocopied, laminated and used in the field. In most rocks there will be a range of grain sizes. Table A1.1 gives the conventional language for classifying the grain size for sedimentary rocks. For igneous and metamorphic rocks the grains size helps to classify what sort of the rock it is – this is described later.

Roundness

Sedimentary particles are abraded during transport. Abrasion acts to smooth angular surfaces. Sedimentary rocks made of well-rounded grains are usually more porous than those made of angular grains, so roundness can be an important factor in determining the hydrogeological properties of sandstone. The grains are usually classified as somewhere in the range between very angular and well rounded. This can be difficult to assess objectively, so reference diagrams can be a great help.

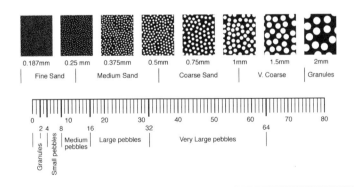

| Figure A1.1 | Grain size chart in mm. |

Table A1.1 Grain size classification in for clasts found in sedimentary rocks

Term	Grain size range (mm)	Field identification
Boulder	>256	Visible to the naked eye
Cobble	64–256	
Very large pebble	32–64	
Large pebble	16–32	
Medium pebble	8–16	
Small pebble	4–8	
Granule (gravel)	2–4	
Very coarse sand	1–2	Visible to the naked eye on freshly broken surface
Coarse sand	0.5–1	
Medium sand	0.25–0.5	
Fine sand	0.125–0.25	
Very fine sand	0.032–0.125	
Silt	0.004–0.032	Only visible with ×10 hand lens. Feels gritty between teeth
Clay	<0.004	Not visible with ×10 hand lens. Feels creamy between teeth

Sorting

Sorting describes the variability of attributes such as rounding and grain size in sedimentary rocks; in well-sorted rocks the component grains are mostly of a similar size, shape and roundness. If a sandstone contains grain sizes from very fine to coarse, porosity is likely to reduce since the pore spaces left by the larger grains will be in filled by the smaller grains.

A1.3.2 Colour

Identifying the colour of chip samples from a borehole can be important for identifying the thickness of the weathered zone, or water inflow horizons. Colour is less important in field samples. The colour should be ideally classified using a standard colour chart; otherwise it is very difficult to know what colour descriptions are referring to. One persons brown could be another's orangey grey! The most commonly used colour chart is the Munsel® chart, which has many different pages with various colours.

Munsel® colours are usually referred to by two or three words, such as 'brownish yellow' or 'light bluish grey', and a number; for example 7.5YR3/3 (which is a kind of dark brown). If colour charts are not available, try to be as consistent as possible. Table A1.2 gives some descriptions that are commonly used.

Table A1.2 Common descriptions for the colour of rocks

	Qualifier colour	Main colour
Light		Pink
Dark	Pinkish	Red
Mottled	Reddish	Yellow
	Yellowish	Brown
	Brownish	Green
	Greenish	Blue
	Bluish	Grey
	Greyish	Black
		White

Table A1.3 Average mineral composition of some common rocks (percentages)

Mineral	Granite	Basalt	Sandstone	Shale	Limestone
Quartz	31.3	—	69.8	31.9	3.7
Feldspar	52.3	46.2	8.4	17.6	2.2
Micas	11.5	—	1.2	18.4	—
Clay minerals	—	—	6.9	10	1.0
Chlorite	—	—	1.1	6.4	—
Amphiboles	2.4	—	—	—	—
Pyroxenes	Rare	36.9	—	—	—
Olivine	—	7.6	—	—	—
Calcite and dolomite	—	—	—	7.9	92.8
Iron oxides	2.0	6.5	10.6	5.4	0.1
Others	0.5	2.8	1.7	2.4	0.3

Source: Duff (1993).

A1.3.3 Identifying minerals

The most common rocks can be adequately described by about 10 different groups of minerals of which the most common are quartz and feldspars (see Table A1.3). Recognizing the different minerals that make up rocks is a specialist skill and is well described in various guides (see resources listed at the end of this appendix). The colour of the minerals can be used as a rough way of distinguishing the two main groups of minerals. Minerals are often divided into mafic and felsic. Felsic minerals are generally pale coloured; quartz and feldspars are the most common felsic minerals. Iron and magnesium rich mafic minerals are commonly dark coloured; the most common include olivine, pyroxenes, dark micas and amphiboles. Rocks rich in mafic minerals are often called basic; rocks rich in felsic minerals are often referred to as acidic.

Some of the more common minerals (such as quartz, feldspars and calcite) can be readily distinguished by their hardness. Table A1.4 shows a very useful scale for measuring the hardness of the different minerals in a rock.

Table A1.4 Moh's revised scale of relative hardness

Hardness	Mineral	Can be scratched by
1	Talc	
2	Gypsum	Fingernail
3	Calcite	Copper coin
4	Fluorite	
5	Apatite	
6	Feldspar	Good knife blade
7	Quartz	
8	Topaz	
9	Corundum (ruby and sapphire)	
10	Diamond	

For example, gypsum can be distinguished from calcite because it can be scratched with your fingernail, whereas calcite cannot.

A1.3.4 Structures and features

It is also useful to describe other features about the rock sample. For example is the rock layered? Are there veins or fractures cutting through the rocks? A basic introduction of what to look for is given below. Sedimentary structures are an important aspect of sedimentary rocks. They can be used to help understand what the original environment of deposition was like and also how groundwater may flow through the rocks. More information on describing structures is given in Tucker (2003). Things to look for are:

- **Bedding and layers**. Measure how thick the layers are and whether they are parallel, cross-bedded, very thin or massive and whether layers include different lithologies (e.g. mudstone and sandstone interbedded).
- **Features on bedding surfaces**. There are many different features than can be found on bedding surfaces (or undersurfaces): ripples, animal burrows, channels shrinkage cracks, etc.
- **Fossils**. Although their study is a specialized skill, the presence of any fossils in the sample should be noted.
- **Banding**. Thinly bedded or laminated sedimentary rocks and some igneous and metamorphic rocks can all be banded in appearance due to variations in the mineral contents of the layers.
- **Veins**. The presence of small veins of rocks or minerals that cut through rocks can be important for understanding the hydrogeology and are often an indication of fracturing. Commonly veins can be made of quartz or calcite.
- **Fractures**. Sometimes fractures can be directly observed from rocks samples. However, rocks often fracture during drilling, coring, or when taking hand specimens. Therefore it is important to look for

signs that show the fracture existed before the sample was taken (for example, discolouration on the fracture surface, slickensides, mineral growths, or the presence of vein material).

A1.3.5 Weathering

The weathering of rocks has an important effect on the availability of groundwater. Weathering can decompose the rocks and form thick and complex soils. In tropical areas weathering can extend to depths of tens or even hundreds of metres. There are two forms of weathering: mechanical disintegration and chemical decomposition. These forms act together, but, depending on climatic regime, one or other may be dominant.

- **Mechanical weathering** results in the formation and opening of discontinuities by fracturing the rocks and minerals and opening grain boundaries.
- **Chemical weathering** results in decomposition of silicate minerals to clay minerals and the dissolution of other minerals such as carbonates or gypsum. Some minerals, e.g. quartz, are resistant to chemical weathering. Geological structures, and in particular, faults, may influence the weathering profile by permitting penetration of weathering agents deep into otherwise fresh rock.

The weathering profile comprises three basic units: soil, weathered rock and fresh rock. The rate and depth of the weathering process is influenced by the presence of open fractures, which allow weathering agencies access into the rock. The initial weathering affects fracture surfaces, followed by inward penetration of weathering until the rock is completely changed to a soil. These various stages are usually observed within a borehole. The top few metres may comprise soil – possibly a complex tropical red soil. Beneath this is decomposed rock, which appears rotten, but still has some resemblance to rock. With depth, the rock becomes harder and less discoloured, until only the edges of fractures are discoloured with iron oxides (this is often seen on the chip samples).

Rock weathering is often described in terms of the distribution and relative proportions of fresh and discoloured rock, decomposed and disintegrated rock. There are excellent detailed resources available for identifying and describing rock weathering (Fookes 1997). Table A1.5 gives a very simple classification that can be used as a rough guide.

The hardness of the rock can also be important in describing how weathered the rock is. Table A1.6 gives a useful method for describing the hardness of a sample.

Table A1.5 Descriptive scheme for weathering grades

Term	Description
Fresh	No visible sign of weathering of the rock material
Discoloured	Colour of the original rock material is changed and may be evidence of weathering. The degree of change from the original colour should be indicated. If the colour change is confined to particular mineral constituents this should be mentioned
Decomposed	The rock is weathered to the condition of a soil in which the original material fabric is still intact, but some or all of the mineral grains are decomposed
Disintegrated	The rock is weathered to the condition of a soil in which the original material fabric is still intact. The rock is friable, but the mineral grains are not decomposed

Table A1.6 Estimating the hardness of a rock sample

Term	Field estimation of hardness
Very soft	Crumbles easily in hand
Soft	Material crumbles from blows with a geological hammer. Can also be cut with a knife
Moderately soft	Thin slabs or edges broken by heavy hand pressure
Moderately hard	Broken by light hammer blows
Hard	Hand held sample can be broken with single blow of a geological hammer
Very hard	More than one blow of geological hammer required to break sample

A1.4 Igneous rocks

Igneous rocks (Table A.17) are formed from molten geological material rising from great depths and cooling to form crystalline rocks either below the ground or at the land surface. Igneous rocks that cool below the earth's surface are called intrusive igneous rocks. They can form large bodies many kilometres across called **plutons**, or small thin sheets called **dykes** or **sills** that may be only a few centimetres across. Igneous rocks that cool on the land surface are known as extrusive igneous rocks. They are formed from various types of volcanic eruptions and include **lava** (molten rock which flows away from the volcano and solidifies) and **pyroclastic rocks**, which are formed by explosive volcanic activity and generally comprise a great deal of ash.

Most igneous rocks are crystalline, and therefore have very limited pore space. They range from very coarse grained pegmatites, where crystals can be hundreds of millimetres across, to obsidian which is a glass. The most common and abundant minerals in igneous rocks are feldspars and quartz (light coloured minerals) and biotite mica, amphibole, pyroxene and olivine (dark coloured minerals). Igneous rocks form characteristically low permeability aquifers where they have been subjected to near surface weathering and/or fracturing.

Table A1.7 A simple classification of igneous rocks

Lithology		Grain size	Colour, texture and occurrence
Coarse grained igneous rocks	Granites	Coarse >2mm	Light coloured, grey, white and pink coarse to very coarse-grained rock containing quartz, feldspar, mica and amphibole. Often occurs as large intrusive masses. Groundwater movement generally indicated by orange weathered zones of rotten and broken granite
Coarse grained igneous rocks	Gabbro	Coarse >2mm	Dark coloured green, black and white coarse to very coarse-grained rock containing feldspar, pyroxene and olivine. Often occurs as large intrusive masses. Groundwater movement generally indicated by orange weathered zones of rotten and broken gabbro
Medium-grained igneous rocks	Micro-granite	Medium 0.25–2mm	Light coloured, medium grained intrusive rock of quartz, feldspar, amphibole and mica. Orange stained zones of groundwater movement in rotten and broken micro-granite
Medium-grained igneous rocks	Dolerite	Medium 0.25–2mm	Dark coloured green, black and white medium grained rock; occurs as dykes and sills. Water occurs in baked margin and zeolite rich rotten dolerite zones
Fine-grained igneous rocks	Rhyolite	Fine <0.25mm	Light coloured, fine grained rock of quartz, feldspar, amphibole and mica; occurs as lava flows or dykes and sills
Fine-grained igneous rocks	Basalt	Fine <0.25mm	Dark coloured green-black, fine grained rock. Can occur in lava flows but also as dykes and sills. Water occurs in intraflow weathered orange-brown soil horizons

Source: adapted from Gillespie and Styles (1999).

Volcanic rocks can be hard to identify and classify. Pyroclastic rocks are sometimes reworked by water, so often contain some features characteristic of both sedimentary and igneous rocks. Agglomerates contain large rock fragments – formed from explosive volcanic eruptions. These can often be rubbly with a high porosity and are good targets for water.

A1.5 Sediments and sedimentary rocks

Sediments are formed by the transport and deposition of material by water and wind. Unconsolidated sediments can become consolidated physically by compaction and chemically by cementation to form rocks. There are various types of sedimentary rocks, based on their composition and grain size. A detailed classification system is given in Hallsworth and Knox (1999), summarized in Table A1.8.

The minerals in sedimentary rocks depends on the composition of the parent rock from which they were eroded or the nature of plant and animal remains (which form some types of sedimentary rocks). Some sedimentary rocks are formed chemically from gels (e.g. flint, chert) or by precipitation to form salts (e.g. halite, gypsum). Sediments should be described according to the methods earlier in this appendix. Information on grain size and texture, cements, etc. should all be carefully recorded.

A1.6 Metamorphic rocks

A1.6.1 Definition

Metamorphic rocks are formed when sedimentary and igneous rocks are subjected to increased heat and pressure at depth in the earth's crust, resulting in changes in mineralogy and/or texture. Most minerals in the original rocks are changed significantly by chemical reactions that take place because of the effects of increased temperature and pressure. Metamorphism occurs over a very wide range of conditions, up to the point at which rocks melt to form magma (see the section on igneous rocks). Thus metamorphic rocks can have very complicated histories and can be difficult to identify and classify.

A1.6.2 Metamorphic minerals

Minerals characteristic of particular ranges of pressure and temperature will grow at the expense of others as reactions take place. Common metamorphic minerals include biotite (a platy mica) and garnet, a ball-shaped mineral that is often a conspicuous pink or red in colour.

A1.6.3 Metamorphic textures

As existing minerals recrystallize and new minerals grow, the textures in the rocks can change significantly. Generally, the higher the temperature

Table A1.8   A simple classification of sediments and sedimentary rocks

Sediments and sedimentary rocks that can be classified by their grain size

	Grain size	Unconsolidated	Consolidated	Volcanoclastic
Rudacious	>2 mm	Gravel	Conglomerate / Breccia if clasts are angular	Clasts > 64 mm Agglomerate or pyroclastic breccia
				Clasts 2–64 mm Lappilli-stone
Arenaceous	0.5–2 mm	Sand	Coarse grained sandstone	Tuff
	0.25–0.5 mm		Medium grained sandstone	
	0.032–0.25 mm		Fine grained sandstone	
Argillacoeous	0.004–0.032	Silt	Siltstone / Mudstone (sometimes called shale)	Fine grained tuff
	<0.004 mm	Clay	Claystone	

Diamicton if poorly sorted (Unconsolidated)

Wacke if poorly sorted (Consolidated)

Table A1.8 contd.

Other sedimentary rocks

Carbonate rocks (rocks with > 50% carbonate material)	Non-carbonate salts	Non-classic sediments	Organic rich (composed of dead plants)
Limestone: if the rock is primarily made up of calcium carbonate (will react with dilute HCl).	Gypsum (calcium sulphate) Softer than a finger nail; often fibrous	Chert; siliceous rocks probably formed from gels. Include flint, agate, jasper etc.	Peat. Unconsolidated, soft dark brown or black.
Chalk is a porous and friable limestone.			
Dolostone: if the rock has significant proportion of magnesium carbonate. (will only react with dilute HCl if powdered)	Halite (rock salt). Often clear or grey with cubic crystals; softer than a finger nail		Coal. Consolidated, black, lightweight, smudgey.
Shelly limestone: a limestone with a high proportion of shell fragments			

and pressure (or grade) of metamorphism, the coarser-grained the resulting metamorphic rock will be, though the resulting textures are dependent on the original grain size, particularly at lower metamorphic grades.

Rocks composed mainly of mud and silt (pelites and semipelites) will be slaty at low metamorphic grades and will split easily along planes formed by the alignment of recrystallized platy clay minerals or new platy micas that grow from clay minerals. In slaty rocks the minerals are generally too small to observe with a hand lens in field specimen. At increasing metamorphic grades, phyllitic and schistose textures develop (schist being more coarse grained than phyllite). Both these rocks will still often split along the fine layering formed by the aligned micas, but not in the clean, smooth way that slaty rocks do. The minerals on these rocks will be readily visible with a hand lens or the naked eye. Some schistose rocks can get very coarse. New minerals like garnet can be very conspicuous in schistose rocks and are often characteristic.

At the higher metamorphic grades, metamorphic processes acting on originally muddy sedimentary rocks cause the minerals quartz and feldspar to segregate from the micas and to become more coarse-grained. The resulting dark and light banded appearance is the texture typical of gneissose ('nice-ose') rocks.

Similar textures will form in metamorphosed sandstones when they are impure and originally contained significant amounts of mud and silt. Clean sandstones composed mainly of quartz and feldspar tend to recrystallize to massive, hard rocks with low porosity.

Metamorphosed intrusive igneous rocks vary considerably in character because of the wide range in original rock composition and grain size. They tend to be affected only by the higher grades of metamorphism. Granitic rocks will become gneissose at high grade – such rocks are typical of many areas of very ancient rocks. In rocks such as basalt, dolerite and gabbro (see the section on igneous rocks), the iron- and magnesium-rich minerals such as pyroxene and olivine are generally replaced by dark green to black amphibole at middle metamorphic grades. The amphibole is commonly aligned, giving the rock a schistose texture. At higher grades, the amphibole is replaced by new pyroxene and garnet and the rocks become coarse, granular and gneissose in texture.

Sedimentary rocks composed of carbonate minerals can undergo very complicated metamorphic reactions, yielding rocks with complex mineralogies and textures, often called marble. They are commonly hard, with a conspicuously banded appearance. The terms 'schistose' and 'gneissose' are less applicable here. Calcite-rich limestones usually form massive granular rocks when metamorphosed in which porosities will be extremely low. These rocks will react readily with 10 per cent HCl. Originally impure carbonate rocks that contain dolomite will form complex metamorphic rocks rich in

Table A1.9 Characteristic metamorphic features of common sedimentary rocks

Original rock type	Metamorphic rock name and mineralogy	Characteristic features when metamorphosed		
		Low grade	Medium grade	High grade
Mudstone	Pelite Quartz, feldspar, mica >40%	Slaty texture, moderately to very fissile, minerals too small to observe with handlens. Often dark in colour. Sedimentary layering may be apparent	Rocks coarsen in grain-size, pervasive phyllitic to schistose texture, fissility increasingly poor. New minerals apparent (e.g. dark micas, garnet). Sedimentary layering increasingly difficult to determine	Rocks very coarse-grained, with strongly schistose to banded, gneissose texture. Original sedimentary layering no longer present
Siltstone, fine muddy sandstones	Semipelite Quartz, feldspar, mica 20–40%	Slaty texture may be developed, fissile, but on a coarse scale than slates. Original layering often readily apparent	As above, though schistose texture is less pervasive and original layering often reasonably well preserved	As above
Sandstones	Psammite Quartz, feldspar, mica <20%	Rocks appear 'indurated' with low porosity, but original layering and sedimentary features well-preserved. Often pale grey to buff in colour	Alignment of micas often conspicuous under a hand lens, but original layering and sedimentary features often still clearly visible. Growth of new minerals will depend on original composition, garnet may be present	Rocks develop a coarse, gneissose texture. Original layering and sedimentary features generally destroyed
Pure limestones, dolostones	Metalimestone/dolostone, 'marble' Dominantly calcitic (white, grey) or dolomitic (creamy to buff grey)	Rocks appear a little recrystallized but fossils and sedimentary commonly still preserved	Largely recrystallized, granular in appearance, often massive. Most original features destroyed, though bedding often still preserved	Recrystallized and coarse grained, massive and featureless. All original textures destroyed

Source: based on Robertson (1999).

Table A1.10 Characteristic metamorphic features of common igneous rocks

Original rock type	Mineralogy	Characteristic features when metamorphosed		
		Low grade	Medium grade	High grade
Basalt	Plagioclase, pyroxene, olivine	Little apparent change, igneous textures preserved	Rocks coarsen in grain-size, pervasive fine rod-like schistose texture. Dark amphibole replaces pyroxene and olivine to form amphibolite. Garnet may appear	Rocks become coarser-grained, strongly schistose to banded, gneissose texture. Pyroxene, olivine and garnet replace amphibole at highest grades, depending on original composition
Gabbro	As above	As above	Coarse amphibolite with some preservation of relict igneous textures	Coarse gneissose rocks with pyroxene, olivine and garnet at the highest grades, depending on original composition
Granitic rocks	Quartz, feldspar, mica, possibly minor amphibole	No change	No significant change	Rocks develop gneissose banding

calc-silicate minerals. They will have low porosity and carbonate may or may not be present. At medium metamorphic grades calc-silicate rich rocks are often very fine-grained. At high metamorphic grades, such rocks can become very coarse, with spectacular minerals developed.

A1.6.4 Describing and identifying metamorphic rocks in the field

Metamorphic rocks have the reputation of being the hardest rocks to deal with in the field. At high metamorphic grades, the boundaries between certain rock types become blurred by the effects of metamorphism. For example, granites and sandstones have broadly similar minerals and compositions and can form very similar looking rocks when they experience metamorphic conditions sufficient to result in the development of gneissose textures. However, a simple approach will help.

- If possible, identify the main minerals and their proportions. This may not be possible in very fine grained rocks: Dark, smooth rocks which are fissile (i.e. split easily) are most likely going to be slaty mudrocks ('slates'). Dark, fine-grained, green and massive, hard rocks are probably going to be lightly metamorphosed igneous rocks rich in iron and magnesium belonging to the basalt family. If you suspect the presence of carbonate, calcite (calcium carbonate) will readily react with 10 per cent HCl, whereas dolomite will only react when powdered.

- Note the texture – is it slaty, schistose or gneissose? Are the rocks conspicuously layered? etc.
- Note the colour – very dark green to black crystalline and schistose rocks with white flecks are likely to be metamorphosed basic igneous rocks like basalts that are termed amphibolites.

If you cannot arrive at a name, then recording the above will at least help describe the rock's chief characteristics. Describe first, name later! Table A1.8 and A1.9 indicate the basic characteristics of metamorphic effects on some of the main rock types.

References, further reading and resources

Bishop, A. Woolley, A.R. and Hamilton, W.R. (1999) *Cambridge guide to minerals rocks and fossils.* Sagebrush Bound, Minnesota, USA.

Duff, D. (1993) *Holmes' principles of physical geology* (4th edition). Chapman & Hall, London.

Fookes, P.G. (1997) *Tropical residual soils.* Professional Handbook Series, Geological Society, London.

Gillespie, M.R. and Styles, M.T. (1999) *BGS Rock classification scheme Volume 1. Classification of igneous rocks* (2nd edition). BGS Research Report RR 99–06. Available at: http://www.bgs.ac.uk

Hallsworth, C.R. and Knox, R.W.O (1999) *BGS Rock classification scheme Volume 3. Classification of sediments and sedimentary rocks.* BGS Research Report RR 99–03. Available at: http://www.bgs.ac.uk

Robertson, S. (1999) *BGS Rock classification scheme Volume 2. Classification of metamorphic rocks.* BGS Research Report RR 99–02. Available at: http://www.bgs.ac.uk

Tucker, M.E. (2003) *Sedimentary rocks in the field.* John Wiley & Sons, Chichester, UK.

Useful websites

Geological Society London. http://www.geolsoc.org.uk/ for links to web based resources on geology.

A1. Tropical red soil containing many iron rich nodules (often called laterite). BGS, © NERC 1998.

A2. Ferricrete: a hard red durable crust that can develop in tropical areas. BGS, © NERC 1998.

A3. A typical tropical red soil profile: red iron-rich layer overlying a paler clay rich horizon. BGS, © NERC 1998.

A4. Tropical black soil: swelling clays sometimes known as mbuga clays or black cotton soils. BGS, © NERC 2002.

A5. Cross bedded unconsolidated sands exposed in a trench in Botswana. BGS, © NERC 1998.

A6. Poorly sorted river gravels in a river bank in Fiji. BGS, © NERC 1990.

A7. A sand river in Tanzania. BGS, © NERC 2002.

A8. Drill chips from a borehole drilled into granite: 0–3 m ferruginous soil; 3–4 m mottle clay; 4–11 m decomposed weathered granite; 11–21 m discoloured and broken granite; 21 m onwards unweathered fresh granite. BGS, © NERC 2000.

A9. Drill chips from a borehole drilled into sandstone: 0–2.5 m ferruginous soil; 2.5–5 m sandy clay; 5 m onwards sandstone. BGS, © NERC 1997.

319

A10. Drill chips from metamorphosed mudstone: 0–2 m ferruginous soil; 2–3.5 m clay; 3.5–10.5 m weathered mudstone; 10.5 onwards unweathered metamorphosed mudstone. BGS, © NERC 1997.

A11. A grey granite composed of grey quartz, white feldspar and black mafic minerals. BGS, © NERC 2002.

A12. A grey granite, containing very large crystals of pink feldpars. BGS, © NERC 2002.

A13. Coarse grained 'red' granite composed of grey quartz, pink feldspars and dark biotite mica. BGS, © NERC 2002.

A14. Rounded granite boulder, typical of many granite environments. BGS, © NERC 2002.

A15. A hill made of granite, with characteristic rounded surfaces. BGS, © NERC 2001.

A16. Gabbro: a coarse grained igneous rock with dark mafic minerals within a groundmass of pale feldspar. BGS, © NERC 2002.

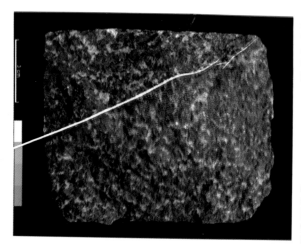

A17. Dolerite: medium grained igneous rock dominated by black mafic minerals. BGS, © NERC 2002.

A18. A dolerite sill exposed in a river bank in Nigeria which has weathered into spheres. BGS, © NERC 1997.

A19. An unweathered surface of dolerite. BGS, © NERC 1999.

A20. A large weathered quartz vein within a darker rock outcrop. BGS, © NERC 2000.

A21. Basaltic lava: the light flecks within basalts are often feldspar crystals or infilled gas bubbles (vesicles). BGS, © NERC 2002.

A22. A weathered rubbly basaltic lava from Ethiopia. BGS, © NERC 2000.

A23. Tuff: consolidated ash from a volcanic eruption. BGS, © NERC 2002.

A24. A pyroclastic rock composed of large rock fragments set in a fine matrix of volcanic ash. BGS, © NERC 2002.

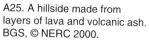

A25. A hillside made from layers of lava and volcanic ash. BGS, © NERC 2000.

A26. Fine to medium-grained well sorted quartz sandstone. BGS, © NERC 2002.

A27. Medium-coarse grained porous sandstone. BGS, © NERC 2002.

A28. Coarse-grained, pebbly sandstone. BGS, © NERC 1999.

A29. Medium-grained cross bedded sandstone. BGS, © NERC 1999.

A30. Interbedded fine-grained sandstones, siltstones and mudstones in a river-bank. BGS, © NERC 1996.

A31. Sandstone cliffs showing flat blocky bedding. BGS, © NERC 2001.

A32. Conglomerate: large pebbles cemented together in a finer grained matrix. BGS, © NERC 1999.

A33. A sample of weathered mudstone from a hand dug well stained by red/brown iron-oxides. BGS, © NERC 1999.

A34. Weathered red mudstones exposed in a river bank. BGS, © NERC 1999

A35. A dark coloured shelly limestone. BGS, © NERC 2002.

A36. A pale coloured limestone containing fossils. BGS, © NERC 2002.

A37. Limestone cliffs. The river emerges from caves at the base of the cliffs. BGS, © NERC 1999.

A38. Distinctive karst weathering on a hard massive limestone. BGS, © NERC 1997.

A39. Phyllitic pelite: metamorphosed mudstones and siltstones with shiny appearance from the mica and platy texture. BGS, © NERC 2002.

A40. Slate (phyllitic pelite): metamorphosed mudstone which can easily split along parallel planes. BGS, © NERC 2002.

A41. A schistose pelite: metamorphosed mudstone and siltstones with a characteristic shiny appearance from the mica. BGS, © NERC 2002.

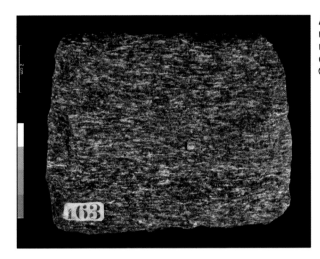

A42. Hornblende schist: metamorphosed mafic rich rocks (such as dolerite and basalt). BGS, © NERC 2002.

A43. Gneiss with a distinctive banded appearance. BGS, © NERC 2002.

A44. Augen gneiss, characterised by large 'eyes' of lighter feldspar crystals. BGS, © NERC 2002.

A45. Marble: metamorphosed limestone. BGS, © NERC 2002.

3 cm

A46. Folded schistose pelites and meta-sandstones in a road cutting in Zambia. BGS, © NERC 2000.

A47. Gneiss rocks exposed in central Tanzania showing distinct banding. BGS, © NERC 2000.

Appendix 2

Village Name..............................   Survey ID..............................

GPS Start.................................   Coil spacing: **10 m / 20 m / 40 m**

Date...   Position receiver: **front / back**

Station	Distance Receiver	Distance midpoint	Vertical coil	Horizontal coil	Comments

EM34 data form

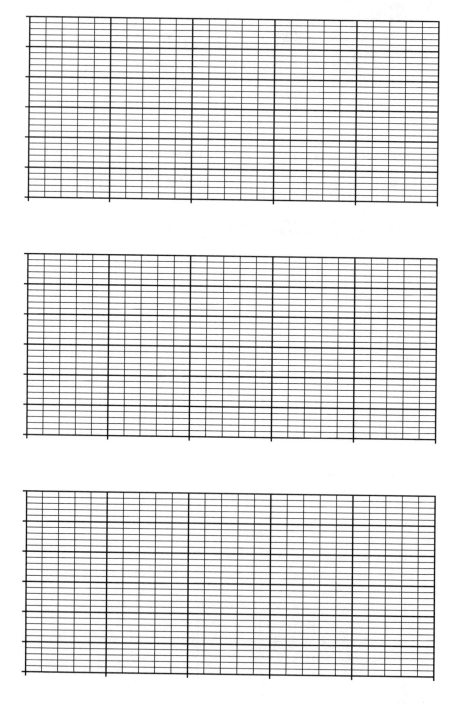

EM34 data form

Apparent resistivity (Ohm-m)

Electrode spacing (m)

Village Name....................................

GPS midpoint...................................

Location...

Survey ID.........................

Date...................................

Direction of line....................

Electrode spacing (m)	Resistance (Ohms)	K value	apparent resistivity (K x resistance)
0.5		3.1	
1		6.3	
1.5		9.4	
2		12.6	
3		18.8	
5		31.4	
7		44	
10		62.8	
15		94.2	
20		126	
30		188	
50		314	
70		440	
100		628	
150		942	

Village Name..........

GPS midpoint..........

Location..........

Survey ID..........

Date..........

Direction of line..........

Outer electrode half spacing (m)	Inner electrode half spacing (m)	Resistance (Ohms)	K value	apparent resistivity (K x resistance)
1	0.2		7.54	
1.5	0.2		17.3	
2	0.2		31.1	
3	0.2		70.3	
5	0.2		196	
7	0.2		384	
10	1.5		102	
7	1.5		48.9	
10	1.5		102	
20	1.5		416	
30	1.5		940	
20	5		118	
30	5		275	
50	5		777	
70	5		1530	
100	5		3130	
70	10		754	
100	10		1550	
150	10		3520	
200	10		6260	

Apparent resistivity (Ohm-m) vs Electrode spacing (m)

Schlumberger data form

Village Name...............................

GPS midpoint..................................

Date..

Survey ID.......................................

Location....................................

Direction of line...................................

Electrode spacing (m)	A	B	C	D1	D2	Resistance (D1+D2)/2	K value	apparent resistivity (K x resistance)
0.5							3.14	
1							6.28	
2							12.6	
4							25.1	
8							50.2	
16							100	
32							2001	
64							402	
128							804	
256							1610	

To check that electrodes and cables are OK then A = B+ C (within 5%)

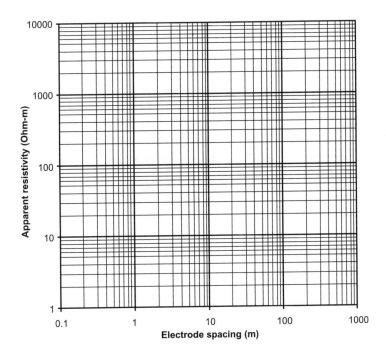

Offset Wenner data form

Village Name............................   **Survey ID**............................

GPS start.................................   **Time start:**...........................

Date.......................................

Station	Distance (m)	Reading	Comments

Magnetic profiling data form

Village Name... Borehole ID............................

GPS borehole... Date.......................................

Drilled Diameter..

Screen diameter.. gravel pack   yes / no

rest water level (always measure from the same spot)...

Number of bails:...............   Period of pumping (mins) (should be 10 minutes):

time since pumping stopped (mins)	water-level (m)	time since pumping stopped (mins)	water-level (m)	time since pumping stopped (mins)	water-level (m)
0.5		21		46	
1		22		47	
1.5		23		48	
2		24		49	
2.5		25		50	
3		26		51	
3.5		27		52	
4		28		53	
4.5		29		54	
5		30		55	
6		31		56	
7		32		57	
8		33		58	
9		34		59	
10		35		60	
11		36		61	
12		37		62	
13		38		63	
14		39		64	
15		40		65	
16		41		66	
17		42		67	
18		43		68	
19		44		69	
20		45		70	

10 minute bailer test form

Pumping rate (litres per minute)	=	volume of bailer (in litres) x number of bails time of pumping in minutes (usually 10)	

Maximum drawdown

A = the earliest reading of water
level after pumping stops

B = the rest water-level

Maximum drawdown = A - B

Time for 75% recovery (t_{75})

Divide the maximum drawdown
by 4

add the rest water-level

t_{75} is the time at which the water
level recovers to the level above

Time for 50% recovery (t_{50})

Divide the maximum drawdown
by 2

add the rest water-level

t_{50} is the time at which the water
level recovers to the level above

Effective borehole diameter

If the borehole is open hole then the drilled
diameter is the effective diameter.

If the borehole is screened with a gravel pack
then the diameter is somewhere between the
drilled and screened diameter. Can be
roughly worked out by:

0.3 x (drilled - screened) + screened.

Estimating success for a borehole with handpump for 250 people with 20 litres each.

Find the pumping rate and the diameter of the borehole on the table below.

If the maximum drawdown, t_{50} and t_{75} are considerably less than those shown on the table, the
borehole will probably be successful

If they are all much greater, the borehole is likely to be unsuccessful.

If some are greater, and some are less, then a constant rate test should be carried out.

Diameter of the borehole ↓	Pumping rate in litres per minute →	7	10.5	14	17.5	21
	(Number of standard bails)*	(16)	(24)	(32)	(40)	(48)
4 inch	Max drawdown (m)	3.5	5.3	7.1	8.8	10.6
	time for half recovery (mins)	6	6	6	6	6
	time for three-quarters recovery (mins)	14	14	14	14	14
5 inch	Max drawdown (m)	2.9	4.3	5.7	7.1	8.5
	time for half recovery (mins)	9	9	9	9	9
	time for three-quarters recovery (mins)	21	21	21	21	21
6 inch	Max drawdown (m)	2.3	3.4	4.6	5.7	6.9
	time for half recovery (mins)	12	12	12	12	12
	time for three-quarters recovery (mins)	28	28	28	28	28
8 inch	Max drawdown (m)	1.5	2.3	3.1	3.8	4.6
	time for half recovery (mins)	19	19	19	19	19
	time for three-quarters recovery (mins)	46	47	47	47	47

*Standard bailer is 4.4 litres (1 m long 3 inch pipe)

10 minute bailer test form

Village Name………………………………… **Borehole ID**…………………………….

GPS borehole…………………………………… **Date**……………………………………….

rest water level (always measure from the same spot)……………………………………..

Average pumping rate for the test………………………………………………

t^1 - time since start of recovery (mins) *measure during test*	t – time since pumping started (mins)	t^1/t	water-level (m) *measure during test*	s^1 (water-level – rest water-level)

Constant rate – recovery form

GPS borehole..   **Date**...

rest water level (always measure from the same spot)...

type of pump...   **depth of pump**...

time since pumping started (mins)	water-level (m)	Comments and pumping rate	time since pumping started (mins)	water-level (m)	Comments and pumping rate

Constant rate – drawdown form

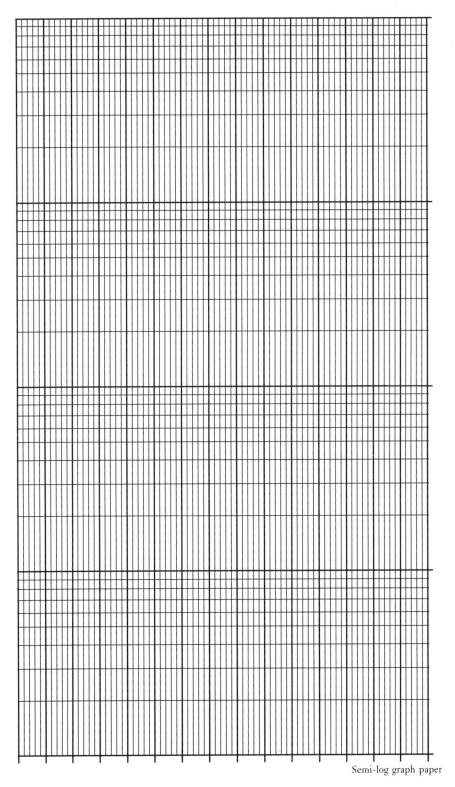

Semi-log graph paper

Glossary

The technical terms used in the manual are generally explained in the text when they appear. However, to further help with the reading of the manual, a selected glossary of various recurring terms is given below. An explanation of the geological terms used in the manual is given in Appendix 1.

Aquifer   A rock formation that is sufficiently porous and **permeable** to be useful for water supply.

Aquitard   A rock formation with a low **permeability** which hinders the movement of **groundwater**.

Baseflow   Natural discharge of groundwater from an aquifer, via springs and seepages, to rivers.

Borehole   A cylindrical hole (usually greater than 20 m deep and less than 0.5 m in diameter) constructed to allow groundwater to be abstracted from an aquifer.

Confined aquifer   An **aquifer** where the water is stored under pressure because of an overlying low-**permeability** layer (**aquitard**). These aquifers are sometimes called artesian.

Contingent valuation   A demand assessment technique in which several options (including costs and levels of service) are described to people, so that people can then state an informed preference.

Cost-effectiveness analysis   An economic appraisal that considers the least cost way of achieving a desired result, such as the drilling of a successful borehole.

Demand   An informed expression of desire for a particular **service**, assessed by the investments people are prepared to make, over the lifetime of the service, to receive and sustain it.

Demand assessment   Any technique used to evaluate **demand** for a particular service.

Demand-responsive approach   An approach to service provision intended to allow consumer **demand** to drive key investment decisions, such that users make choices and commit resources in support of these choices.

Enabling environment   The policies, institutions and legal frameworks that support the design and implementation of projects and their subsequent sustainability. Includes the objectives and targets set by government for rural water supply, the institutional arrangements for service delivery and support, and legal matters relating to the ownership of assets and the status of water committees, or user groups.

Focus group   A small group of individuals with a similar social, cultural or economic background, brought together to discuss a particular issue, such as what they want from an improved service, and how much they would be prepared to pay for it.

Fracture flow   The preferential flow of groundwater through dilated cracks, joints, bedding planes or other features of secondary **porosity** within an aquifer.

Groundwater   The name given to water stored in an aquifer in pore spaces or fractures in rocks or sediments. Sometimes written as 'ground water'.

Hydraulic conductivity   A measure of how easily groundwater flows through a rock or soil. Usually reported, in m/day it is the velocity that groundwater would flow through the rock under a pressure gradient of 1 m per metre.

Hydrogeology   The study of groundwater.

Intergranular flow   The flow of groundwater through pore spaces in rocks rather than cracks or joints.

Permeability   Generally, the term is used loosely to mean the ease with which a rock or soil can transmit groundwater. However, the term also has a precise definition: the ease with which a rock can transmit any fluid under an unequal pressure.

Piezometric level   A way of expressing the pressure in a confined aquifer. It is the level at which water would rise in a borehole drilled into the confined aquifer.

Porosity   A measure of the void spaces in a rock or sediment. It is measured as the ratio of the volume of the spaces to the total volume of rock, usually expressed as a percentage. The term **primary porosity** is often used for porosity from pore spaces; **secondary porosity** refers to void spaces caused by cracks or joints.

Recharge   The quantity of water that is added to groundwater resources from sources such as the direct infiltration of rainfall or leakage from streams and rivers.

Service   The system that provides users with a particular function, such as an improved water supply. It includes the physical infrastructure of water supply (e.g. a borehole with a handpump), as well as the management, contribution and support systems that help sustain it.

Service level   A term used to describe the relative quality of the service provided to users. This may be related to physical infrastructure (from a communal well to a yard tap or in-house private connection, for example), and to the quantity, quality and reliability of water supply.

Spring   A place where groundwater naturally overflows at the ground surface.

Storage coefficient (*S*)   The storage coefficient is a truer measure than **porosity** of the amount of usable groundwater stored in an **aquifer**. It is defined as the amount of groundwater released from storage per square metre of aquifer when the water-table falls by 1 m.

Transmissivity (*T*)   Describes the ability of an aquifer to transmit volumes of groundwater throughout its entire thickness and is calculated by multiplying the **hydraulic conductivity** by the aquifer thickness. It is usually measured in m^2/day.

Unconfined aquifer   A partially saturated aquifer which contains a **water table** that is free to fluctuate under atmospheric pressure in response to discharge or **recharge**.

Unsaturated zone   The zone between the land surface and the **water table**.

Water table   The upper surface of a groundwater body in an **unconfined aquifer**. It can be measured by the static water level in a well or borehole in an unconfined aquifer.

Well   A large-diameter hole (usually greater than 1 m) dug to access groundwater. Usually (but not always) less than 20 m deep.

Willingness to pay   The financial or economic contribution that people are willing to make to receive and sustain a particular **service**. It can be gauged through several different **demand assessment** techniques.

Yield   The volume of water produced by a **spring, borehole** or **well**. Usually measured in m^3/day or l/second.

Abbreviations

EM	electromagnetic
BGS	British Geological Survey
DRA	Demand Responsive Approaches
FEM	frequency domain electromagnetic
IAH	International Association of Hydrogeologists
M&E	monitoring and evaluation
NGO	non-governmental organization
O&M	operations and maintenance
PRA	participatory rural appraisal
TEM	time domain electromagnetic
UN	United Nations
UNICEF	United Nations International Children's Fund
VES	vertical electric sounding
VLF	very low frequency
WHO	World Health Organization

Index